Hadoop Real-World Solutions Cookbook

Realistic, simple code examples to solve problems at scale with Hadoop and related technologies

Jonathan R. Owens

Jon Lentz

Brian Femiano

BIRMINGHAM - MUMBAI

Hadoop Real-World Solutions Cookbook

First published: February 2013

Production Reference: 1280113

Published by Packt Publishing Ltd.
Livery Place
35 Livery Street
Birmingham B3 2PB, UK.

ISBN 978-1-84951-912-0

www.packtpub.com

Cover Image by iStockPhoto

Credits

Authors

Jonathan R. Owens

Jon Lentz

Brian Femiano

Reviewers

Edward J. Cody

Daniel Jue

Bruce C. Miller

Acquisition Editor

Robin de Jongh

Lead Technical Editor

Azharuddin Sheikh

Technical Editor

Dennis John

Copy Editors

Brandt D'Mello

Insiya Morbiwala

Aditya Nair

Alfida Paiva

Ruta Waghmare

Project Coordinator

Abhishek Kori

Proofreader

Stephen Silk

Indexer

Monica Ajmera Mehta

Graphics

Conidon Miranda

Layout Coordinator

Conidon Miranda

Cover Work

Conidon Miranda

About the Authors

Jonathan R. Owens has a background in Java and C++, and has worked in both private and public sectors as a software engineer. Most recently, he has been working with Hadoop and related distributed processing technologies.

Currently, he works for comScore, Inc., a widely regarded digital measurement and analytics company. At comScore, he is a member of the core processing team, which uses Hadoop and other custom distributed systems to aggregate, analyze, and manage over 40 billion transactions per day.

I would like to thank my parents James and Patricia Owens, for their support and introducing me to technology at a young age.

Jon Lentz is a Software Engineer on the core processing team at comScore, Inc., an online audience measurement and analytics company. He prefers to do most of his coding in Pig. Before working at comScore, he developed software to optimize supply chains and allocate fixed-income securities.

To my daughter, Emma, born during the writing of this book. Thanks for the company on late nights.

Brian Femiano has a B.S. in Computer Science and has been programming professionally for over 6 years, the last two of which have been spent building advanced analytics and Big Data capabilities using Apache Hadoop. He has worked for the commercial sector in the past, but the majority of his experience comes from the government contracting space. He currently works for Potomac Fusion in the DC/Virginia area, where they develop scalable algorithms to study and enhance some of the most advanced and complex datasets in the government space. Within Potomac Fusion, he has taught courses and conducted training sessions to help teach Apache Hadoop and related cloud-scale technologies.

I'd like to thank my co-authors for their patience and hard work building the code you see in this book. Also, my various colleagues at Potomac Fusion, whose talent and passion for building cutting-edge capability and promoting knowledge transfer have inspired me.

About the Reviewers

Edward J. Cody is an author, speaker, and industry expert in data warehousing, Oracle Business Intelligence, and Hyperion EPM implementations. He is the author and co-author respectively of two books with Packt Publishing, titled *The Business Analyst's Guide to Oracle Hyperion Interactive Reporting 11* and *The Oracle Hyperion Interactive Reporting 11 Expert Guide*. He has consulted to both commercial and federal government clients throughout his career, and is currently managing large-scale EPM, BI, and data warehouse implementations.

> I would like to commend the authors of this book for a job well done, and would like to thank Packt Publishing for the opportunity to assist in the editing of this publication.

Daniel Jue is a Sr. Software Engineer at Sotera Defense Solutions and a member of the Apache Software Foundation. He has worked in peace and conflict zones to showcase the hidden dynamics and anomalies in the underlying "Big Data", with clients such as ACSIM, DARPA, and various federal agencies. Daniel holds a B.S. in Computer Science from the University of Maryland, College Park, where he also specialized in Physics and Astronomy. His current interests include merging distributed artificial intelligence techniques with adaptive heterogeneous cloud computing.

> I'd like to thank my beautiful wife Wendy, and my twin sons Christopher and Jonathan, for their love and patience while I research and review. I owe a great deal to Brian Femiano, Bruce Miller, and Jonathan Larson for allowing me to be exposed to many great ideas, points of view, and zealous inspiration.

Bruce Miller is a Senior Software Engineer for Sotera Defense Solutions, currently employed at DARPA, with most of his 10-year career focused on Big Data software development. His non-work interests include functional programming in languages like Haskell and Lisp dialects, and their application to real-world problems.

www.packtpub.com

Support files, eBooks, discount offers and more

You might want to visit www.packtpub.com for support files and downloads related to your book.

Did you know that Packt offers eBook versions of every book published, with PDF and ePub files available? You can upgrade to the eBook version at www.packtpub.com and as a print book customer, you are entitled to a discount on the eBook copy. Get in touch with us at service@packtpub.com for more details.

At www.packtpub.com, you can also read a collection of free technical articles, sign up for a range of free newsletters and receive exclusive discounts and offers on Packt books and eBooks.

http://packtLib.packtPub.com

Do you need instant solutions to your IT questions? PacktLib is Packt's online digital book library. Here, you can access, read and search across Packt's entire library of books.

Why Subscribe?

- Fully searchable across every book published by Packt
- Copy and paste, print and bookmark content
- On demand and accessible via web browser

Free Access for Packt account holders

If you have an account with Packt at www.packtpub.com, you can use this to access PacktLib today and view nine entirely free books. Simply use your login credentials for immediate access.

Table of Contents

Preface

Hadoop Real-World Solutions Cookbook helps developers become more comfortable with, and proficient at solving problems in, the Hadoop space. Readers will become more familiar with a wide variety of Hadoop-related tools and best practices for implementation.

This book will teach readers how to build solutions using tools such as Apache Hive, Pig, MapReduce, Mahout, Giraph, HDFS, Accumulo, Redis, and Ganglia.

This book provides in-depth explanations and code examples. Each chapter contains a set of recipes that pose, and then solve, technical challenges and that can be completed in any order. A recipe breaks a single problem down into discrete steps that are easy to follow. This book covers unloading/loading to and from HDFS, graph analytics with Giraph, batch data analysis using Hive, Pig, and MapReduce, machine-learning approaches with Mahout, debugging and troubleshooting MapReduce jobs, and columnar storage and retrieval of structured data using Apache Accumulo.

This book will give readers the examples they need to apply the Hadoop technology to their own problems.

What this book covers

Chapter 1, Hadoop Distributed File System – Importing and Exporting Data, shows several approaches for loading and unloading data from several popular databases that include MySQL, MongoDB, Greenplum, and MS SQL Server, among others, with the aid of tools such as Pig, Flume, and Sqoop.

Chapter 2, HDFS, includes recipes for reading and writing data to/from HDFS. It shows how to use different serialization libraries, including Avro, Thrift, and Protocol Buffers. Also covered is how to set the block size and replication, and enable LZO compression.

Chapter 3, Extracting and Transforming Data, includes recipes that show basic Hadoop ETL over several different types of data sources. Different tools, including Hive, Pig, and the Java MapReduce API, are used to batch-process data samples and produce one or more transformed outputs.

Chapter 4, Performing Common Tasks Using Hive, Pig, and MapReduce, focuses on how to leverage certain functionality in these tools to quickly tackle many different classes of problems. This includes string concatenation, external table mapping, simple table joins, custom functions, and dependency distribution across the cluster.

Chapter 5, Advanced Joins, contains recipes that demonstrate more complex and useful join techniques in MapReduce, Hive, and Pig. These recipes show merged, replicated, and skewed joins in Pig as well as Hive map-side and full outer joins. There is also a recipe that shows how to use Redis to join data from an external data store.

Chapter 6, Big Data Analysis, contains recipes designed to show how you can put Hadoop to use to answer different questions about your data. Several of the Hive examples will demonstrate how to properly implement and use a custom function (UDF) for reuse in different analytics. There are two Pig recipes that show different analytics with the Audioscrobbler dataset and one MapReduce Java API recipe that shows Combiners.

Chapter 7, Advanced Big Data Analysis, shows recipes in Apache Giraph and Mahout that tackle different types of graph analytics and machine-learning challenges.

Chapter 8, Debugging, includes recipes designed to aid in the troubleshooting and testing of MapReduce jobs. There are examples that use MRUnit and local mode for ease of testing. There are also recipes that emphasize the importance of using counters and updating task status to help monitor the MapReduce job.

Chapter 9, System Administration, focuses mainly on how to performance-tune and optimize the different settings available in Hadoop. Several different topics are covered, including basic setup, XML configuration tuning, troubleshooting bad data nodes, handling NameNode failure, and performance monitoring using Ganglia.

Chapter 10, Persistence Using Apache Accumulo, contains recipes that show off many of the unique features and capabilities that come with using the NoSQL datastore Apache Accumulo. The recipes leverage many of its unique features, including iterators, combiners, scan authorizations, and constraints. There are also examples for building an efficient geospatial row key and performing batch analysis using MapReduce.

What you need for this book

Readers will need access to a pseudo-distributed (single machine) or fully-distributed (multi-machine) cluster to execute the code in this book. The various tools that the recipes leverage need to be installed and properly configured on the cluster. Moreover, the code recipes throughout this book are written in different languages; therefore, it's best if readers have access to a machine with development tools they are comfortable using.

Who this book is for

This book uses concise code examples to highlight different types of real-world problems you can solve with Hadoop. It is designed for developers with varying levels of comfort using Hadoop and related tools. Hadoop beginners can use the recipes to accelerate the learning curve and see real-world examples of Hadoop application. For more experienced Hadoop developers, many of the tools and techniques might expose them to new ways of thinking or help clarify a framework they had heard of but the value of which they had not really understood.

Conventions

In this book, you will find a number of styles of text that distinguish between different kinds of information. Here are some examples of these styles, and an explanation of their meaning.

Code words in text are shown as follows: "All of the Hadoop filesystem shell commands take the general form `hadoop fs -COMMAND`."

A block of code is set as follows:

```
weblogs = load '/data/weblogs/weblog_entries.txt' as
                (md5:chararray,
                 url:chararray,
                 date:chararray,
                 time:chararray,
                 ip:chararray);

md5_grp = group weblogs by md5 parallel 4;

store md5_grp into '/data/weblogs/weblogs_md5_groups.bcp';
```

When we wish to draw your attention to a particular part of a code block, the relevant lines or items are set in bold:

```
weblogs = load '/data/weblogs/weblog_entries.txt' as
                (md5:chararray,
                 url:chararray,
                 date:chararray,
                 time:chararray,
                 ip:chararray);

md5_grp = group weblogs by md5 parallel 4;

store md5_grp into '/data/weblogs/weblogs_md5_groups.bcp';
```

Any command-line input or output is written as follows:

```
hadoop distcp -m 10 hdfs://namenodeA/data/weblogs hdfs://namenodeB/data/
weblogs
```

New terms and **important words** are shown in bold. Words that you see on the screen, in menus or dialog boxes for example, appear in the text like this: "To build the JAR file, download the Jython java installer, run the installer, and select **Standalone** from the installation menu".

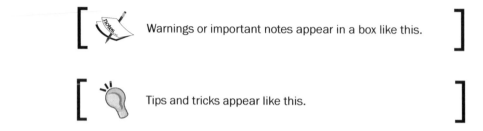

Warnings or important notes appear in a box like this.

Tips and tricks appear like this.

Reader feedback

Feedback from our readers is always welcome. Let us know what you think about this book—what you liked or may have disliked. Reader feedback is important for us to develop titles that you really get the most out of.

To send us general feedback, simply send an e-mail to feedback@packtpub.com, and mention the book title via the subject of your message.

If there is a topic that you have expertise in and you are interested in either writing or contributing to a book, see our author guide on www.packtpub.com/authors.

Customer support

Now that you are the proud owner of a Packt book, we have a number of things to help you to get the most from your purchase.

Downloading the example code

You can download the example code files for all Packt books you have purchased from your account at http://www.packtpub.com. If you purchased this book elsewhere, you can visit http://www.packtpub.com/support and register to have the files e-mailed directly to you.

Errata

Although we have taken every care to ensure the accuracy of our content, mistakes do happen. If you find a mistake in one of our books—maybe a mistake in the text or the code—we would be grateful if you would report this to us. By doing so, you can save other readers from frustration and help us improve subsequent versions of this book. If you find any errata, please report them by visiting http://www.packtpub.com/support, selecting your book, clicking on the **errata submission form** link, and entering the details of your errata. Once your errata are verified, your submission will be accepted and the errata will be uploaded on our website, or added to any list of existing errata, under the Errata section of that title. Any existing errata can be viewed by selecting your title from http://www.packtpub.com/support.

Piracy

Piracy of copyright material on the Internet is an ongoing problem across all media. At Packt, we take the protection of our copyright and licenses very seriously. If you come across any illegal copies of our works, in any form, on the Internet, please provide us with the location address or website name immediately so that we can pursue a remedy.

Please contact us at copyright@packtpub.com with a link to the suspected pirated material.

We appreciate your help in protecting our authors, and our ability to bring you valuable content.

Questions

You can contact us at questions@packtpub.com if you are having a problem with any aspect of the book, and we will do our best to address it.

1
Hadoop Distributed File System – Importing and Exporting Data

In this chapter we will cover:

- ▶ Importing and exporting data into HDFS using the Hadoop shell commands
- ▶ Moving data efficiently between clusters using Distributed Copy
- ▶ Importing data from MySQL into HDFS using Sqoop
- ▶ Exporting data from HDFS into MySQL using Sqoop
- ▶ Configuring Sqoop for Microsoft SQL Server
- ▶ Exporting data from HDFS into MongoDB
- ▶ Importing data from MongoDB into HDFS
- ▶ Exporting data from HDFS into MongoDB using Pig
- ▶ Using HDFS in a Greenplum external table
- ▶ Using Flume to load data into HDFS

Introduction

In a typical installation, Hadoop is the heart of a complex flow of data. Data is often collected from many disparate systems. This data is then imported into the **Hadoop Distributed File System** (**HDFS**). Next, some form of processing takes place using MapReduce or one of the several languages built on top of MapReduce (Hive, Pig, Cascading, and so on). Finally, the filtered, transformed, and aggregated results are exported to one or more external systems.

For a more concrete example, a large website may want to produce basic analytical data about its hits. Weblog data from several servers is collected and pushed into HDFS. A MapReduce job is started, which runs using the weblogs as its input. The weblog data is parsed, summarized, and combined with the IP address geolocation data. The output produced shows the URL, page views, and location data by each cookie. This report is exported into a relational database. Ad hoc queries can now be run against this data. Analysts can quickly produce reports of total unique cookies present, pages with the most views, breakdowns of visitors by region, or any other rollup of this data.

The recipes in this chapter will focus on the process of importing and exporting data to and from HDFS. The sources and destinations include the local filesystem, relational databases, NoSQL databases, distributed databases, and other Hadoop clusters.

Importing and exporting data into HDFS using Hadoop shell commands

HDFS provides shell command access to much of its functionality. These commands are built on top of the HDFS FileSystem API. Hadoop comes with a shell script that drives all interaction from the command line. This shell script is named `hadoop` and is usually located in `$HADOOP_BIN`, where `$HADOOP_BIN` is the full path to the Hadoop binary folder. For convenience, `$HADOOP_BIN` should be set in your `$PATH` environment variable. All of the Hadoop filesystem shell commands take the general form `hadoop fs -COMMAND`.

To get a full listing of the filesystem commands, run the `hadoop` shell script passing it the `fs` option with no commands.

```
hadoop fs
```

```
[cloudera@localhost Desktop]$ hadoop fs
Usage: hadoop fs [generic options]
        [-cat [-ignoreCrc] <src> ...]
        [-chgrp [-R] GROUP PATH...]
        [-chmod [-R] <MODE[,MODE]... | OCTALMODE> PATH...]
        [-chown [-R] [OWNER][:[GROUP]] PATH...]
        [-copyFromLocal <localsrc> ... <dst>]
        [-copyToLocal [-ignoreCrc] [-crc] <src> ... <localdst>]
        [-count [-q] <path> ...]
        [-cp <src> ... <dst>]
        [-df [-h] [<path> ...]]
        [-du [-s] [-h] <path> ...]
        [-expunge]
        [-get [-ignoreCrc] [-crc] <src> ... <localdst>]
        [-getmerge [-nl] <src> <localdst>]
        [-help [cmd ...]]
        [-ls [-d] [-h] [-R] [<path> ...]]
        [-mkdir [-p] <path> ...]
        [-moveFromLocal <localsrc> ... <dst>]
        [-moveToLocal <src> <localdst>]
        [-mv <src> ... <dst>]
        [-put <localsrc> ... <dst>]
        [-rm [-f] [-r|-R] [-skipTrash] <src> ...]
        [-rmdir [--ignore-fail-on-non-empty] <dir> ...]
        [-setrep [-R] [-w] <rep> <path/file> ...]
        [-stat [format] <path> ...]
        [-tail [-f] <file>]
        [-test -[ezd] <path>]
        [-text [-ignoreCrc] <src> ...]
        [-touchz <path> ...]
        [-usage [cmd ...]]
```

These command names along with their functionality closely resemble Unix shell commands. To get more information about a particular command, use the `help` option.

```
hadoop fs -help ls
```

```
[cloudera@localhost Desktop]$ hadoop fs -help ls
-ls [-d] [-h] [-R] [<path> ...]:        List the contents that match the specified file pattern. If
                path is not specified, the contents of /user/<currentUser>
                will be listed. Directory entries are of the form
                        dirName (full path) <dir>
                and file entries are of the form
                        fileName(full path) <r n> size
                where n is the number of replicas specified for the file
                and size is the size of the file, in bytes.
                -d  Directories are listed as plain files.
                -h  Formats the sizes of files in a human-readable fashion
                    rather than a number of bytes.
                -R  Recursively list the contents of directories.
[cloudera@localhost Desktop]$
```

The shell commands and brief descriptions can also be found online in the official documentation located at `http://hadoop.apache.org/common/docs/r0.20.2/hdfs_shell.html`

In this recipe, we will be using Hadoop shell commands to import data into HDFS and export data from HDFS. These commands are often used to load ad hoc data, download processed data, maintain the filesystem, and view the contents of folders. Knowing these commands is a requirement for efficiently working with HDFS.

Getting ready

You will need to download the `weblog_entries.txt` dataset from the Packt website `http://www.packtpub.com/support`.

How to do it...

Complete the following steps to create a new folder in HDFS and copy the `weblog_entries.txt` file from the local filesystem to HDFS:

1. Create a new folder in HDFS to store the `weblog_entries.txt` file:

   ```
   hadoop fs -mkdir /data/weblogs
   ```

2. Copy the `weblog_entries.txt` file from the local filesystem into the new folder created in HDFS:

   ```
   hadoop fs -copyFromLocal weblog_entries.txt /data/weblogs
   ```

3. List the information in the `weblog_entires.txt` file:

   ```
   hadoop fs -ls /data/weblogs/weblog_entries.txt
   ```

   ```
   [cloudera@localhost Desktop]$ hadoop fs -ls /data/weblogs
   Found 1 items
   -rw-r--r--   1 cloudera supergroup     254129 2012-12-31 11:06 /data/weblogs/weblog_entries.txt
   [cloudera@localhost Desktop]$
   ```

 The result of a job run in Hadoop may be used by an external system, may require further processing in a legacy system, or the processing requirements might not fit the MapReduce paradigm. Any one of these situations will require data to be exported from HDFS. One of the simplest ways to download data from HDFS is to use the Hadoop shell.

4. The following code will copy the `weblog_entries.txt` file from HDFS to the local filesystem's current folder:

   ```
   hadoop fs -copyToLocal /data/weblogs/weblog_entries.txt ./weblog_entries.txt
   ```

   ```
   [cloudera@localhost data]$ hadoop fs -copyToLocal /data/weblogs/weblog_entries.txt ./w
   eblog_entries.txt
   [cloudera@localhost data]$ ls -ltr
   total 252
   -rwxr-xr-x 1 cloudera cloudera 254129 Dec 31 11:15 weblog_entries.txt
   [cloudera@localhost data]$
   ```

When copying a file from HDFS to the local filesystem, keep in mind the space available on the local filesystem and the network connection speed. It's not uncommon for HDFS to have file sizes in the range of terabytes or even tens of terabytes. In the best case scenario, a ten terabyte file would take almost 23 hours to be copied from HDFS to the local filesystem over a 1-gigabit connection, and that is if the space is available!

Downloading the example code for this book

You can download the example code files for all the Packt books you have purchased from your account at http://www.packtpub.com. If you purchased this book elsewhere, you can visit http://www.packtpub.com/support and register to have the files e-mailed directly to you.

How it works...

The Hadoop shell commands are a convenient wrapper around the HDFS FileSystem API. In fact, calling the hadoop shell script and passing it the fs option sets the Java application entry point to the org.apache.hadoop.fs.FsShell class. The FsShell class then instantiates an org.apache.hadoop.fs.FileSystem object and maps the filesystem's methods to the fs command-line arguments. For example, hadoop fs -mkdir /data/weblogs, is equivalent to FileSystem.mkdirs(new Path("/data/weblogs")). Similarly, hadoop fs -copyFromLocal weblog_entries.txt /data/weblogs is equivalent to FileSystem.copyFromLocal(new Path("weblog_entries.txt"), new Path("/data/weblogs")). The same applies to copying the data from HDFS to the local filesystem. The copyToLocal Hadoop shell command is equivalent to FileSystem.copyToLocal(new Path("/data/weblogs/weblog_entries.txt"), new Path("./weblog_entries.txt")). More information about the FileSystem class and its methods can be found on its official Javadoc page: http://hadoop.apache.org/docs/r0.20.2/api/org/apache/hadoop/fs/FileSystem.html.

The mkdir command takes the general form of hadoop fs -mkdir PATH1 PATH2. For example, hadoop fs -mkdir /data/weblogs/12012012 /data/weblogs/12022012 would create two folders in HDFS: /data/weblogs/12012012 and /data/weblogs/12022012, respectively. The mkdir command returns 0 on success and -1 on error:

```
hadoop fs -mkdir /data/weblogs/12012012 /data/weblogs/12022012

hadoop fs -ls /data/weblogs
```

```
[cloudera@localhost data]$ hadoop fs -mkdir /data/weblogs/12012012 /data/weblogs/12022
012
[cloudera@localhost data]$ hadoop fs -ls /data/weblogs
Found 3 items
drwxr-xr-x   - cloudera supergroup          0 2012-12-31 11:18 /data/weblogs/12012012
drwxr-xr-x   - cloudera supergroup          0 2012-12-31 11:18 /data/weblogs/12022012
-rw-r--r--   1 cloudera supergroup     254129 2012-12-31 11:06 /data/weblogs/weblog_en
tries.txt
[cloudera@localhost data]$ 
```

The `copyFromLocal` command takes the general form of `hadoop fs -copyFromLocal LOCAL_FILE_PATH URI`. If the URI is not explicitly given, a default is used. The default value is set using the `fs.default.name` property from the `core-site.xml` file. `copyFromLocal` returns `0` on success and `-1` on error.

The `copyToLocal` command takes the general form of `hadoop fs -copyToLocal [-ignorecrc] [-crc] URI LOCAL_FILE_PATH`. If the URI is not explicitly given, a default is used. The default value is set using the `fs.default.name` property from the `core-site.xml` file. The `copyToLocal` command does a **Cyclic Redundancy Check (CRC)** to verify that the data copied was unchanged. A failed copy can be forced using the optional `-ignorecrc` argument. The file and its CRC can be copied using the optional `-crc` argument.

There's more...

The command `put` is similar to `copyFromLocal`. Although `put` is slightly more general, it is able to copy multiple files into HDFS, and also can read input from stdin.

The `get` Hadoop shell command can be used in place of the `copyToLocal` command. At this time they share the same implementation.

When working with large datasets, the output of a job will be partitioned into one or more parts. The number of parts is determined by the `mapred.reduce.tasks` property which can be set using the `setNumReduceTasks()` method on the `JobConf` class. There will be one part file for each reducer task. The number of reducers that should be used varies from job to job; therefore, this property should be set at the job and not the cluster level. The default value is `1`. This means that the output from all map tasks will be sent to a single reducer. Unless the cumulative output from the map tasks is relatively small, less than a gigabyte, the default value should not be used. Setting the optimal number of reduce tasks can be more of an art than science. In the JobConf documentation it is recommended that one of the two formulae be used:

*0.95 * NUMBER_OF_NODES * mapred.tasktracker.reduce.tasks.maximum*

Or

*1.75 * NUMBER_OF_NODES * mapred.tasktracker.reduce.tasks.maximum*

For example, if your cluster has 10 nodes running a task tracker and the `mapred.tasktracker.reduce.tasks.maximum` property is set to have a maximum of five reduce slots, the formula would look like this *0.95 * 10 * 5 = 47.5*. Since the number of reduce slots must be a nonnegative integer, this value should be rounded or trimmed.

The JobConf documentation provides the following rationale for using these multipliers at `http://hadoop.apache.org/docs/current/api/org/apache/hadoop/mapred/JobConf.html#setNumReduceTasks(int)`:

> *With 0.95 all of the reducers can launch immediately and start transferring map outputs as the maps finish. With 1.75 the faster nodes will finish their first round of reduces and launch a second wave of reduces doing a much better job of load balancing.*

The partitioned output can be referenced within HDFS using the folder name. A job given the folder name will read each part file when processing. The problem is that the `get` and `copyToLocal` commands only work on files. They cannot be used to copy folders. It would be cumbersome and inefficient to copy each part file (there could be hundreds or even thousands of them) and merge them locally. Fortunately, the Hadoop shell provides the `getmerge` command to merge all of the distributed part files into a single output file and copy that file to the local filesystem.

The following Pig script illustrates the `getmerge` command:

```
weblogs = load '/data/weblogs/weblog_entries.txt' as
                (md5:chararray,
                 url:chararray,
                 date:chararray,
                 time:chararray,
                 ip:chararray);

md5_grp = group weblogs by md5 parallel 4;

store md5_grp into '/data/weblogs/weblogs_md5_groups.bcp';
```

The Pig script can be executed from the command line by running the following command:

```
pig -f weblogs_md5_group.pig
```

This Pig script reads in each line of the `weblog_entries.txt` file. It then groups the data by the `md5` value. `parallel 4` is the Pig-specific way of setting the number of `mapred.reduce.tasks`. Since there are four reduce tasks that will be run as part of this job, we expect four part files to be created. The Pig script stores its output into `/data/weblogs/weblogs_md5_groups.bcp`.

```
[cloudera@localhost data]$ hadoop fs -ls /data/weblogs
Found 4 items
drwxr-xr-x   - cloudera supergroup          0 2012-12-31 11:18 /data/weblogs/12012012
drwxr-xr-x   - cloudera supergroup          0 2012-12-31 11:18 /data/weblogs/12022012
-rw-r--r--   1 cloudera supergroup     254129 2012-12-31 11:06 /data/weblogs/weblog_entries.txt
drwxr-xr-x   - cloudera supergroup          0 2012-12-31 11:27 /data/weblogs/weblogs_md5_groups.bcp
[cloudera@localhost data]$
```

Notice that `weblogs_md5_groups.bcp` is actually a folder. Listing that folder will show the following output:

```
[cloudera@localhost data]$ hadoop fs -ls /data/weblogs/weblogs_md5_groups.bcp
Found 5 items
-rw-r--r--   1 cloudera supergroup          0 2012-12-31 11:27 /data/weblogs/weblogs_md5_groups.bcp/
_SUCCESS
-rw-r--r--   1 cloudera supergroup      85435 2012-12-31 11:27 /data/weblogs/weblogs_md5_groups.bcp/
part-r-00000
-rw-r--r--   1 cloudera supergroup      91250 2012-12-31 11:27 /data/weblogs/weblogs_md5_groups.bcp/
part-r-00001
-rw-r--r--   1 cloudera supergroup      87885 2012-12-31 11:27 /data/weblogs/weblogs_md5_groups.bcp/
part-r-00002
-rw-r--r--   1 cloudera supergroup      90017 2012-12-31 11:27 /data/weblogs/weblogs_md5_groups.bcp/
part-r-00003
[cloudera@localhost data]$ 
```

Within the `/data/weblogs/weblogs_md5_groups.bcp` folder, there are four part files: `part-r-00000`, `part-r-00001`, `part-r-00002`, and `part-r-00003`.

The `getmerge` command can be used to merge all four of the part files and then copy the singled merged file to the local filesystem as shown in the following command line:

```
hadoop fs –getmerge /data/weblogs/weblogs_md5_groups.bcp weblogs_md5_groups.bcp
```

Listing the local folder we get the following output:

```
[cloudera@localhost data]$ hadoop fs -getmerge /data/weblogs/weblogs_md5_groups.bcp weblogs_md5_grou
ps.bcp
[cloudera@localhost data]$ ls -ltr
total 600
-rwxr-xr-x 1 cloudera cloudera 254129 Dec 31 11:15 weblog_entries.txt
-rwxr-xr-x 1 cloudera cloudera 354587 Dec 31 15:25 weblogs_md5_groups.bcp
[cloudera@localhost data]$ 
```

See also

- The *Reading and writing data to HDFS* recipe in *Chapter 2, HDFS* shows how to use the FileSystem API directly.

- The following links show the different filesystem shell commands and the Java API docs for the `FileSystem` class:

  - `http://hadoop.apache.org/common/docs/r0.20.2/hdfs_shell.html`

  - `http://hadoop.apache.org/docs/r0.20.2/api/org/apache/hadoop/fs/FileSystem.html`

Moving data efficiently between clusters using Distributed Copy

Hadoop Distributed Copy (`distcp`) is a tool for efficiently copying large amounts of data within or in between clusters. It uses the MapReduce framework to do the copying. The benefits of using MapReduce include parallelism, error handling, recovery, logging, and reporting. The Hadoop Distributed Copy command (`distcp`) is useful when moving data between development, research, and production cluster environments.

Getting ready

The source and destination clusters must be able to reach each other.

The source cluster should have speculative execution turned off for map tasks. In the `mapred-site.xml` configuration file, set `mapred.map.tasks.speculative.execution` to `false`. This will prevent any undefined behavior from occurring in the case where a map task fails.

The source and destination cluster must use the same RPC protocol. Typically, this means that the source and destination cluster should have the same version of Hadoop installed.

How to do it...

Complete the following steps to copy a folder from one cluster to another:

1. Copy the weblogs folder from cluster A to cluster B:

   ```
   hadoop distcp hdfs://namenodeA/data/weblogs hdfs://namenodeB/data/
   weblogs
   ```

2. Copy the weblogs folder from cluster A to cluster B, overwriting any existing files:

   ```
   hadoop distcp -overwrite hdfs://namenodeA/data/weblogs hdfs://
   namenodeB/data/weblogs
   ```

3. Synchronize the weblogs folder between cluster A and cluster B:

   ```
   hadoop distcp -update hdfs://namenodeA/data/weblogs hdfs://
   namenodeB/data/weblogs
   ```

How it works...

On the source cluster, the contents of the folder being copied are treated as a large temporary file. A map-only MapReduce job is created, which will do the copying between clusters. By default, each mapper will be given a 256-MB block of the temporary file. For example, if the weblogs folder was 10 GB in size, 40 mappers would each get roughly 256 MB to copy. `distcp` also has an option to specify the number of mappers.

```
hadoop distcp -m 10 hdfs://namenodeA/data/weblogs hdfs://namenodeB/data/
weblogs
```

In the previous example, 10 mappers would be used. If the weblogs folder was 10 GB in size, then each mapper would be given roughly 1 GB to copy.

There's more...

While copying between two clusters that are running different versions of Hadoop, it is generally recommended to use `HftpFileSystem` as the source. `HftpFileSystem` is a read-only filesystem. The `distcp` command has to be run from the destination server:

```
hadoop distcp hftp://namenodeA:port/data/weblogs hdfs://namenodeB/data/
weblogs
```

In the preceding command, `port` is defined by the `dfs.http.address` property in the `hdfs-site.xml` configuration file.

Importing data from MySQL into HDFS using Sqoop

Sqoop is an Apache project that is part of the broader Hadoop ecosphere. In many ways Sqoop is similar to `distcp` (See the *Moving data efficiently between clusters using Distributed Copy* recipe of this chapter). Both are built on top of MapReduce and take advantage of its parallelism and fault tolerance. Instead of moving data between clusters, Sqoop was designed to move data from and into relational databases using a JDBC driver to connect.

Its functionality is extensive. This recipe will show how to use Sqoop to import data from MySQL to HDFS using the weblog entries as an example.

Getting ready

This example uses Sqoop v1.3.0.

If you are using CDH3, you already have Sqoop installed. If you are not running CDH3, you can find instructions for your distro at `https://ccp.cloudera.com/display/CDHDOC/Sqoop+Installation`.

This recipe assumes that you have a MySQL instance up and running that can reach your Hadoop cluster. The `mysql.user` table is configured to accept a user connecting from the machine where you will be running Sqoop. Visit `http://dev.mysql.com/doc/refman//5.5/en/installing.html` for more information on installing and configuring MySQL.

The MySQL JDBC driver JAR file has been copied to `$SQOOP_HOME/libs`. The driver can be downloaded from `http://dev.mysql.com/downloads/connector/j/`.

How to do it...

Complete the following steps to transfer data from a MySQL table to an HDFS file:

1. Create a new database in the MySQL instance:

   ```
   CREATE DATABASE logs;
   ```

2. Create and load the weblogs table:

   ```
   USE logs;
   CREATE TABLE weblogs(
       md5             VARCHAR(32),
       url             VARCHAR(64),
       request_date    DATE,
       request_time    TIME,
       ip              VARCHAR(15)
   );
   LOAD DATA INFILE '/path/weblog_entries.txt' INTO TABLE weblogs
   FIELDS TERMINATED BY '\t' LINES TERMINATED BY '\r\n';
   ```

3. Select a count of rows from the weblogs table:

```
mysql> select count(*) from weblogs;
```

The output would be:

```
+----------+
| count(*) |
+----------+
|     3000 |
+----------+
1 row in set (0.01 sec)
```

4. Import the data from MySQL to HDFS:

```
sqoop import -m 1 --connect jdbc:mysql://<HOST>:<PORT>/logs
--username hdp_usr --password test1 --table weblogs --target-dir /
data/weblogs/import
```

The output would be:

```
INFO orm.CompilationManager: Writing jar file:
/tmp/sqoop-jon/compile/f57ad8b208643698f3d01954eedb2e4d/weblogs.
jar
```

WARN manager.MySQLManager: It looks like you are importing from mysql.

WARN manager.MySQLManager: This transfer can be faster! Use the --direct

WARN manager.MySQLManager: option to exercise a MySQL-specific fast path.

...

INFO mapred.JobClient: Map input records=3000

INFO mapred.JobClient: Spilled Records=0

INFO mapred.JobClient: Total committed heap usage (bytes)=85000192

INFO mapred.JobClient: Map output records=3000

INFO mapred.JobClient: SPLIT_RAW_BYTES=87

INFO mapreduce.ImportJobBase: Transferred 245.2451 KB in 13.7619 seconds (17.8206 KB/sec)

INFO mapreduce.ImportJobBase: Retrieved 3000 records.

How it works...

Sqoop loads the JDBC driver defined in the `--connect` statement from `$SQOOP_HOME/libs`, where `$SQOOP_HOME` is the full path to the location where Sqoop is installed. The `--username` and `--password` options are used to authenticate the user issuing the command against the MySQL instance. The `mysql.user` table must have an entry for the `--username` option and the host of each node in the Hadoop cluster; or else Sqoop will throw an exception indicating that the host is not allowed to connect to the MySQL Server.

```
mysql> USE mysql;
mysql> select host, user from user;
```

The output would be:

```
+-------------+-------------+
| user        | host        |
+-------------+-------------+
| hdp_usr     | hdp01       |
| hdp_usr     | hdp02       |
| hdp_usr     | hdp03       |
| hdp_usr     | hdp04       |
| root        | 127.0.0.1   |
| root        | ::1         |
| root        | localhost   |
+-------------+-------------+
7 rows in set (1.04 sec)
```

In this example, we connected to the MySQL server using `hdp_usr`. Our cluster has four machines, `hdp01`, `hdp02`, `hdp03`, and `hdp04`.

The `--table` argument tells Sqoop which table to import. In our case, we are looking to import the weblogs table into HDFS. The `--target-dir` argument is passed the folder path in HDFS where the imported table will be stored:

```
hadoop fs -ls /data/weblogs/import
```

The output would be:

```
-rw-r--r--   1   hdp_usr hdp_grp    0      2012-06-08  23:47 /data/
weblogs/import/_SUCCESS
drwxr-xr-x   -   hdp_usr hdp_grp    0      2012-06-08  23:47 /data/
weblogs/import/_logs
-rw-r--r--   1   hdp_usr hdp_grp    251131 2012-06-08  23:47 /data/
weblogs/import/part-m-00000
```

By default, the imported data will be split on the primary key. If the table being imported does not have a primary key, the `-m` or `--split-by` arguments must be used to tell Sqoop how to split the data. In the preceding example, the `-m` argument was used. The `-m` argument controls the number of mappers that are used to import the data. Since `-m` was set to 1, a single mapper was used to import the data. Each mapper used will produce a part file.

This one line hides an incredible amount of complexity. Sqoop uses the metadata stored by the database to generate the `DBWritable` classes for each column. These classes are used by `DBInputFormat`, a Hadoop input format with the ability to read the results of arbitrary queries run against a database. In the preceding example, a MapReduce job is started using the `DBInputFormat` class to retrieve the contents from the weblogs table. The entire weblogs table is scanned and stored in `/data/weblogs/import`.

There's more...

There are many useful options for configuring how Sqoop imports data. Sqoop can import data as Avro or Sequence files using the `--as-avrodatafile` and `--as-sequencefile` arguments respectively. The data can be compressed while being imported as well using the `-z` or `--compress` arguments. The default codec is GZIP, but any Hadoop compression codec can be used by supplying the `--compression-codec <CODEC>` argument. See the *Compressing data using LZO* recipe in *Chapter 2, HDFS*. Another useful option is `--direct`. This argument instructs Sqoop to use native import/export tools if they are supported by the configured database. In the preceding example, if `--direct` was added as an argument, Sqoop would use `mysqldump` for fast exporting of the weblogs table. The `--direct` argument is so important that in the preceding example, a warning message was logged as follows:

```
WARN manager.MySQLManager: It looks like you are importing from mysql.
WARN manager.MySQLManager: This transfer can be faster! Use the --direct
WARN manager.MySQLManager: option to exercise a MySQL-specific fast path.
```

See also

- ▶ *Exporting data from HDFS into MySQL using Sqoop*

Exporting data from HDFS into MySQL using Sqoop

Sqoop is an Apache project that is part of the broader Hadoop ecosphere. In many ways Sqoop is similar to `distcp` (See the *Moving data efficiently between clusters using Distributed Copy* recipe of this chapter). Both are built on top of MapReduce and take advantage of its parallelism and fault tolerance. Instead of moving data between clusters, Sqoop was designed to move data from and into relational databases using a JDBC driver to connect.

Its functionality is extensive. This recipe will show how to use Sqoop to export data from HDFS to MySQL using the weblog entries as an example.

Getting ready

This example uses Sqoop v1.3.0.

If you are using CDH3, you already have Sqoop installed. If you are not running CDH3 you can find instructions for your distro at `https://ccp.cloudera.com/display/CDHDOC/Sqoop+Installation`.

This recipe assumes that you have a MySQL instance up and running that can reach your Hadoop cluster. The `mysql.user` table is configured to accept a user connecting from the machine where you will be running Sqoop. Visit `http://dev.mysql.com/doc/refman/5.5/en/installing.html` for more information on installing and configuring MySQL.

The MySQL JDBC driver JAR file has been copied to `$SQOOP_HOME/libs`. The driver can be downloaded from `http://dev.mysql.com/downloads/connector/j/`.

Follow the *Importing and exporting data into HDFS using the Hadoop shell commands* recipe of this chapter to load the `weblog_entires.txt` file into HDFS.

How to do it...

Complete the following steps to transfer data from HDFS to a MySQL table:

1. Create a new database in the MySQL instance:

    ```
    CREATE DATABASE logs;
    ```

2. Create the `weblogs_from_hdfs` table:

```
USE logs;
CREATE TABLE weblogs_from_hdfs (
        md5                 VARCHAR(32),
        url                 VARCHAR(64),
        request_date        DATE,
        request_time        TIME,
        ip                  VARCHAR(15)
);
```

3. Export the `weblog_entries.txt` file from HDFS to MySQL:

```
sqoop export -m 1 --connect jdbc:mysql://<HOST>:<PORT>/logs
--username hdp_usr --password test1 --table weblogs_from_hdfs
--export-dir /data/weblogs/05102012 --input-fields-terminated-by
'\t' --mysql-delmiters
```

The output is as follows:

```
INFO mapreduce.ExportJobBase: Beginning export of weblogs_from_
hdfs

input.FileInputFormat: Total input paths to process : 1

input.FileInputFormat: Total input paths to process : 1

mapred.JobClient: Running job: job_201206222224_9010

INFO mapred.JobClient:    Map-Reduce Framework

INFO mapred.JobClient:     Map input records=3000

INFO mapred.JobClient:     Spilled Records=0

INFO mapred.JobClient:     Total committed heap usage
(bytes)=85000192

INFO mapred.JobClient:     Map output records=3000

INFO mapred.JobClient:     SPLIT_RAW_BYTES=133

INFO mapreduce.ExportJobBase: Transferred 248.3086 KB in 12.2398
seconds (20.287 KB/sec)

INFO mapreduce.ExportJobBase: Exported 3000 records.
```

How it works...

Sqoop loads the JDBC driver defined in the `--connect` statement from `$SQOOP_HOME/libs`, where `$SQOOP_HOME` is the full path to the location where Sqoop is installed. The `--username` and `--password` options are used to authenticate the user issuing the command against the MySQL instance. The `mysql.user` table must have an entry for the `--username` and the host of each node in the Hadoop cluster; or else Sqoop will throw an exception indicating that the host is not allowed to connect to the MySQL Server.

```
mysql> USE mysql;
mysql> select host, user from user;

+----------------+-----------+
| user           | host      |
+----------------+-----------+
| hdp_usr        | hdp01     |
| hdp_usr        | hdp02     |
| hdp_usr        | hdp03     |
| hdp_usr        | hdp04     |
| root           | 127.0.0.1 |
| root           | ::1       |
| root           | localhost |
+----------------+-----------+
7 rows in set (1.04 sec)
```

In this example, we connected to the MySQL server using `hdp_usr`. Our cluster has four machines, `hdp01`, `hdp02`, `hdp03`, and `hdp04`.

The `--table` argument identifies the MySQL table that will receive the data from HDFS. This table must be created before running the Sqoop `export` command. Sqoop uses the metadata of the table, the number of columns, and their types, to validate the data coming from the HDFS folder and to create `INSERT` statements. For example, the export job can be thought of as reading each line of the `weblogs_entries.txt` file in HDFS and producing the following output:

```
INSERT INTO weblogs_from_hdfs
VALUES('aabba15edcd0c8042a14bf216c5', '/jcwbtvnkkujo.html', '2012-05-
10', '21:25:44', '148.113.13.214');

INSERT INTO weblogs_from_hdfs
VALUES('e7d3f242f111c1b522137481d8508ab7', '/ckyhatbpxu.html', '2012-
05-10', '21:11:20', '4.175.198.160');
```

```
INSERT INTO weblogs_from_hdfs
VALUES('b8bd62a5c4ede37b9e77893e043fc1', '/rr.html', '2012-05-10',
'21:32:08', '24.146.153.181');
...
```

By default, Sqoop `export` creates `INSERT` statements. If the `--update-key` argument is specified, `UPDATE` statements will be created instead. If the preceding example had used the argument `--update-key md5`, the generated code would have run like the following:

```
UPDATE weblogs_from_hdfs SET url='/jcwbtvnkkujo.html', request_
date='2012-05-10'request_time='21:25:44'
ip='148.113.13.214'WHERE md5='aabba15edcd0c8042a14bf216c5'

UPDATE weblogs_from_hdfs SET url='/jcwbtvnkkujo.html', request_
date='2012-05-10'request_time='21:11:20' ip='4.175.198.160' WHERE
md5='e7d3f242f111c1b522137481d8508ab7'

UPDATE weblogs_from_hdfs SET url='/jcwbtvnkkujo.html', request_
date='2012-05-10'request_time='21:32:08' ip='24.146.153.181' WHERE
md5='b8bd62a5c4ede37b9e77893e043fc1'
```

In the case where the `--update-key` value is not found, setting the `--update-mode` to `allowinsert` will insert the row.

The `-m` argument sets the number of map jobs reading the file splits from HDFS. Each mapper will have its own connection to the MySQL Server. It will insert up to 100 records per statement. After it has completed 100 `INSERT` statements, that is 10,000 records in total, it will commit the current transaction. It is possible that a map task failure could cause data inconsistency resulting in possible insert collisions or duplicated data. These issues can be overcome with the use of the `--staging-table` argument. This will cause the job to insert into a staging table, and then in one transaction, move the data from the staging table to the table specified by the `--table` argument. The `--staging-table` argument must have the same format as `--table`. The `--staging-table` argument must be empty, or else the `--clear-staging-table` argument must be used.

See also

▶ *Importing data from MySQL into HDFS using Sqoop*

Configuring Sqoop for Microsoft SQL Server

This recipe shows how to configure Sqoop to connect with Microsoft SQL Server databases. This will allow data to be efficiently loaded from a Microsoft SQL Server database into HDFS.

Getting ready

This example uses Sqoop v1.3.0.

If you are using CDH3, you already have Sqoop installed. If you are not running CDH3, you can find instructions for your distro at `https://ccp.cloudera.com/display/CDHDOC/Sqoop+Installation`.

This recipe assumes that you have an instance of SQL Server up and running that can connect to your Hadoop cluster.

How to do it...

Complete the following steps to configure Sqoop to connect with Microsoft SQL Server:

1. Download the Microsoft SQL Server JDBC Driver 3.0 from the following site `http://download.microsoft.com/download/D/6/A/D6A241AC-433E-4CD2-A1CE-50177E8428F0/1033/sqljdbc_3.0.1301.101_enu.tar.gz`.

    This download contains the SQL Server JDBC driver (`sqljdbc4.jar`). Sqoop connects to relational databases using JDBC drivers.

2. Uncompress and extract the TAR file:

    ```
    gzip -d sqljdbc_3.0.1301.101_enu.tar.gz
    tar -xvf sqljdbc_3.0.1301.101_enu.tar
    ```

    This will result in a new folder being created, `sqljdbc_3.0`.

3. Copy `sqljdbc4.jar` to `$SQOOP_HOME/lib`:

    ```
    cp sqljdbc_3.0/enu/sqljdbc4.jar $SQOOP_HOME/lib
    ```

    Sqoop now has access to the `sqljdbc4.jar` file and will be able to use it to connect to a SQL Server instance.

4. Download the Microsoft SQL Server Connector for Apache Hadoop from the site `http://download.microsoft.com/download/B/E/5/BE5EC4FD-9EDA-4C3F-8B36-1C8AC4CE2CEF/sqoop-sqlserver-1.0.tar.gz`.

5. Uncompress and extract the TAR file:

```
gzip -d sqoop-sqlserver-1.0.tar.gz

tar -xvf sqoop-sqlserver-1.0.tar
```

   This will result in a new folder being created, `sqoop-sqlserver-1.0`.

6. Set the `MSSQL_CONNECTOR_HOME` environment variable:

```
export MSSQL_CONNECTOR_HOME=/path/to/sqoop-sqlserver-1.0
```

7. Run the installation script:

```
./install.sh
```

8. For importing and exporting data, see the *Importing data from MySQL into HDFS using Sqoop* and *Exporting data from HDFS into MySQL using Sqoop* recipes of this chapter. These recipes apply to SQL Server as well. The `--connect` argument must be changed to `--connect jdbc:sqlserver://<HOST>:<PORT>`.

How it works...

Sqoop communicates with databases using JDBC. After adding the `sqljdbc4.jar` file to the `$SQOOP_HOME/lib` folder, Sqoop will be able to connect to SQL Server instances using `--connect jdbc:sqlserver://<HOST>:<PORT>`. In order for SQL Server to have full compatibility with Sqoop, some configuration changes are necessary. The configurations are updated by running the `install.sh` script.

Exporting data from HDFS into MongoDB

This recipe will use the `MongoOutputFormat` class to load data from an HDFS instance into a MongoDB collection.

Getting ready

The easiest way to get started with the Mongo Hadoop Adaptor is to clone the Mongo-Hadoop project from GitHub and build the project configured for a specific version of Hadoop. A Git client must be installed to clone this project.

This recipe assumes that you are using the CDH3 distribution of Hadoop.

The official Git Client can be found at `http://git-scm.com/downloads`.

GitHub for Windows can be found at `http://windows.github.com/`.

GitHub for Mac can be found at `http://mac.github.com/`.

The Mongo Hadoop Adaptor can be found on GitHub at `https://github.com/mongodb/mongo-hadoop`. This project needs to be built for a specific version of Hadoop. The resulting JAR file must be installed on each node in the `$HADOOP_HOME/lib` folder.

The Mongo Java Driver is required to be installed on each node in the `$HADOOP_HOME/lib` folder. It can be found at `https://github.com/mongodb/mongo-java-driver/downloads`.

How to do it...

Complete the following steps to copy data form HDFS into MongoDB:

1. Clone the `mongo-hadoop` repository with the following command line:

   ```
   git clone https://github.com/mongodb/mongo-hadoop.git
   ```

2. Switch to the stable release 1.0 branch:

   ```
   git checkout release-1.0
   ```

3. Set the Hadoop version which `mongo-hadoop` should target. In the folder that `mongo-hadoop` was cloned to, open the `build.sbt` file with a text editor. Change the following line:

   ```
   hadoopRelease in ThisBuild := "default"
   ```

   to

   ```
   hadoopRelease in ThisBuild := "cdh3"
   ```

4. Build `mongo-hadoop`:

   ```
   ./sbt package
   ```

   This will create a file named `mongo-hadoop-core_cdh3u3-1.0.0.jar` in the `core/target` folder.

5. Download the MongoDB Java Driver Version 2.8.0 from `https://github.com/mongodb/mongo-java-driver/downloads`.

6. Copy `mongo-hadoop` and the MongoDB Java Driver to `$HADOOP_HOME/lib` on each node:

   ```
   cp mongo-hadoop-core_cdh3u3-1.0.0.jar mongo-2.8.0.jar $HADOOP_HOME/lib
   ```

7. Create a Java MapReduce program that will read the `weblog_entries.txt` file from HDFS and write them to MongoDB using the `MongoOutputFormat` class:

```java
import java.io.*;

import org.apache.commons.logging.*;
import org.apache.hadoop.conf.*;
import org.apache.hadoop.fs.Path;
import org.apache.hadoop.io.*;
import org.apache.hadoop.mapreduce.lib.input.FileInputFormat;
import org.apache.hadoop.mapreduce.lib.input.TextInputFormat;
import org.apache.hadoop.mapreduce.*;
import org.bson.*;
import org.bson.types.ObjectId;


import com.mongodb.hadoop.*;
import com.mongodb.hadoop.util.*;

public class ExportToMongoDBFromHDFS {

    private static final Log log =
LogFactory.getLog(ExportToMongoDBFromHDFS.class);

    public static class ReadWeblogs extends Mapper<LongWritable,
Text, ObjectId, BSONObject>{

        public void map(Text key, Text value, Context context)
throws IOException, InterruptedException{

            System.out.println("Key: " + key);
            System.out.println("Value: " + value);

            String[] fields = value.toString().split("\t");

            String md5 = fields[0];
            String url = fields[1];
            String date = fields[2];
            String time = fields[3];
            String ip = fields[4];

            BSONObject b = new BasicBSONObject();
            b.put("md5", md5);
            b.put("url", url);
            b.put("date", date);
```

```
            b.put("time", time);
            b.put("ip", ip);

            context.write( new ObjectId(), b);
    }
    }

    public static void main(String[] args) throws Exception{

        final Configuration conf = new Configuration();
MongoConfigUtil.setOutputURI(conf,"mongodb://<HOST>:<PORT>/test.
weblogs");

        System.out.println("Configuration: " + conf);

        final Job job = new Job(conf, "Export to Mongo");

        Path in = new Path("/data/weblogs/weblog_entries.txt");
        FileInputFormat.setInputPaths(job, in);

        job.setJarByClass(ExportToMongoDBFromHDFS.class);
        job.setMapperClass(ReadWeblogs.class);

        job.setOutputKeyClass(ObjectId.class);
        job.setOutputValueClass(BSONObject.class);

        job.setInputFormatClass(TextInputFormat.class);
        job.setOutputFormatClass(MongoOutputFormat.class);

        job.setNumReduceTasks(0);

        System.exit(job.waitForCompletion(true) ? 0 : 1 );

    }

}
```

8. Export as a runnable JAR file and run the job:

```
hadoop jar ExportToMongoDBFromHDFS.jar
```

9. Verify that the weblogs MongoDB collection was populated from the Mongo shell:

```
db.weblogs.find();
```

How it works...

The Mongo Hadoop Adaptor provides a new Hadoop compatible filesystem implementation, `MongoInputFormat`, and `MongoOutputFormat`. These abstractions make working with MongoDB similar to working with any Hadoop compatible filesystem.

Importing data from MongoDB into HDFS

This recipe will use the `MongoInputFormat` class to load data from a MongoDB collection into HDFS.

Getting ready

The easiest way to get started with the Mongo Hadoop Adaptor is to clone the `mongo-hadoop` project from GitHub and build the project configured for a specific version of Hadoop. A Git client must be installed to clone this project.

This recipe assumes that you are using the CDH3 distribution of Hadoop.

The official Git Client can be found at `http://git-scm.com/downloads`.

GitHub for Windows can be found at `http://windows.github.com/`.

GitHub for Mac can be found at `http://mac.github.com/`.

The Mongo Hadoop Adaptor can be found on GitHub at `https://github.com/mongodb/mongo-hadoop`. This project needs to be built for a specific version of Hadoop. The resulting JAR file must be installed on each node in the `$HADOOP_HOME/lib` folder.

The Mongo Java Driver is required to be installed on each node in the `$HADOOP_HOME/lib` folder. It can be found at `https://github.com/mongodb/mongo-java-driver/downloads`.

How to do it...

Complete the following steps to copy data from MongoDB into HDFS:

1. Clone the `mongo-hadoop` repository:

    ```
    git clone https://github.com/mongodb/mongo-hadoop.git
    ```

2. Switch to the stable release 1.0 branch:

    ```
    git checkout release-1.0
    ```

3. Set the Hadoop version which `mongo-hadoop` should target. In the folder that `mongo-hadoop` was cloned to, open the `build.sbt` file with a text editor. Change the following line:

```
hadoopRelease in ThisBuild := "default"
```

to

```
hadoopRelease in ThisBuild := "cdh3"
```

4. Build `mongo-hadoop`:

```
./sbt package
```

This will create a file named `mongo-hadoop-core_cdh3u3-1.0.0.jar` in the `core/target` folder.

5. Download the Mongo Java Driver Version 2.8.0 from `https://github.com/mongodb/mongo-java-driver/downloads`.

6. Copy `mongo-hadoop` and the MongoDB Java Driver to `$HADOOP_HOME/lib` on each node:

```
cp mongo-hadoop-core_cdh3u3-1.0.0.jar mongo-2.8.0.jar $HADOOP_
HOME/lib
```

7. Create a Java MapReduce program that will read the weblogs file from a MongoDB collection and write them to HDFS:

```java
import java.io.*;

import org.apache.commons.logging.*;
import org.apache.hadoop.conf.*;
import org.apache.hadoop.fs.Path;
import org.apache.hadoop.io.*;
import org.apache.hadoop.mapreduce.lib.output.*;
import org.apache.hadoop.mapreduce.*;
import org.bson.*;

import com.mongodb.hadoop.*;
import com.mongodb.hadoop.util.*;

public class ImportWeblogsFromMongo {

    private static final Log log = LogFactory.
getLog(ImportWeblogsFromMongo.class);

    public static class ReadWeblogsFromMongo extends Mapper<Object,
BSONObject, Text, Text>{
```

```java
    public void map(Object key, BSONObject value, Context
context) throws IOException, InterruptedException{

        System.out.println("Key: " + key);
        System.out.println("Value: " + value);

        String md5 = value.get("md5").toString();
        String url = value.get("url").toString();
        String date = value.get("date").toString();
        String time = value.get("time").toString();
        String ip = value.get("ip").toString();
        String output = "\t" + url + "\t" + date + "\t" +
                        time + "\t" + ip;
        context.write( new Text(md5), new Text(output));
    }
}


    public static void main(String[] args) throws Exception{

        final Configuration conf = new Configuration();
        MongoConfigUtil.setInputURI(conf,
"mongodb://<HOST>:<PORT>/test.weblogs");
        MongoConfigUtil.setCreateInputSplits(conf, false);
        System.out.println("Configuration: " + conf);

        final Job job = new Job(conf, "Mongo Import");

        Path out = new Path("/data/weblogs/mongo_import");
        FileOutputFormat.setOutputPath(job, out);
        job.setJarByClass(ImportWeblogsFromMongo.class);
        job.setMapperClass(ReadWeblogsFromMongo.class);
         job.setOutputKeyClass(Text.class);
        job.setOutputValueClass(Text.class);

        job.setInputFormatClass(MongoInputFormat.class);
        job.setOutputFormatClass(TextOutputFormat.class);

        job.setNumReduceTasks(0);

        System.exit(job.waitForCompletion(true) ? 0 : 1 );

    }

}
```

This map-only job uses several classes provided by the Mongo Hadoop Adaptor. Data that is read in from HDFS is converted to a `BSONObject`. This class represents a binary format `JSON` value. MongoDB uses these `BSON` objects to efficiently serialize, transfer, and store data. The Mongo Hadoop Adaptor also provides a convenient `MongoConfigUtil` class to help set up the job to connect to MongoDB as if it were a filesystem.

8. Export as runnable JAR file and run the job:

   ```
   hadoop jar ImportWeblogsFromMongo.jar
   ```

9. Verify that the weblogs were imported from MongoDB:

   ```
   hadoop fs -ls /data/weblogs/mongo_import
   ```

How it works...

The Mongo Hadoop Adaptor provides a new Hadoop compatible filesystem implementation, `MongoInputFormat` and `MongoOutputFormat`. These abstractions make working with MongoDB similar to working with any Hadoop compatible filesystem.

Exporting data from HDFS into MongoDB using Pig

MongoDB is a NoSQL database that was designed for storing and retrieving large amounts of data. MongoDB is often used for user-facing data. This data must be cleaned and formatted before it can be made available. Apache Pig was designed, in part, with this kind of work in mind. The `MongoStorage` class makes it extremely convenient to bulk process the data in HDFS using Pig and then load this data directly into MongoDB. This recipe will use the `MongoStorage` class to store data from HDFS into a MongoDB collection.

Getting ready

The easiest way to get started with the Mongo Hadoop Adaptor is to clone the `mongo-hadoop` project from GitHub and build the project configured for a specific version of Hadoop. A Git client must be installed to clone this project.

This recipe assumes that you are using the CDH3 distribution of Hadoop.

The official Git Client can be found at `http://git-scm.com/downloads`.

GitHub for Windows can be found at `http://windows.github.com/`.

GitHub for Mac can be found at `http://mac.github.com/`.

The Mongo Hadoop Adaptor can be found on GitHub at `https://github.com/mongodb/mongo-hadoop`. This project needs to be built for a specific version of Hadoop. The resulting JAR file must be installed on each node in the `$HADOOP_HOME/lib` folder.

The Mongo Java Driver is required to be installed on each node in the `$HADOOP_HOME/lib` folder. It can be found at `https://github.com/mongodb/mongo-java-driver/downloads`.

How to do it...

Complete the following steps to copy data from HDFS to MongoDB:

1. Clone the `mongo-hadoop` repository:

   ```
   git clone https://github.com/mongodb/mongo-hadoop.git
   ```

2. Switch to the stable release 1.0 branch:

   ```
   git checkout release-1.0
   ```

3. Set the Hadoop version which `mongo-hadoop` should target. In the folder that `mongo-hadoop` was cloned to, open the `build.sbt` file with a text editor. Change the following line:

   ```
   hadoopRelease in ThisBuild := "default"
   ```

   to

   ```
   hadoopRelease in ThisBuild := "cdh3"
   ```

4. Build `mongo-hadoop`:

   ```
   ./sbt package
   ```

   This will create a file named `mongo-hadoop-core_cdh3u3-1.0.0.jar` in the `core/target` folder. It will also create a file named `mongo-hadoop-pig_cdh3u3-1.0.0.jar` in the `pig/target` folder.

5. Download the Mongo Java Driver Version 2.8.0 from: `https://github.com/mongodb/mongo-java-driver/downloads`.

6. Copy `mongo-hadoop-core`, `mongo-hadoop-pig`, and the MongoDB Java Driver to `$HADOOP_HOME/lib` on each node:

   ```
   cp mongo-hadoop-core_cdh3u3-1.0.0.jar mongo-2.8.0.jar $HADOOP_HOME/lib
   ```

7. Create a Pig script that will read the weblogs from HDFS and store them into a MongoDB Collection:

```
register /path/to/mongo-hadoop/mongo-2.8.0.jar

register /path/to/mongo-hadoop/core/target/mongo-hadoop-core-
1.0.0.jar

register /path/to/mongo-hadoop/pig/target/mongo-hadoop-pig-
1.0.0.jar


define MongoStorage com.mongodb.hadoop.pig.MongoStorage();


weblogs = load '/data/weblogs/weblog_entries.txt' as
              (md5:chararray, url:chararry, date:chararray,
time:chararray, ip:chararray);


store weblogs into 'mongodb://<HOST>:<PORT>/test.weblogs_from_pig'
using MongoStorage();
```

How it works...

The Mongo Hadoop Adaptor provides a new Hadoop compatible filesystem implementation, `MongoInputFormat` and `MongoOutputFormat`. These abstractions make working with MongoDB similar to working with any Hadoop compatible filesystem. `MongoStorage` converts Pig types to the `BasicDBObjectBuilder` object type, which is used by MongoDB.

Using HDFS in a Greenplum external table

Greenplum is a parallel database that distributes data and queries to one or more PostgreSQL instances. It complements Hadoop by providing real-time or near real-time access to large amounts of data. It supports using HDFS files as external tables. External tables are a good solution for working with data that lives outside of the Greenplum cluster. Since data in external tables must first travel over the network, they should be infrequently used in queries with other data that lives inside of the Greenplum cluster. This recipe will cover creating read-only and read/write external tables.

Getting ready

This recipe assumes that you are using the CDH3 distribution of Hadoop.

Run an instance of Greenplum that must be able to reach the Hadoop cluster found at `http://www.greenplum.com/products/greenplum-database`.

Configure Greenplum with the following:

- ▸ `gp_hadoop_target_version` set to `cdh3u2`
- ▸ `gp_hadoop_home` set to the full path of `$HADOOP_HOME`

Java 1.6 or above must be installed on each node in the Greenplum cluster.

How to do it...

Create an external table from the weblogs file in HDFS:

```
CREATE EXTERNAL TABLE weblogs(
    md5             text,
    url             text,
    request_date    date,
    request_time    time,
    ip              inet
)
LOCATION ('gphdfs://<NAMENODE_HOST>:<NAMENODE_PORT>/data/weblogs/
weblog_entries.txt')
FORMAT 'TEXT' (DELIMITER '\t');
```

How it works...

Greenplum has native support for loading data from HDFS in parallel. When a query is run against the `weblog_entries.txt` table, the `weblog_entries.txt` file is loaded into a temporary Greenplum table. The query then executes against this table. After the query finishes the table is discarded.

There's more...

Greenplum external tables also support writing of data. This requires the `WRITABLE` keyword while creating the table:

```
CREATE WRITABLE EXTERNAL TABLE weblogs(
    md5             text,
    url             text,
    request_date    date,
    request_time    time,
    ip              inet
)
LOCATION ('gphdfs://<NAMENODE_HOST>:<NAMENODE_PORT>/data/weblogs/
weblog_entries.txt')
FORMAT 'TEXT' (DELIMITER '\t');
```

More information can be found in the Greenplum administrator's handbook at `http://media.gpadmin.me/wp-content/uploads/2011/05/GP-4100-AdminGuide.pdf`

Using Flume to load data into HDFS

Apache Flume is a project in the Hadoop community, consisting of related projects designed to efficiently and reliably load streaming data from many different sources into HDFS. A common use case for Flume is loading the weblog data from several sources into HDFS. This recipe will cover loading the weblog entries into HDFS using Flume.

Getting ready

This recipe assumes that you have Flume installed and configured.

Flume can be downloaded from its Apache page at `http://incubator.apache.org/flume/`.

If you are using CDH3, Flume Version 0.9.4+25.43 is installed by default.

How to do it...

Complete the following steps to load the weblogs data into HDFS:

1. Use the `dump` command to test that Flume is configured properly:

    ```
    flume dump 'text("/path/to/weblog_entries.txt")'
    ```

2. Use the Flume shell to execute a configuration:

    ```
    flume shell -c<MASTER_HOST>:<MASTER_PORT> -e 'exec config text("/
    path/to/weblog_entries.txt") | collectorSink("hdfs://<NAMENODE_
    HOST>:<NAMENODE_PORT>/data/weblogs/flume")'
    ```

How it works...

Flume uses **Sources** and **Sinks** abstractions and a pipe-like data flow to link them together. In the example, `text` is a source which takes a path to a file as an argument and sends the contents of that file to the configured sink. The `dump` command uses the console as a sink. With this configuration the `weblog_entries.txt` file is read by `text` and written to the console.

In step 2, the Flume shell is used to configure and execute a job. The `-c` argument tells Flume where to connect to the Flume Master node. Flume will execute the command after the `-e` argument. As mentioned previously, `text` is a source which reads all of the contents of the file it is passed. `collectorSink` is a sink which can be passed a local filesystem path or a path in HDFS. In the preceding example, a HDFS path is given. The result of this command will be to load the `weblog_entries.txt` into HDFS.

There's more...

Flume comes with several predefined Sources and Sinks. A few of the many basic Sources include:

- ▶ `null`: This opens, closes, and returns null
- ▶ `stdin`: This reads from stdin
- ▶ `rpcSource`: This reads either Thrift or Avro RPC
- ▶ `text`: This reads the contents of a file
- ▶ `tail`: This reads a file and stays open, reading data that is appended to the file

A few of the many basic Sinks include:

- ▶ `null`: This drops the events
- ▶ `collectorSink`: This writes to the local filesystem or HDFS
- ▶ `console`: This writes to the console
- ▶ `formatDfs`: This writes to HDFS in a specified format Sequence File, Avro, Thrift, and so on
- ▶ `rpcSink`: This writes either Thrift or Avro RPC

2
HDFS

In this chapter we will cover:

- ▸ Reading and writing data to HDFS
- ▸ Compressing data using LZO
- ▸ Reading and writing data to SequenceFiles
- ▸ Using Apache Avro to serialize data
- ▸ Using Apache Thrift to serialize data
- ▸ Using Protocol Buffers to serialize data
- ▸ Setting the replication factor for HDFS
- ▸ Setting the block size for HDFS

Introduction

Hadoop Distributed File System (**HDFS**) is a fault-tolerant distributed filesystem designed to run on "off-the-shelf" hardware. It has been optimized for streaming reads on large files whereas I/O throughput is favored over low latency. In addition, HDFS uses a simple model for data consistency where files can only be written to once.

HDFS assumes disk failure as an eventuality and uses a concept called **block replication** to replicate data across nodes in the cluster. HDFS uses a much larger block size when compared to desktop filesystems. For example, the default block size for HDFS is 64 MB. Once a file has been placed into HDFS, the file is divided into one or more data blocks and is distributed to nodes in the cluster. In addition, copies of the data blocks are made, which again are distributed to nodes in the cluster to ensure high data availability in case of a disk failure. The number of copies HDFS makes of each data block is determined by the **replication factor** setting. The default replication factor is 3, meaning three replicas of a data block will be distributed across the nodes in the cluster.

Finally, applications using HDFS can achieve high throughput because the Hadoop framework was designed to move computation to the data. In other words, applications can run on the nodes where the data resides instead of moving the data to the application. This concept is known as **data locality**.

HDFS consists of three services:

HDFS Application	Purpose
NameNode	This maintains a catalog of all block locations in the cluster
Secondary NameNode	This periodically synchronizes with the NameNode block index. During the synchronizing process, the Secondary NameNode retrieves the current NameNode image and edit logs, merges them together, and then sends the merged image back to the NameNode. The Secondary NameNode is not a "hot" backup of the NameNode. It cannot be used in the event of a NameNode failure.
DataNode	This manages the data blocks it receives from the NameNode. It is unaware of any other DataNodes in the cluster and only communicates with the NameNode.

This chapter will use the FileSystem API, MapReduce, and advanced serialization libraries to efficiently write and store data in HDFS.

 Version 0.20.x does not support append operations

Reading and writing data to HDFS

There are many ways to read data from and write data to HDFS. We will start by using the FileSystem API to create and write to a file in HDFS, followed by an application to read a file from HDFS and write it back to the local filesystem.

Getting ready

You will need to download the `weblog_entries.txt` dataset from the Packt website, `http://www.packtpub.com/support`.

How to do it...

Carry out the following steps to read and write data to HDFS:

1. Once you have downloaded the test dataset, we can write an application to read a file from the local filesystem and write the contents to HDFS.

```
public class HdfsWriter extends Configured implements Tool {

    public int run(String[] args) throws Exception {

        String localInputPath = args[0];
        Path outputPath = new Path(args[1]);
        Configuration conf = getConf();
        FileSystem fs = FileSystem.get(conf);
        OutputStream os = fs.create(outputPath);
        InputStream is = new BufferedInputStream(
            new FileInputStream(localInputPath));
        IOUtils.copyBytes(is, os, conf);
        return 0;
    }

    public static void main(String[] args) throws Exception {
        int returnCode = ToolRunner.run(
            new HdfsWriter(), args);
        System.exit(returnCode);
    }
}
```

2. Next, we write an application to read the file we just created in HDFS and write its contents back to the local filesystem.

```
public class HdfsReader extends Configured implements Tool {

    public int run(String[] args) throws Exception {

        Path inputPath = new Path(args[0]);
        String localOutputPath = args[1];
        Configuration conf = getConf();
        FileSystem fs = FileSystem.get(conf);
        InputStream is = fs.open(inputPath);
        OutputStream os = new BufferedOutputStream(
            new FileOutputStream(localOutputPath));
        IOUtils.copyBytes(is, os, conf);
        return 0;
    }

    public static void main(String[] args) throws Exception {
        int returnCode = ToolRunner.run(
            new HdfsReader(), args);
        System.exit(returnCode);
    }
}
```

How it works...

`FileSystem` is an abstract class that represents a generic filesystem. Most Hadoop filesystem implementations can be accessed and manipulated through the `FileSystem` object. To create an instance of the Hadoop Distributed File System, you call the method `FileSystem.get()`. The `FileSystem.get()` method will look at the URI assigned to the `fs.default.name` parameter of the Hadoop configuration files on your classpath and choose the correct implementation of the `FileSystem` class to instantiate. The `fs.default.name` parameter of HDFS has the value `hdfs://`.

Once an instance of the `FileSystem` class has been created, the `HdfsWriter` class calls the `create()` method to create a file (or overwrite if it already exists) in HDFS. The `create()` method returns an `OutputStream` object, which can be manipulated using normal Java I/O methods. Similarly, `HdfsReader` calls the method `open()` to open a file in HDFS, which returns an `InputStream` object that can be used to read the contents of the file.

There's more...

The `FileSystem` API is extensive. To demonstrate some of the other methods available in the API, we can add some error checking to the `HdfsWriter` and `HdfsReader` classes we created.

To check whether the file exists before we call `create()`, use:

```
boolean exists = fs.exists(inputPath);
```

To check whether the path is a file, use:

```
boolean isFile = fs.isFile(inputPath);
```

To rename a file that already exists, use:

```
boolean renamed = fs.rename(inputPath, new Path("old_file.txt"));
```

Compressing data using LZO

Hadoop supports a number of compression algorithms, including:

- bzip2
- gzip
- DEFLATE

Hadoop provides Java implementations of these algorithms, and therefore, files can be easily compressed/decompressed using the `FileSystem` API or MapReduce input and output formats.

However, there is a drawback to storing data in HDFS using the compression formats listed previously. These formats are not *splittable*. Meaning, once a file is compressed using any of the codecs that Hadoop provides, the file cannot be decompressed without the whole file being read.

To understand why this is a drawback, you must first understand how Hadoop MapReduce determines the number of mappers to launch for a given task. The number of mappers launched is roughly equal to the input size divided by `dfs.block.size` (the default block size is 64 MB). The blocks of work that each mapper will receive are called **input splits**. For example, if the input to a MapReduce job was an uncompressed file that was 128 MB, this would probably result in two mappers being launched (128 MB/64 MB).

Since files compressed using the bzip2, gzip, and DEFLATE codecs cannot be split, the whole file must be given as a single input split to the mapper. Using the previous example, if the input to a MapReduce job was a gzip compressed file that was 128 MB, the MapReduce framework would only launch one mapper.

Now, where does LZO fit in to all of this? Well, the LZO algorithm was designed to have fast decompression speeds while having a similar compression speed as compared to DEFLATE. In addition, thanks to the hard work of the Hadoop community, LZO compressed files are splittable.

 bzip2 is splittable as of Hadoop Version 0.21.0; however, the algorithm does have some performance limitations and should be investigated thoroughly before being used in a production environment.

Getting ready

You will need to download the LZO codec implementation for Hadoop from `https://github.com/kevinweil/hadoop-lzo`.

How to do it...

Perform the following steps to set up LZO and then compress and index a text file:

1. First, install the `lzo` and `lzo-devel` packages.

   On Red Hat Linux, use:

   ```
   # yum install liblzo-devel
   ```

   On Ubuntu, use:

   ```
   # apt-get install liblzo2-devel
   ```

2. Navigate to the directory where you extracted the `hadoop-lzo` source, and build the project.

```
# cd kevinweil-hadoop-lzo-6bb1b7f/
# export JAVA_HOME=/path/to/jdk/ # ./setup.sh
```

3. If the build was successful, you should see:

```
BUILD SUCCESSFUL
```

4. Copy the build JAR files to the Hadoop `lib` folder on your cluster.

```
# cp build/hadoop-lzo*.jar /path/to/hadoop/lib/
```

5. Copy the native libraries to the Hadoop native `lib` folder on your cluster.

```
# tar -cBf - -C build/hadoop-lzo-0.4.15/lib/native/ . | tar -xBvf
- -C /path/to/hadoop/lib/native
```

6. Next, update `core-site.xml` to use the LZO codec classes.

```
<property>
<name>io.compression.codecs</name>
<value>org.apache.hadoop.io.compress.GzipCodec,
          org.apache.hadoop.io.compress.DefaultCodec,
org.apache.hadoop.io.compress.BZip2Codec,
com.hadoop.compression.lzo.LzoCodec,
com.hadoop.compression.lzo.LzopCodec
   </value>
</property>
<property>
   <name>io.compression.codec.lzo.class</name>
   <value>com.hadoop.compression.lzo.LzoCodec</value>
</property>
```

7. Finally, update the following environment variables in your `hadoop-env.sh` script:

```
export HADOOP_CLASSPATH=/path/to/hadoop/lib/hadoop-lzo-X.X.XX.jar
```

```
export JAVA_LIBRARY_PATH=/path/to/hadoop/lib/native/hadoop-lzo-
native-lib:/path/to/hadoop/lib/native/other-native-libs
```

Now test the installation of the LZO library.

8. Compress the test dataset:

```
$ lzop weblog_entries.txt
```

9. Put the compressed `weblog_entries.txt.lzo` file into HDFS:

   ```
   $ hadoop fs -put weblog_entries.txt.lzo /test/weblog_entries.txt.
   lzo
   ```

10. Run the MapReduce LZO indexer to index the `weblog_entries.txt.lzo` file:

    ```
    $ hadoop jar /usr/lib/hadoop/lib/hadoop-lzo-0.4.15.jar com.hadoop.
    compression.lzo.DistributedLzoIndexer /test/weblog_entries.txt.lzo
    ```

You should now see two files in the `/test` folder

```
$ hadoop fs -ls /test
$ /test/weblog_entries.txt.lzo
$ /test/weblog_entries.txt.lzo.index
```

How it works...

This recipe involved a lot of steps. After we moved the LZO JAR files and native libraries into place, we updated the `io.compression.codecs` property in `core-site.xml`. Both HDFS and Hadoop MapReduce share this configuration file, and the value of the `io.compression.codecs` property will be used to determine which codecs are available to the system.

Finally, we ran `DistributedLzoIndexer`. This is a MapReduce application that will read one or more LZO compressed files and index the LZO block boundaries of each file. Once this application has been run on an LZO file, the LZO file can be split and sent to multiple mappers by using the included input format `LzoTextInputFormat`.

There's more...

In addition to `DistributedLzoIndexer`, the Hadoop LZO library also includes a class named `LzoIndexer`. `LzoIndexer` launches a standalone application to index LZO files in HDFS. To index the `weblog_entries.txt.lzo` in HDFS, run the following command:

```
$ hadoop jar /usr/lib/hadoop/lib/hadoop-lzo-0.4.15.jar com.hadoop.
compression.lzo.LzoIndexer /test/weblog_entries.txt.lzo
```

See also

- ▶ *Using Apache Thrift to serialize data*
- ▶ *Using Protocol Buffers to serialize data*

Reading and writing data to SequenceFiles

The **SequenceFile** format is a flexible format included with the Hadoop distribution. It is capable of storing both text and binary data. SequenceFiles store data as binary key-value pairs. The binary pairs are then grouped together into blocks. This format supports compressing the value portion of a record or an entire block of key-value pairs. SequenceFiles are splittable even when using a compression codec that is not normally splittable, such as `GzipCodec`. SequenceFiles are able to do this because individual values (or blocks) are compressed, not the entire SequenceFile.

This recipe will demonstrate how to write and read to SequenceFiles.

Getting ready

You will need to download the `weblog_entries.txt` dataset from the Packt website, `http://www.packtpub.com/support`. Also, `weblog_entries.txt` should be available in HDFS. You can place the `weblog_entries.txt` file in HDFS using the Hadoop FS shell as follows:

```
$ hadoop fs -put /path/on/local/filesystem/weblog_entries.txt /path/in/
hdfs
```

How to do it...

1. Once you have downloaded the test dataset, we can write an application to read a plain text file from HDFS and write the contents to a SequenceFile in HDFS using MapReduce.

```
public class SequenceWriter extends Configured implements Tool {

    public int run(String[] args) throws Exception {

        Path inputPath = new Path(args[0]);
        Path outputPath = new Path(args[1]);

        Configuration conf = getConf();
        Job weblogJob = new Job(conf);
        weblogJob.setJobName("Sequence File Writer");
        weblogJob.setJarByClass(getClass());
        weblogJob.setNumReduceTasks(0);
        weblogJob.setMapperClass(IdentityMapper.class);
        weblogJob.setMapOutputKeyClass(LongWritable.class);
        weblogJob.setMapOutputValueClass(Text.class);
        weblogJob.setOutputKeyClass(LongWritable.class);
        weblogJob.setOutputValueClass(Text.class);
```

```
        weblogJob.setInputFormatClass(TextInputFormat.class);
        weblogJob.setOutputFormatClass(
    SequenceFileOutputFormat.class);

        FileInputFormat.setInputPaths(weblogJob, inputPath);
        SequenceFileOutputFormat.setOutputPath(
    weblogJob, outputPath);


        if(weblogJob.waitForCompletion(true)) {
            return 0;
        }
        return 1;
    }

    public static void main(String[] args) throws Exception {
        int returnCode = ToolRunner.run(
    new SequenceWriter(), args);
        System.exit(returnCode);
    }
}
```

2. Now, use the MapReduce job to read a SequenceFile from HDFS and transform it back to normal text:

```
public class SequenceReader extends Configured implements Tool {

    public int run(String[] args) throws Exception {

        Path inputPath = new Path(args[0]);
        Path outputPath = new Path(args[1]);

        Configuration conf = getConf();
        Job weblogJob = new Job(conf);
        weblogJob.setJobName("Sequence File Reader");
        weblogJob.setJarByClass(getClass());
        weblogJob.setNumReduceTasks(0);
        weblogJob.setMapperClass(IdentityMapper.class);
        weblogJob.setMapOutputKeyClass(LongWritable.class);
        weblogJob.setMapOutputValueClass(Text.class);
        weblogJob.setOutputKeyClass(LongWritable.class);
        weblogJob.setOutputValueClass(Text.class);
        weblogJob.setInputFormatClass(
    SequenceFileInputFormat.class);
        weblogJob.setOutputFormatClass(
    TextOutputFormat.class);
```

```
          SequenceFileInputFormat.addInputPath(
weblogJob, inputPath);
          FileOutputFormat.setOutputPath(
weblogJob, outputPath);

          if(weblogJob.waitForCompletion(true)) {
              return 0;
          }
          return 1;
     }

     public static void main(String[] args) throws Exception {
          int returnCode = ToolRunner.run(
new SequenceReader(), args);
          System.exit(returnCode);
     }
}
```

How it works...

MapReduce is an efficient way to transform data in HDFS. These two MapReduce jobs are very simple to code and are capable of transforming data using the distributed processing power of the cluster.

First, both MapReduce jobs are "map-only" jobs. This means that Hadoop will launch only mappers to process the test data. This is achieved by setting the number of reducers to 0, as shown in the following line of code:

```
weblogJob.setNumReduceTasks(0);
```

Next, we want the sequence writer job to read text input and save its output as a SequenceFile. To do this, the `SequenceWriter` class sets the input format class to `TextInputFormat.class`, as shown in the following line of code:

```
weblogJob.setInputFormatClass(TextInputFormat.class);
```

And we also set the output format class to `SequenceFileInputFormat.class`, as shown in the following lines of code:

```
weblogJob.setOutputFormatClass(
SequenceFileOutputFormat.class);
```

For the next application, we wanted to read a sequence file and write a normal text file. To do this, we reversed the input and output formats we used for the sequence writer job.

In the sequence reader job, set the input format to read SequenceFiles.

```
weblogJob.setInputFormatClass(
SequenceFileInputFormat.class);
```

Set the output format to plain text.

```
weblogJob.setOutputFormatClass(
TextOutputFormat.class);
```

There's more...

SequenceFiles have three compression options:

- **Uncompressed**: Key-value pairs are stored uncompressed
- **Record compression**: The value emitted from a mapper or reducer is compressed
- **Block compression**: An entire block of key-value pairs is compressed

You can compress SequenceFiles using the following methods when you set up your job:

```
SequenceFileOutputFormat.setOutputCompression(job, true);
```

Next, set the compression option you want to use; the following code sets the record compression option:

```
SequenceFileOutputFormat.setOutputCompressionType(weblogJob,
SequenceFile.CompressionType.RECORD);
```

Or set the block compression option:

```
SequenceFileOutputFormat.setOutputCompressionType(weblogJob,
SequenceFile.CompressionType.BLOCK);
```

Finally, choose a compression codec class, for example gzip:

```
SequenceFileOutputFormat.setOutputCompressorClass(weblogJob,
GzipCodec.class);
```

See also

In the following recipes, we will continue to explore different data serialization libraries and formats:

- *Using Apache Avro to serialize data*
- *Using Apache Thrift to serialize data*
- *Using Protocol Buffers to serialize data*

Using Apache Avro to serialize data

The description from the Apache Avro site defines Avro as a "data serialization system". Apache Avro supports a language-independent file format and includes serialization and RPC mechanisms. One of the neat features of Avro is that you do not need to compile any type of interface or protocol definition files in order to use the serialization features of the framework.

In this recipe, we will use Avro to serialize and write Java objects to a file in HDFS using MapReduce.

Getting ready

You will need to download/compile/install the following:

▶ Version 1.5.4 of the `avro` and the `avro-mapred` JAR files, from `http://avro.apache.org`

▶ The test data file `weblog_entries.txt`, from `http://www.packtpub.com/support`

How to do it...

1. The following is a Java class that represents a row from the `weblog_entries.txt` dataset:

```
public class WeblogRecord {
    private String cookie;
    private String page;
    private Date date;
    private String ip;

    public WeblogRecord() {

    }
    public WeblogRecord(String cookie, String page, Date date,
String ip) {
        this.cookie = cookie;
        this.page = page;
        this.date = date;
        this.ip = ip;
    }
    //getters and setters

    @Override
    public String toString() {
```

```
        return cookie + "\t" + page + "\t" + date.toString() +
"\t" + ip;
    }

}
```

2. This will be a map-only job, like the job that was created to generate and read SequenceFiles. However, instead of using `IdentityMapper`, we will write a mapper that reads a row from `weblog_entries.txt` and creates an instance of `WeblogRecord`.

```
public class WeblogMapper extends MapReduceBase implements
Mapper<LongWritable, Text, AvroWrapper, NullWritable> {

    private AvroWrapper<WeblogRecord> outputRecord = new
AvroWrapper<WeblogRecord>();

    private WeblogRecord weblogRecord = new WeblogRecord();

    SimpleDateFormat dateFormatter = new SimpleDateFormat("yyyy-
MM-dd:HH:mm:ss");

    public void map(LongWritable key, Text value,
OutputCollector<AvroWrapper, NullWritable> oc, Reporter rprtr)
throws IOException {
            String[] tokens = value.toString().split("\t");
            String cookie = tokens[0];
            String page = tokens[1];
            String date = tokens[2];
            String time = tokens[3];
            String formattedDate = date + ":" + time;
            Date timestamp = null;
            try {
                timestamp = dateFormatter.parse(formattedDate);
            } catch(ParseException ex) {
                // ignore records with invalid dates
                return;
            }
            String ip = tokens[4];

            weblogRecord.setCookie(cookie);
            weblogRecord.setDate(timestamp);
            weblogRecord.setIp(ip);
            weblogRecord.setPage(page);
            outputRecord.datum(weblogRecord);
            oc.collect(outputRecord, NullWritable.get());
    }

}
```

3. Now, use the MapReduce job to read a text file, and then serialize and persist the
   WeblogRecord object:

```
public class AvroWriter extends Configured implements Tool {

    public int run(String[] args) throws Exception {

        Path inputPath = new Path(args[0]);
        Path outputPath = new Path(args[1]);

        Schema schema = ReflectData.get().getSchema(WeblogRecord.
class);

        Configuration conf = getConf();
        JobConf weblogJob = new JobConf(conf, getClass());
        weblogJob.setJobName("Avro Writer");
        weblogJob.setNumReduceTasks(0);
        weblogJob.setMapperClass(WeblogMapper.class);
        weblogJob.setMapOutputKeyClass(AvroWrapper.class);
        weblogJob.setMapOutputValueClass(NullWritable.class);
        weblogJob.setInputFormat(TextInputFormat.class);
        AvroJob.setOutputSchema(weblogJob, schema);
        FileInputFormat.setInputPaths(weblogJob, inputPath);
        FileOutputFormat.setOutputPath(weblogJob, outputPath);

        RunningJob job = JobClient.runJob(weblogJob);
        if(job.isSuccessful()) {
            return 0;
        }
        return 1;
    }

    public static void main(String[] args) throws Exception {
        int returnCode = ToolRunner.run(new AvroWriter(), args);
        System.exit(returnCode);
    }
}
```

How it works...

The `AvroWriter` MapReduce job reads a plain text file and serializes the `WeblogRecord`
class into an Avro file. The first step is to set up a MapReduce job to read the text file and
write the output file using the Avro file format.

Set the input format to read a text file:

```
weblogJob.setInputFormat(TextInputFormat.class);
```

Build an Avro schema based on the `WeblogRecord` class, and then set the output schema:

```
Schema schema = ReflectData.get().getSchema(WeblogRecord.class);
AvroJob.setOutputSchema(weblogJob, schema);
```

Next, we use the old Hadoop MapReduce API to write the mapper and emit the `WeblogRecord` object by using the `AvroWrapper` class.

Members emitted of the `WeblogMapper` class are:

```
private AvroWrapper<WeblogRecord> outputRecord = new
AvroWrapper<WeblogRecord>();
private WeblogRecord weblogRecord = new WeblogRecord();
```

Data emitted from the `WeblogMapper` `map()` method are:

```
outputRecord.datum(weblogRecord);
oc.collect(outputRecord, NullWritable.get());
```

The output of this map-only job is stored in the Avro file format.

There's more...

To read the Avro file format produced by the `AvroWriter` job, we just need to change the input format and the mapper class. First, set the input format and the input schema.

```
JobConf weblogJob = new JobConf(conf, getClass());
Schema schema = ReflectData.get().getSchema(WeblogRecord.class);
AvroJob.setReflect(weblogJob);
```

Next, create a mapper class with the following definition:

```
public class WeblogMapperAvro extends MapReduceBase
            implements Mapper<AvroWrapper<WeblogRecord>, NullWritable,
Text, NullWritable>
{
 public void map(AvroWrapper<WeblogRecord> key, NullWritable value,
OutputCollector<Text, NullWritable> oc, Reporter rprtr) throws
IOException {
        WeblogRecord weblogRecord = key.datum();
      //process the web log record
    }
}
```

See also

The following recipes will demonstrate additional data serialization libraries that can be used with Hadoop:

- ▶ *Using Apache Thrift to serialize data*
- ▶ *Using Protocol Buffers to serialize data*

Using Apache Thrift to serialize data

Apache Thrift is a cross-language serialization and RPC services framework. Thrift uses an interface definition file to generate bindings in many languages, including Java.

This recipe demonstrates the defining of a Thrift interface, the generation of the corresponding Java bindings, and the use of these bindings to serialize a Java object to HDFS using MapReduce.

Getting ready

You will need to download/compile/install the following:

- ▶ Hadoop LZO library
- ▶ Apache Thrift Version 0.7.0, from `http://thrift.apache.org/`
- ▶ The latest version of Elephant Bird, from `https://github.com/kevinweil/elephant-bird`
- ▶ The test data file `weblog_entries.txt`, from `http://www.packtpub.com/support`

To compile and install Apache Thrift, first ensure that you have all the required dependencies using Yum:

```
# yum install automake libtool flex bison pkgconfig gcc-c++ boost-devel
libevent-devel zlib-devel python-devel ruby-devel openssl-devel
```

Next, build Elephant Bird.

```
$ cd /path/to/elephant-bird
$ ant
```

Copy the `elephant-bird-X.X.X.jar` file to the classpath of your development environment.

How to do it...

1. Set up the directory structure.

```
$ mkdir test-thrift
$ mkdir test-thrift/src
$ mkdir test-thrift/src/thrift
$ mkdir test-thrift/src/java
$ cd test-thrift/src/thrift
```

2. Next, create an interface definition:

```
namespace java com.packt.hadoop.hdfs.ch2.thrift

struct WeblogRecord {
  1: optional string cookie,
  2: string page,
  3: i64 timestamp,
  4: string ip
}
```

Save the file as `weblog_record.thrift` in the `test-thrift/src/thrift/` folder.

3. Compile and generate the `.java` file:

```
# thrift --gen java -o src/java/ src/thrift/weblog_record.thrift
```

Thrift should have generated a file named `WeblogRecord.java` in the `src/java/` folder.

4. Now, we will write a MapReduce application to read `weblog_entries.txt` from HDFS and use Elephant-Bird's `LzoThriftBlockOutputFormat` class to serialize the `WeblogRecord` object to an LZO compressed file

```
public class ThriftMapper extends Mapper<Object, Text,
NullWritable, ThriftWritable<WeblogRecord>> {

    private ThriftWritable<WeblogRecord> thriftRecord =
ThriftWritable.newInstance(WeblogRecord.class);
    private WeblogRecord record = new WeblogRecord();
    private SimpleDateFormat dateFormatter = new
SimpleDateFormat("yyyy-MM-dd:HH:mm:ss");

    @Override
```

```
        protected void map(Object key, Text value, Context context)
    throws IOException, InterruptedException {
            String[] tokens = value.toString().split("\t");
            String cookie = tokens[0];
            String page = tokens[1];
            String date = tokens[2];
            String time = tokens[3];
            String formatedDate = date + ":" + time;
            Date timestamp = null;
            try {
                timestamp = dateFormatter.parse(formatedDate);
            } catch(ParseException ex) {
                return;
            }
            String ip = tokens[4];
            record.setCookie(cookie);
            record.setPage(page);
            record.setTimestamp(timestamp.getTime());
            record.setIp(ip);
            thriftRecord.set(record);
            context.write(NullWritable.get(), thriftRecord);
        }
    }
```

5. Finally, we will configure the MapReduce job.

```
    public class ThriftWriter extends Configured implements Tool {

        public int run(String[] args) throws Exception {

            Path inputPath = new Path(args[0]);
            Path outputPath = new Path(args[1]);

            Configuration conf = getConf();
            Job weblogJob = new Job(conf);
            weblogJob.setJobName("ThriftWriter");
            weblogJob.setJarByClass(getClass());
            weblogJob.setNumReduceTasks(0);
            weblogJob.setMapperClass(ThriftMapper.class);
            weblogJob.setMapOutputKeyClass(LongWritable.class);
            weblogJob.setMapOutputValueClass(Text.class);
            weblogJob.setOutputKeyClass(LongWritable.class);
            weblogJob.setOutputValueClass(Text.class);
            weblogJob.setInputFormatClass(TextInputFormat.class);
            weblogJob.setOutputFormatClass(
```

```
LzoThriftBlockOutputFormat.class);

        FileInputFormat.setInputPaths(weblogJob, inputPath);
        LzoThriftBlockOutputFormat.setClassConf(
WeblogRecord.class, weblogJob.getConfiguration());
        LzoThriftBlockOutputFormat.setOutputPath(weblogJob,
outputPath);

        if (weblogJob.waitForCompletion(true)) {
            return 0;
        }
        return 1;
    }

    public static void main( String[] args ) throws Exception {
        int returnCode = ToolRunner.run(
new ThriftWriter(), args);
        System.exit(returnCode);
    }
}
```

How it works...

The first task required us to define and compile a Thrift interface definition. This definition file can be used to generate bindings in any language that Thrift supports.

Next, we used Elephant Bird to build a MapReduce application to serialize the `WeblogRecord` object that Thrift generated. To set up the MapReduce job, we set the input format to read a normal text file:

```
weblogJob.setInputFormatClass(TextInputFormat.class);
```

Then the output format was configured to use Thrift block format compression with LZO to store the output records.

```
LzoThriftBlockOutputFormat.setClassConf(
WeblogRecord.class, weblogJob.getConfiguration());
        LzoThriftBlockOutputFormat.setOutputPath(weblogJob,
outputPath);
```

In the mapper, we use the `ThriftWritable` class of Elephant Bird to wrap the `WeblogRecord` object. The `ThriftWritable` class is derived from the `WritableComparable` class of Hadoop, which must be implemented by all the keys emitted in MapReduce. Every time we generate any type of binding using Thrift, the `ThriftWritable` class helps avoid having to write a custom `WritableComparable` class.

In the mapper, we instantiate both `ThriftWritable` and `WeblogRecord` instances:

```
private ThriftWritable<WeblogRecord> thriftRecord =
    ThriftWritable.newInstance(WeblogRecord.class);
private WeblogRecord record = new WeblogRecord();
```

Then, we call the set method of the `thriftRecord` object with an instance of `WeblogRecord`. Finally, the mapper emits the `thriftRecord` object, which contains an instance of `WeblogRecord`.

```
thriftRecord.set(record);
context.write(NullWritable.get(), thriftRecord);
```

See also

The following recipe will demonstrate another popular serialization framework developed by Google:

▸ *Using Protocol Buffers to serialize Data*

Using Protocol Buffers to serialize data

Protocol Buffers is a cross-language data format. Protocol Buffers uses an interface definition file to generate bindings in many languages, including Java.

This recipe will demonstrate how to define a Protocol Buffers message, generate the corresponding Java bindings, and use these bindings to serialize a Java object to HDFS using MapReduce.

Getting ready

You will need to download/compile/install the following:

▸ Hadoop LZO library

▸ Google Protocol Buffers Version 2.3.0 from `http://code.google.com/p/protobuf/`

▸ Elephant Bird (see the previous recipe)

▸ The test data file `weblog_entries.txt`, from `http://www.packtpub.com/support`

 Note that you will need to have a GNU C/C++ compiler collection installed to compile the protocol buffer source. We will be compiling the source code for Protocol Buffers.

To install GNU C/C++ using Yum, run the following command as the root user from a bash shell:

```
# yum install gcc gcc-c++ autoconf automake
```

To compile and install Protocol Buffers, type the following lines of code:

```
$ cd /path/to/protobuf
$ ./configure
$ make
$ make check
# make install
# ldconfig
```

How to do it...

1. Set up the directory structure.

   ```
   $ mkdir test-protobufs
   $ mkdir test-protobufs/src
   $ mkdir test-protobufs/src/proto
   $ mkdir test-protobufs/src/java
   $ cd test-protobufs/src/proto
   ```

2. Next, create the protocol format.

   ```
   package example;

   option java_package = "com.packt.hadoop.hdfs.ch2";
   option java_outer_classname = "WeblogRecord";

   message Record {
     optional string cookie = 1;
     required string page = 2;
     required int64 timestamp = 3;
     required string ip = 4;
   }
   ```

   Save the file as `weblog_record.proto` in the `test-protobufs/src/proto/` folder.

3. Compile the protocol format from the `test-protobufs` folder. `WeblogRecord.java` is generated in `src/java/` by `protoc`:

   ```
   $ cd ../../
   $ protoc --proto_path=src/proto/ --java_out=src/java/ src/proto/weblog_record.proto
   ```

4. Now, we will write a MapReduce application to read `weblog_entries.txt` from HDFS and use Elephant Bird's `LzoProtobufBlockOutputFormat` class to serialize the `WeblogRecord` object to an LZO compressed file:

```
public class ProtobufMapper extends Mapper<Object, Text,
NullWritable, ProtobufWritable<WeblogRecord.Record>> {

    private ProtobufWritable<WeblogRecord.Record> protobufRecord =
ProtobufWritable.newInstance(WeblogRecord.Record.class);
    private SimpleDateFormat dateFormatter = new
SimpleDateFormat("yyyy-MM-dd:HH:mm:ss");

    @Override
    protected void map(Object key, Text value, Context context)
throws IOException, InterruptedException {
        String[] tokens = value.toString().split("\t");
        String cookie = tokens[0];
        String page = tokens[1];
        String date = tokens[2];
        String time = tokens[3];
        String formatedDate = date + ":" + time;
        Date timestamp = null;
        try {
            timestamp = dateFormatter.parse(formatedDate);
        } catch(ParseException ex) {
            return;
        }
        String ip = tokens[4];
        protobufRecord.set(WeblogRecord.Record.newBuilder()
                .setCookie(cookie)
                .setPage(page)
                .setTimestamp(timestamp.getTime())
                .setIp(ip)
                .build());
        context.write(NullWritable.get(), protobufRecord);
    }
}
```

5. Finally, we will configure the MapReduce job.

```java
public class ProtobufWriter extends Configured implements Tool {

    public int run(String[] args) throws Exception {

        Path inputPath = new Path(args[0]);
        Path outputPath = new Path(args[1]);

        Configuration conf = getConf();
        Job weblogJob = new Job(conf);
        weblogJob.setJobName("ProtobufWriter");
        weblogJob.setJarByClass(getClass());
        weblogJob.setNumReduceTasks(0);
        weblogJob.setMapperClass(ProtobufMapper.class);
        weblogJob.setMapOutputKeyClass(LongWritable.class);
        weblogJob.setMapOutputValueClass(Text.class);
        weblogJob.setOutputKeyClass(LongWritable.class);
        weblogJob.setOutputValueClass(Text.class);
        weblogJob.setInputFormatClass(TextInputFormat.class);
        weblogJob.setOutputFormatClass(
LzoProtobufBlockOutputFormat.class);

        FileInputFormat.setInputPaths(weblogJob, inputPath);
        LzoProtobufBlockOutputFormat.setClassConf(WeblogRecord.
Record.class, weblogJob.getConfiguration());
        LzoProtobufBlockOutputFormat.setOutputPath(weblogJob,
outputPath);


        if(weblogJob.waitForCompletion(true)) {
            return 0;
        }
        return 1;
    }

    public static void main( String[] args ) throws Exception {
        int returnCode = ToolRunner.run(
new ProtobufWriter(), args);
        System.exit(returnCode);
    }
}
```

How it works...

The first task is to define and compile a Protocol Buffers message definition. This definition file can be used to generate bindings in any language the Protocol Buffers compiler supports. There are a couple of things to note about the format of the message.

First, the package definition `package example;` is not related to Java packages. It is the namespace of the message defined in the `*.proto` file. Second, the `option java_package` declaration is a Java package definition. Finally, the `option java_outer_classname` declaration is the output class name that will be used. Within `java_outer_classname`, the `Record` class will be defined.

Next, we wrote a MapReduce application to serialize the `WeblogRecord` object generated by the Protocol Buffers compiler. To set up the MapReduce job, we set the input format to read a normal text file.

```
weblogJob.setInputFormatClass(TextInputFormat.class);
```

Then, the output format was set to store the records produced from the job in the Protocol Buffers block format, compressed using LZO.

```
LzoProtobufBlockOutputFormat.setClassConf(WeblogRecord.Record.class,
weblogJob.getConfiguration());
        LzoProtobufBlockOutputFormat.setOutputPath(weblogJob,
outputPath);
```

In the mapper, we use the `ProtobufWritable` class of Elephant Bird to wrap the `WeblogRecord.Record` object. The `ProtobufWritable` class is derived from the `WritableComparable` class of Hadoop, which all keys emitted in MapReduce must implement. Every time we generate any type of binding using `protoc`, the `ProtobufWritable` class helps avoid having to write a custom `WritableComparable` class.

In the mapper, we instantiate a `ProtobufWritable` instance.

```
    private ProtobufWritable<WeblogRecord.Record> protobufRecord =
ProtobufWritable.newInstance(WeblogRecord.Record.class);
```

Then, we call the set method of the `protobufRecord` object with a new instance of `WeblogRecord.Record`. Finally, the mapper emits the `protobufRecord` object:

```
protobufRecord.set(WeblogRecord.Record.newBuilder()
                .setCookie(cookie)
                .setPage(page)
                .setTimestamp(timestamp.getTime())
                .setIp(ip)
                .build());
    context.write(NullWritable.get(), protobufRecord);
```

Setting the replication factor for HDFS

HDFS stores files as data blocks and distributes these blocks across the entire cluster. As HDFS was designed to be fault-tolerant and to run on commodity hardware, blocks are replicated a number of times to ensure high data availability. The replication factor is a property that can be set in the HDFS configuration file that will allow you to adjust the global replication factor for the entire cluster. For each block stored in HDFS, there will be *n - 1* duplicated blocks distributed across the cluster. For example, if the replication factor was set to 3 there would be one original block and two replicas.

Getting ready

Open the `hdfs-site.xml` file. This file is usually found in the `conf/` folder of the Hadoop installation directory.

How to do it...

Change or add the following property to `hdfs-site.xml`:

```
<property>
<name>dfs.replication<name>
<value>3<value>
<description>Block Replication<description>
<property>
```

How it works...

`hdfs-site.xml` is used to configure HDFS. Changing the `dfs.replication` property in `hdfs-site.xml` will change the default replication for all files placed in HDFS.

There's more...

You can also change the replication factor on a per-file basis using the Hadoop FS shell.

```
$ hadoop fs -setrep -w 3 /my/file
```

Alternatively, you can change the replication factor of all the files under a directory.

```
$ hadoop fs -setrep -w 3 -R /my/dir
```

See also

▶ The *Setting the block size for HDFS* recipe in this chapter; it will explain how to set the block size for HDFS

Setting the block size for HDFS

HDFS was designed to hold and manage large amounts of data; therefore typical HDFS block sizes are significantly larger than the block sizes you would see for a traditional filesystem (for example, the filesystem on my laptop uses a block size of 4 KB). The block size setting is used by HDFS to divide files into blocks and then distribute those blocks across the cluster. For example, if a cluster is using a block size of 64 MB, and a 128-MB text file was put in to HDFS, HDFS would split the file into two blocks (128 MB/64 MB) and distribute the two chunks to the data nodes in the cluster.

Getting ready

Open the `hdfs-site.xml` file. This file is usually found in the `conf/` folder of the Hadoop installation directory.

How to do it...

Set the following property in `hdfs-size.xml`:

```
<property>
<name>dfs.block.size<name>
<value>134217728<value>
<description>Block size<description>
<property>
```

How it works...

`hdfs-site.xml` is used to configure HDFS. Changing the `dfs.block.size` property in `hdfs-site.xml` will change the default block size for all the files placed into HDFS. In this case, we set the `dfs.block.size` to 128 MB. Changing this setting will not affect the block size of any files currently in HDFS. It will only affect the block size of files placed into HDFS after this setting has taken effect.

3
Extracting and Transforming Data

In this chapter, we will cover:

- ▶ Transforming Apache logs into TSV format using MapReduce
- ▶ Using Apache Pig to filter bot traffic from web server logs
- ▶ Using Apache Pig to sort web server log data by timestamp
- ▶ Using Apache Pig to sessionize web server log data
- ▶ Using Python to extend Apache Pig functionality
- ▶ Using MapReduce and secondary sort to calculate page views
- ▶ Using Hive and Python to clean and transform geographical event data
- ▶ Using Python and Hadoop Streaming to perform a time series analytic
- ▶ Using MultipleOutputs in MapReduce to name output files
- ▶ Creating custom Hadoop Writable and InputFormat to read geographical event data

Introduction

Parsing and formatting large amounts of data to meet business requirements is a challenging task. The software and the architecture must meet strict scalability, reliability, and run-time constraints. Hadoop is an ideal environment for extracting and transforming large-scale data. Hadoop provides a scalable, reliable, and distributed processing environment that is ideal for large-scale data processing. This chapter will demonstrate methods to extract and transform data using MapReduce, Apache Pig, Apache Hive, and Python.

Transforming Apache logs into TSV format using MapReduce

MapReduce is an excellent tool for transforming data into **tab-separated values** (**TSV**). Once the input data is loaded into HDFS, the entire Hadoop cluster can be utilized to transform large datasets in parallel. This recipe will demonstrate the method to extract records from Apache access logs and store those records as tab-separated values in HDFS.

Getting ready

You will need to download the `apache_clf.txt` dataset from the support page of the Packt website, `http://www.packtpub.com/support`, and place the file in HDFS.

How to do it...

Perform the following steps to transform Apache logs to TSV format using MapReduce:

1. Build a regular expression pattern to parse the Apache combined log format:

```
private Pattern p = Pattern.compile("^([\\d.]+) (\\S+) (\\S+) \\
[([\\w:/]+\\s[+\\-]\\d{4})\\] \"(\\w+) (.+?) (.+?)\" (\\d+) (\\d+)
\"([^\"]+|(.+?))\" \"([^\"]+|(.+?))\"", Pattern.DOTALL);
```

2. Create a mapper class to read the log files. The mapper should emit IP address as the key, and the following as values: timestamp, page, http status, bytes returned to the client, and the user agent of the client:

```
public class CLFMapper extends Mapper<Object, Text, Text, Text>{

    private SimpleDateFormat dateFormatter =
            new SimpleDateFormat("dd/MMM/yyyy:HH:mm:ss Z");
    private Pattern p =
            Pattern.compile("^([\\d.]+) (\\S+) (\\S+) "
        + " \\[([\\w:/]+\\s[+\\-]\\d{4})\\] \"(\\w+) (.+?)
(.+?)\" "
        + "(\\d+) (\\d+) \"([^\"]+|(.+?))\"
\"([^\"]+|(.+?))\"",
            Pattern.DOTALL);

    private Text outputKey = new Text();
    private Text outputValue = new Text();
    @Override
    protected void map(Object key, Text value, Context
      context) throws IOException, InterruptedException {
        String entry = value.toString();
```

```
        Matcher m = p.matcher(entry);
        if (!m.matches()) {
            return;
        }
        Date date = null;
        try {
            date = dateFormatter.parse(m.group(4));
        } catch (ParseException ex) {
            return;
        }
        outputKey.set(m.group(1)); //ip
        StringBuilder b = new StringBuilder();
        b.append(date.getTime()); //timestamp
        b.append('\t');
        b.append(m.group(6)); //page
        b.append('\t');
        b.append(m.group(8)); //http status
        b.append('\t');
        b.append(m.group(9)); //bytes
        b.append('\t');
        b.append(m.group(12)); //useragent
        outputValue.set(b.toString());
        context.write(outputKey, outputValue);
    }

}
```

3. Now, create a map-only job to apply the transformation:

```
public class ParseWeblogs extends Configured implements Tool {

  public int run(String[] args) throws Exception {

    Path inputPath = new Path(args[0]);
    Path outputPath = new Path(args[1]);

    Configuration conf = getConf();
    Job weblogJob = new Job(conf);
    weblogJob.setJobName("Weblog Transformer");
    weblogJob.setJarByClass(getClass());
    weblogJob.setNumReduceTasks(0);
    weblogJob.setMapperClass(CLFMapper.class);
    weblogJob.setMapOutputKeyClass(Text.class);
    weblogJob.setMapOutputValueClass(Text.class);
    weblogJob.setOutputKeyClass(Text.class);
```

```
weblogJob.setOutputValueClass(Text.class);
weblogJob.setInputFormatClass(TextInputFormat.class);
weblogJob.setOutputFormatClass(TextOutputFormat.class);

FileInputFormat.setInputPaths(weblogJob, inputPath);
FileOutputFormat.setOutputPath(weblogJob, outputPath);


if(weblogJob.waitForCompletion(true)) {
  return 0;
}
return 1;
}

public static void main( String[] args ) throws Exception {
    int returnCode = ToolRunner.run(new ParseWeblogs(), args);
    System.exit(returnCode);
}

}
```

4. Finally, launch the MapReduce job:

```
$ hadoop jar myjar.jar com.packt.ch3.etl.ParseWeblogs /user/
hadoop/apache_clf.txt /user/hadoop/apache_clf_tsv
```

How it works...

We first created a mapper that was responsible for the extraction of the desired information we from the Apache weblogs and for emitting the extracted fields in a tab-separated format.

Next, we created a map-only job to transform the web server log data into a tab-separated format. The key-value pairs emitted from the mapper were stored in a file in HDFS.

There's more...

By default, the `TextOutputFormat` class uses a tab to separate the key and value pairs. You can change the default separator by setting the `mapred.textoutputformat. separator` property. For example, to separate the IP and the timestamp by a ',', we could re-run the job using the following command:

```
$ hadoop jar myjar.jar com.packt.ch3.etl.ParseWeblogs -Dmapred.
textoutputformat.separator=',' /user/hadoop/apache_clf.txt /user/hadoop/
csv
```

See also

The tab-separated output from this recipe will be used in the following recipes:

▶ *Using Apache Pig to filter bot traffic from web server logs*

▶ *Using Apache Pig to sort web server log data by timestamp*

▶ *Using Apache Pig to sessionize web server log data*

▶ *Using Python to extend Apache Pig functionality*

▶ *Using MapReduce and secondary sort to calculate page views*

Using Apache Pig to filter bot traffic from web server logs

Apache Pig is a high-level language for creating MapReduce applications. This recipe will use Apache Pig and a Pig user-defined filter function (UDF) to remove all bot traffic from a sample web server log dataset. **Bot traffic** is the non-human traffic that visits a webpage, such as **spiders**.

Getting ready

You will need to download/compile/install the following:

▶ Version 0.8.1 or better of Apache Pig from `http://pig.apache.org/`

▶ Test data: `apache_tsv.txt` and `useragent_blacklist.txt` from the support page on the Packt website, `http://www.packtpub.com/support`

▶ Place `apache_tsv.txt` in HDFS and put `useragent_blacklist.txt` in your current working directory

How to do it...

Carry out the following steps to filter bot traffic using an Apache Pig UDF:

1. First, write a Pig UDF that extends the Pig `FilterFunc` abstract class. This class will be used to filter records in the weblogs dataset by using the user agent string.

```
public class IsUseragentBot extends FilterFunc {

    private Set<String> blacklist = null;

    private void loadBlacklist() throws IOException {
        blacklist = new HashSet<String>();
        BufferedReader in = new BufferedReader(new
```

```
            FileReader("blacklist"));
        String userAgent = null;
        while ((userAgent = in.readLine()) != null) {
            blacklist.add(userAgent);
        }
    }

    @Override
    public Boolean exec(Tuple tuple) throws IOException {
        if (blacklist == null) {
            loadBlacklist();
        }
        if (tuple == null || tuple.size() == 0) {
            return null;
        }

        String ua = (String) tuple.get(0);
        if (blacklist.contains(ua)) {
            return true;
        }
        return false;
    }

}
```

2. Next, create a Pig script in your current working directory. At the beginning of the Pig script, give the MapReduce framework the path to useragent_blacklist.txt in HDFS:

```
set mapred.cache.files '/user/hadoop/blacklist.txt#blacklist';
set mapred.create.symlink 'yes';
```

3. Register the JAR file containing the IsUseragentBot class with Pig, and write the Pig script to filter the weblogs by the user agent:

```
register myudfjar.jar;


all_weblogs = LOAD '/user/hadoop/apache_tsv.txt' AS (ip:
chararray, timestamp:long, page:chararray, http_status:int,
payload_size:int, useragent:chararray);
```

```
nobots_weblogs = FILTER all_weblogs BY NOT com.packt.ch3.etl.pig.
IsUseragentBot(useragent);


STORE nobots_weblogs INTO '/user/hadoop/nobots_weblogs';
```

To run the Pig job, put `myudfjar.jar` into the same folder as the Pig script and execute it.

```
$ ls
$ myudfjar.jar filter_bot_traffic.pig
$ pig -f filter_bot_traffic.pig
```

How it works...

Apache Pig is extendable through the use of user-defined functions (UDF). One way to create a UDF is through the use of the Java abstract classes and interfaces that come with the Apache Pig distribution. In this recipe, we wanted to remove all records that contain known bot user agent strings. One way to do this is to create our own Pig filter.

The `IsUseragentBot` class extends the abstract class `FilterFunc`, which allows us to override the `exec(Tuple t)` method. A Pig Tuple is an ordered list of fields that can be any Pig primitive, or null. At runtime, Pig will feed the `exec(Tuple t)` method of the `IsUseragentBot` class with the user agent strings from our dataset. The UDF will extract the user agent string by accessing the first field in the Tuple, and it will return `true` if we find the user agent string is a bot, otherwise the UDF returns `false`.

In addition, the `IsUseragentBot` UDF reads a file called `blacklist` and loads the contents into a `HashSet` instance. The file named `blacklist` is a symbolic link to `blacklist.txt`, which has been distributed to the nodes in the cluster using the **distributed cache** mechanism. To place a file into the distributed cache, and to create the symbolic link, set the following MapReduce properties:

```
set mapred.cache.files '/user/hadoop/blacklist.txt#blacklist';
set mapred.create.symlink 'yes';
```

It is important to note that these properties are not Pig properties. These properties are used by the MapReduce framework, so you can use these properties to load a file to the distributed cache for any MapReduce job.

Next, we told Pig where to find the JAR file containing the `IsUseragentBot` UDF:

```
register myudfjar.jar;
```

Finally, we call the UDF using the Java class name. When the job runs, Pig will instantiate an instance of the `IsUseragentBot` class and feed the `exec(Tuple t)` method with records from the `all_weblogs` relation.

There's more...

Starting in Pig Version 0.9, Pig UDFs can access the distributed cache without setting the `mapred.cache.files` and `mapred.create.symlink` properties. Most abstract Pig classes that used to create UDFs now have a method named `List<String> getCacheFiles()` that can be overridden to load files from HDFS into the distributed cache. For example, the `IsUseragentBot` class can be modified to load the `blacklist.txt` file to the distributed cache by adding the following method:

```
@Override
public List<String> getCacheFiles() {
        List<String> list = new ArrayList<String>();
        list.add("/user/hadoop/blacklist.txt#blacklist");
        return list;
}
```

See also

Apache Pig will be used with the following recipes in this chapter:

▸ *Using Apache Pig to sort web server log data by timestamp*

▸ *Using Apache Pig to sessionize web server log data*

▸ *Using Python to extend Apache Pig functionality*

▸ *Using MapReduce and secondary sort to calculate page views*

Using Apache Pig to sort web server log data by timestamp

Sorting data is a common data transformation technique. In this recipe, we will demonstrate the method of writing a simple Pig script to sort a dataset using the distributed processing power of the Hadoop cluster.

Getting ready

You will need to download/compile/install the following:

▸ Version 0.8.1 or better of Apache Pig from `http://pig.apache.org/`

▸ Test data: `apache_nobots_tsv.txt` from `http://www.packtpub.com/support`

How to do it...

Perform the following steps to sort data using Apache Pig:

1. First load the web server log data into a Pig relation:

```
nobots_weblogs = LOAD '/user/hadoop/apache_nobots_tsv.txt' AS
(ip: chararray, timestamp:long, page:chararray, http_status:int,
payload_size:int, useragent:chararray);
```

2. Next, order the web server log records by the `timestamp` field in the ascending order:

```
ordered_weblogs = ORDER nobots BY timestamp;
```

3. Finally, store the sorted results in HDFS:

```
STORE ordered_weblogs INTO '/user/hadoop/ordered_weblogs';\
```

4. Run the Pig job:

```
$ pig -f ordered_weblogs.pig
```

How it works...

Sorting data in a distributed, share-nothing environment is non-trivial. The Pig relational operator ORDER BY has the capability to provide total ordering of a dataset. This means any record that appears in the output file `part-00000`, will have a timestamp less than the timestamp in the output file `part-00001` (since our data was sorted by `timestamp`).

There's more...

The Pig ORDER BY relational operator sorts data by multiple fields, and also supports sorting data in the descending order. For example, to sort the `nobots` relationship by the `ip` and `timestamp` fields, we would use the following expression:

```
ordered_weblogs = ORDER nobots BY ip, timestamp;
```

To sort the `nobots` relationship by `timestamp` in the descending order, use the `desc` option:

```
ordered_weblogs = ORDER nobots timestamp desc;
```

See also

The following recipes will use Apache Pig:

- *Using Apache Pig to sessionize web server log data*
- *Using Python to extend Apache Pig functionality*
- *Using MapReduce and secondary sort to calculate page views*

Using Apache Pig to sessionize web server log data

A session represents a user's continuous interaction with a website, and the user session ends when an arbitrary activity timeout has occurred. A new session begins once the user returns to the website after a period of inactivity. This recipe will use Apache Pig and a Pig user-defined function (UDF) to generate a subset of records from `apache_nobots_tsv.txt` that marks the beginning of a session for a specific IP.

Getting ready

You will need to download/compile/install the following:

▸ Version 0.8.1 or better of Apache Pig from `http://pig.apache.org/`

▸ Test data: `apache_nobots_tsv.txt` from `http://www.packtpub.com/support`

How to do it...

The following are the steps to create an Apache Pig UDF to sessionize web server log data:

1. Start by creating a Pig UDF to emit only the first record of a session. The UDF extends the Pig abstract class `EvalFunc` and implements the Pig interface, `Accumulator`. This class is responsible for applying the session logic on the web server log dataset:

```
public class Sessionize extends EvalFunc<DataBag> implements
Accumulator<DataBag> {

    private long sessionLength = 0;
    private Long lastSession = null;
    private DataBag sessionBag = null;

    public Sessionize(String seconds) {
        sessionLength = Integer.parseInt(seconds) * 1000;
        sessionBag = BagFactory.getInstance().newDefaultBag();
    }

    @Override
    public DataBag exec(Tuple tuple) throws IOException {
        accumulate(tuple);
```

```
            DataBag bag = getValue();
            cleanup();
            return bag;
        }


        @Override
        public void accumulate(Tuple tuple) throws IOException {
            if (tuple == null || tuple.size() == 0) {
                return;
            }
            DataBag inputBag = (DataBag) tuple.get(0);
            for(Tuple t: inputBag) {
                Long timestamp = (Long)t.get(1);
                if (lastSession == null) {
                    sessionBag.add(t);
                }
                else if ((timestamp - lastSession) >= sessionLength) {
                    sessionBag.add(t);
                }
                lastSession = timestamp;
            }
        }


        @Override
        public DataBag getValue() {
            return sessionBag;
        }    @Override
        public void cleanup() {
            lastSession = null;
            sessionBag = BagFactory.getInstance().newDefaultBag();
        }
    }
```

2. Next, create a Pig script to load and group the web server log records by IP address:

```
register myjar.jar;
define Sessionize com.packt.ch3.etl.pig.Sessionize('1800'); /* 30
minutes */

nobots_weblogs = LOAD '/user/hadoop/apache_nobots_tsv.txt' AS
(ip: chararray, timestamp:long, page:chararray, http_status:int,
payload_size:int, useragent:chararray);

ip_groups = GROUP nobots_weblogs BY ip;
```

3. Finally, write the Pig expression to order all of the records associated with a specific IP by timestamp. Then, send the ordered records to the `Sessionize` UDF:

```
sessions = FOREACH ip_groups {
            ordered_by_timestamp = ORDER nobots_weblogs BY
timestamp;
            GENERATE FLATTEN(Sessionize(ordered_by_
timestamp));
        }

STORE sessions INTO '/user/jowens/sessions';
```

4. Copy the JAR file containing the `Sessionize` class to the current working directory, and run the Pig script:

```
$ pig -f sessionize.pig
```

How it works...

We first created a UDF that extended the `EvalFunc` abstract class and implemented the `Accumulator` interface. The `EvalFunc` class is used to create our own function that can be used within a Pig script. Data will be passed to the UDF via the `exec(Tuple t)` method, where it is processed. The `Accumulator` interface is optional for custom `eval` functions, and allows Pig to optimize the data flow and memory utilization of the UDF. Instead of passing the whole dataset, similar to how the `EvalFunc` class works, the `Accumulator` interface allows for subsets of the data to be passed to the UDF.

Next, we wrote a Pig script to group all of the web server log records by IP, and sort the records by timestamp. We need the data sorted by timestamp because the `Sessionize` UDF uses the sorted order of the timestamps to determine the start of each session.

Then, we generated all of the sessions associated with a specific IP by calling the `Sessionize` alias.

Finally, we used the `FLATTEN` operator to unnest the Tuples in the DataBags emitted from the UDF.

See also

▶ *Using Python to extend Apache Pig functionality*

Using Python to extend Apache Pig functionality

In this recipe, we will use Python to create a simple Apache Pig user-defined function (UDF) to count the number of records in a Pig DataBag.

Getting ready

You will need to download/compile/install the following:

▶ Jython 2.5.2 from `http://www.jython.org/`

▶ Version 0.8.1 or better of Apache Pig from `http://pig.apache.org/`

▶ Test data: `apache_nobots_tsv.txt` from `http://www.packtpub.com/support`

This recipe requires the Jython standalone JAR file. To build the file, download the Jython java installer, run the installer, and select **Standalone** from the installation menu.

```
$ java -jar jython_installer-2.5.2.jar
```

Add the Jython standalone JAR file to Apache Pig's classpath:

```
$ export PIG_CLASSPATH=$PIG_CLASSPATH:/path/to/jython2.5.2/jython.jar
```

How to do it...

The following are the steps to create an Apache Pig UDF using Python:

1. Start by creating a simple Python function to count the number of records in a Pig DataBag:

```python
#!/usr/bin/python

@outputSchema("hits:long")
def calculate(inputBag):
    hits = len(inputBag)
    return hits
```

2. Next, create a Pig script to group all of the web server log records by IP and page. Then send the grouped web server log records to the Python function:

```
register 'count.py' using jython as count;

nobots_weblogs = LOAD '/user/hadoop/apache_nobots_tsv.txt' AS
(ip: chararray, timestamp:long, page:chararray, http_status:int,
payload_size:int, useragent:chararray);

ip_page_groups = GROUP nobots_weblogs BY (ip, page);

ip_page_hits = FOREACH ip_page_groups GENERATE FLATTEN(group),
count.calculate(nobots_weblogs);

STORE ip_page_hits INTO '/user/hadoop/ip_page_hits';
```

How it works...

First, we created a simple Python function to calculate the length of a Pig DataBag. In addition, the Python script contained the Python decorator, `@outputSchema("hits:long")`, that instructs Pig on how to interpret the data returned by the Python function. In this case, we want Pig to store the data returned by this function as a Java Long in a field named `hits`.

Next, we wrote a Pig script that registers the Python UDF using the statement:

```
register 'count.py' using jython as count;
```

Finally, we called the `calculate()` function using the alias `count`, in the Pig DataBag:

```
count.calculate(nobots_weblogs);
```

Using MapReduce and secondary sort to calculate page views

In a typical MapReduce job, key-value pairs are emitted from the mappers, shuffled, and sorted, and then finally passed to the reducers. There is no attempt by the MapReduce framework to sort the values passed to the reducers for processing. However, there are cases when we need the values passed to the reducers to be sorted, such as in the case of counting page views.

To calculate page views, we need to calculate distinct IPs by page. One way to calculate this is to have the mappers emit the key-value pairs: page and IP. Then, in the reducer, we can store all of the IPs associated with a page in a set. However, this approach is not scalable. What happens if the weblogs contain a large number of distinct IPs visiting a single page? We might not be able to fit the entire set of distinct IPs in memory.

The MapReduce framework provides a way to work around this complication. In this recipe, we will write a MapReduce application that allows us to sort the values going to a reducer using an approach known as the **secondary sort**. Instead of holding all of the distinct IPs in memory, we can keep track of the last IP we saw while processing the values in the reducer, and we can maintain a counter to calculate distinct IPs.

Getting ready

You will need to download the `apache_nobots_tsv.txt` dataset from `http://www.packtpub.com/support` and place the file into HDFS.

How to do it...

The following steps show how to implement a secondary sort in MapReduce to calculate page views:

1. Create a class that implements the Hadoop `WritableComparable` interface. We will use this class to store the key and sort fields:

```
public class CompositeKey implements WritableComparable {

    private Text first = null;
    private Text second = null;

    public CompositeKey() {

    }

    public CompositeKey(Text first, Text second) {
        this.first = first;
        this.second = second;
    }

    //...getters and setters

    public void write(DataOutput d) throws IOException {
        first.write(d);
        second.write(d);
    }
```

```
public void readFields(DataInput di) throws IOException {
    if (first == null) {
        first = new Text();
    }
    if (second == null) {
        second = new Text();
    }
    first.readFields(di);
    second.readFields(di);
}

public int compareTo(Object obj) {
    CompositeKey other = (CompositeKey) obj;
    int cmp = first.compareTo(other.getFirst());
    if (cmp != 0) {
        return cmp;
    }
    return second.compareTo(other.getSecond());
}

@Override
public boolean equals(Object obj) {
    CompositeKey other = (CompositeKey)obj;
    return first.equals(other.getFirst());
}

@Override
public int hashCode() {
    return first.hashCode();
}
}
```

2. Next, write the `Mapper` and `Reducer` classes. The `Mapper` class will use the `CompositeKey` class to store two fields. The first will be the `page` field, which is used to group and partition the data leaving the mapper. The second is the `ip` field, which is used to sort the values passed to the reducer.

```
public class PageViewMapper extends Mapper<Object, Text,
CompositeKey, Text> {
    private CompositeKey compositeKey = new CompositeKey();
    private Text first = new Text();
    private Text second = new Text();
    private Text outputValue = new Text();
    @Override
```

```java
        protected void map(Object key, Text value, Context
          context) throws IOException, InterruptedException {
            String[] tokens = value.toString().split("\t");
            if (tokens.length > 3) {
                String page = tokens[2];
                String ip = tokens[0];
                first.set(page);
                second.set(ip);
                compositeKey.setFirst(first);
                compositeKey.setSecond(second);
                outputValue.set(ip);
                context.write(compositeKey, outputValue);
            }
        }
    }
}

public class PageViewReducer extends Reducer<CompositeKey, Text,
Text, LongWritable> {
    private LongWritable pageViews = new LongWritable();

    @Override
    protected void reduce(CompositeKey key, Iterable<Text>
      values, Context context)
      throws IOException, InterruptedException {
        String lastIp = null;
        long pages = 0;
        for(Text t : values) {
            String ip = t.toString();
            if (lastIp == null) {
                lastIp = ip;
                pages++;
            }
            else if (!lastIp.equals(ip)) {
                lastIp = ip;
                pages++;
            }
            else if (lastIp.compareTo(ip) > 0) {
                throw new IOException("secondary sort failed");
            }
        }
        pageViews.set(pages);
        context.write(key.getFirst(), pageViews);
    }
}
```

3. Create three classes to partition, group, and sort the data leaving the mapper. These classes are used by the MapReduce framework. First, write a class to partition the data emitted from the mapper by the `page` field:

```
static class CompositeKeyParitioner extends
Partitioner<CompositeKey, Writable> {

        @Override
        public int getPartition(CompositeKey key, Writable value,
    int numParition) {
            return (key.getFirst().hashCode() &  0x7FFFFFFF) %
    numParition;
        }
    }
```

4. Next, write a Comparator that will group all of the keys together:

```
static class GroupComparator extends WritableComparator {
        public GroupComparator() {
            super(CompositeKey.class, true);
        }

        @Override
        public int compare(WritableComparable a,
    WritableComparable b) {
            CompositeKey lhs = (CompositeKey)a;
            CompositeKey rhs = (CompositeKey)b;
            return lhs.getFirst().compareTo(rhs.getFirst());
        }
    }
```

5. Write a second Comparator that will sort the values passed to the reducer:

```
static class SortComparator extends WritableComparator {
        public SortComparator() {
            super(CompositeKey.class, true);
        }

        @Override
        public int compare(WritableComparable a,
    WritableComparable b) {
            CompositeKey lhs = (CompositeKey)a;
            CompositeKey rhs = (CompositeKey)b;
            int cmp = lhs.getFirst().compareTo(rhs.getFirst());
            if (cmp != 0) {
                return cmp;
            }
```

```
                 return lhs.getSecond().compareTo(rhs.getSecond());
        }
    }
```

6. Finally, write the code to set up a normal MapReduce job, but tell the MapReduce framework to use our own partitioner and comparator classes:

```
public int run(String[] args) throws Exception {

        Path inputPath = new Path(args[0]);
        Path outputPath = new Path(args[1]);

        Configuration conf = getConf();
        Job weblogJob = new Job(conf);
        weblogJob.setJobName("PageViews");
        weblogJob.setJarByClass(getClass());
        weblogJob.setMapperClass(PageViewMapper.class);
        weblogJob.setMapOutputKeyClass(CompositeKey.class);
        weblogJob.setMapOutputValueClass(Text.class);

        weblogJob.setPartitionerClass(CompositeKeyParitioner.
class);
        weblogJob.setGroupingComparatorClass(GroupComparator.
class);
        weblogJob.setSortComparatorClass(SortComparator.class);

        weblogJob.setReducerClass(PageViewReducer.class);
        weblogJob.setOutputKeyClass(Text.class);
        weblogJob.setOutputValueClass(Text.class);
        weblogJob.setInputFormatClass(TextInputFormat.class);
        weblogJob.setOutputFormatClass(TextOutputFormat.class);

        FileInputFormat.setInputPaths(weblogJob, inputPath);
        FileOutputFormat.setOutputPath(weblogJob, outputPath);


        if(weblogJob.waitForCompletion(true)) {
            return 0;
        }
        return 1;
    }
```

How it works...

We first created a class named `CompositeKey`. This class extends the Hadoop `WritableComparable` interface so that we can use the `CompositeKey` class just like any normal Hadoop `WritableComparable` interface (for example, `Text` and `IntWritable`). The `CompositeKey` class holds two `Text` objects. The first `Text` object is used to partition and group the key-value pairs emitted from the mapper. The second `Text` object is used to perform the secondary sort.

Next, we wrote a mapper class to emit the key-value pair `CompositeKey` (which consists of page and IP) as the key, and IP as the value. In addition, we wrote a reducer class that receives a `CompositeKey` object and a sorted list of IPs. The distinct IP count is calculated by incrementing a counter whenever we see an IP that does not equal a previously seen IP.

After writing the mapper and reducer classes, we created three classes to partition, group, and sort the data. The `CompositeKeyPartitioner` class is responsible for partitioning the data emitted from the mapper. In this recipe, we want all of the same pages to go to the same partition. Therefore, we calculate the partition location based only on the first field of the `CompositeKey` class.

Next, we created a `GroupComparator` class that uses the same logic as `CompositeKeyPartitioner`. We want all of the same page keys grouped together for processing by a reducer. Therefore, the group comparator only inspects the first member of the `CompositeKey` class for comparison.

Finally, we created the `SortComparator` class. This class is responsible for sorting all of the values that are sent to the reducer. As you can see from the method signature, `compare(WritableComparable a, WritableComparable b)`, we only receive the keys that are sent to each reducer, which is why we needed to include the IP with each and every key the mapper emitted. The `SortComparator` class compares both the first and second members of the `CompositeKey` class to ensure that the values a reducer receives are sorted.

See also

 ▸   *Creating custom Hadoop Writable and InputFormat to read geographical event data*

Using Hive and Python to clean and transform geographical event data

This recipe uses certain operators in Hive to input/output data through a custom Python script. The script performs a few simple pruning operations over each row, and outputs a slightly modified version of the row into a Hive table.

Getting ready

You will need to download/compile/install the following:

- ► Version 0.7.1 of Apache Hive from `http://hive.apache.org/`
- ► Test data: `Nigeria_ACLED.csv`, `Nigeria_ACLED_cleaned.tsv` from `http://www.packtpub.com/support`
- ► Python 2.7 or greater

This recipe requires the `Nigera_ACLED.csv` file to be loaded into a Hive table named `acled_nigeria` with the following fields mapped to the respective data types.

Issue the following command to the Hive client:

```
describe acled_nigeria
```

You should see the following response:

```
OK
loc string
event_date    string
year    string
event_type    string
actor    string
latitude    double
longitude double
source string
fatalities    string
```

How to do it...

Follow these steps to use Python and Hive to transform data:

1. Create a file named `clean_and_transform_acled.hql` in your local working directory and add the inline creation and transformation syntax:

```
SET mapred.child.java.opts=-Xmx512M;

DROP TABLE IF EXISTS acled_nigeria_cleaned;
CREATE TABLE acled_nigeria_cleaned (
    loc STRING,
    event_date STRING,
    event_type STRING,
```

```
    actor STRING,
    latitude DOUBLE,
    longitude DOUBLE,
    source STRING,
    fatalities INT
) ROW FORMAT DELIMITED;

ADD FILE ./clean_acled_nigeria.py;
INSERT OVERWRITE TABLE acled_nigeria_cleaned
    SELECT TRANSFORM(
            if(loc != "", loc, 'Unknown'),
            event_date,
            year,
            event_type,
            actor,
            latitude,
            longitude,
            source,
            if(fatalities != "", fatalities, 'ZERO_FLAG'))
    USING 'python clean_acled_nigeria.py'
    AS (loc, event_date, event_type, actor, latitude, longitude,
source, fatalities)
    FROM acled_nigeria;
```

2. Next, create another file named `clean_acled_nigeria.py` in the same working directory as `clean_and_transform_acled.hql` and add the following Python code to read from stdin:

```python
#!/usr/bin/env python
import sys

for line in sys.stdin:
    (loc, event_date, year, event_type, actor, lat, lon, src,
fatalities) = line.strip().split('\t')
  if loc != 'LOCATION': #remove header row
    if fatalities == 'ZERO_FLAG':
    fatalities = '0'
      print '\t'.join([loc, event_date, event_type, \ actor, lat,
lon, src, fatalities]) #strip out year
```

It is important to note that Python is sensitive to inconsistent indentation. Be careful if you are copying and pasting Python code.

3. Run the script from the operating system shell by supplying the −f option to the Hive client:

```
$ hive -f clean_and_transform_acled.hql
```

4. To verify that the script finished properly, run the following command using the −e option to the Hive client.

```
hive -e "select count(1) from acled_nigeria_cleaned"
```

Hive should count 2931 rows.

How it works...

Let's start with the Hive script that we created. The first line is simply to force a certain JVM heap size in our execution. You can set this to any size that may be appropriate for your cluster. For the ACLED Nigeria dataset, a 512 MB memory is more than enough.

Immediately following this, we drop any tables with the name acled_nigeria_cleaned and create a table by the same name. We can omit the fields delimited by ',' and rows delimited by '\n' since they are the default field and row delimiters assumed by ROW FORMAT, and the ACLED Nigeria data is in that format.

Once we have our receiving table defined, we need to define the SELECT statement that will transform and output the data. The common convention is to add scripts required by SELECT before the statement. The command ADD FILE ./clean_acled_nigeria.py tells Hive to load the script from the local filesystem into the distributed cache for use by the MapReduce tasks.

The SELECT statement uses the Hive TRANSFORM operator to separate each column by tabs and to cast all columns as String with nulls as '\n'. The columns loc and fatalities are conditionally checked for empty strings; and if found to be empty, are set to a default value.

We specify the USING operator to provide a custom script to work with the TRANSFORM operator. Hive requires that scripts that make a call to the USING operator for row transformation need to first invoke TRANSFORM with the appropriate columns. If the file has been placed on the distributed cache, and each node in the cluster has Python installed, the MapReduce JVM tasks will be able to execute the script and read the rows in parallel. The AS operator contains a list of named fields corresponding to the columns found in the receiving Hive table, acled_nigeria_cleaned.

The Python script is very straightforward. The `#!/usr/bin/env python` statement is a hint to tell the shell how to execute the script. Each row from the table is passed in as a line over standard input. The call to `strip()` method removes any leading/trailing whitespace, and then we tokenize it into an array of named variables. Each field from the row is put in a named variable. The raw ACLED Nigeria data was used to create the input Hive table, and contains a header row we wish to discard. The first condition will check for `'LOCATION'` as the value of `loc`, which indicates the header row we want to ignore.

If the row passes this check, we look for the presence of `'ZERO_FLAG'` as the value for `fatalities`, which we set in our Hive script. If the script detects this value for `fatalities`, we set the value of `fatalities` to the string `'0'`.

Finally, we output each field excluding `year` in the same order as it was input. Each row will be placed into the table `acled_nigeria_cleaned`.

There's more...

There is a lot going on in this recipe. The following are a few additional explanations that will help you with Hive `TRANSFORM/USING/AS` operations and ETL in general.

Making every column type String

This is a bit counterintuitive and certainly not found anywhere in the Hive documentation. If your initial Hive staging table for the incoming data maps each delimited field as a string, it will aid tremendously in data validation and debugging. You can use the Hive `STRING` type to successfully represent almost any input into a cleansing script or direct Hive `QL` statement. Trying to perfectly map datatypes over expected values is not flexible to an erroneous input. There may be malformed characters for fields where you expect numeric values, and other similar hang-ups that make it impossible to perform certain analytics. Using strings over the raw data fields will allow a custom script to inspect the invalid data and decide how to respond. Moreover, when dealing with CSV or tab-separated data, a slightly misaligned `INT` or `FLOAT` type mapping in your Hive table declaration, where the data has a `STRING`, could lead to `NULL` mappings per row. String mappings for every field in the raw table will show you column misalignment failures such as these, very quickly. This is just a matter of preference, and only applies to tables designed for holding the raw or dirty input for immediate validation and transformation into other Hive tables.

Type casing values using the AS keyword

This recipe only outputs strings from the Python script for use over standard output. Hive will attempt to cast them to the appropriate type in the receiving table. The advantage to this is the time and coding space saved by not having to explicitly cast every field with the `AS` operator. The disadvantage is that this will not fail should a value be cast to an incompatible type. For instance, outputting `HI THERE` to a numeric field will insert `NULL` for the field value for that row. This can lead to undesirable behavior for subsequent `SELECT` statements over the table.

Testing the script locally

This one is pretty self-explanatory. It is much easier to debug your script directly on the command line than it is across MapReduce task error logs. It likely will not prevent you from having to troubleshoot issues dealing with scale or data validity, but it will eliminate a large majority of the compile time and control flow issues.

Using Python and Hadoop Streaming to perform a time series analytic

This recipe shows how to use Hadoop Streaming with Python to perform a basic time series analysis over the cleansed ACLED Nigeria dataset. The program is designed to output a list of dates in sorted order for each location where the government in Nigeria regained territory.

For this recipe, we will use structured Nigerian conflict data provided by Armed Conflict Location and Event dataset collections team.

Getting ready

You will need to download/compile/install the following:

- ▸ Version 0.7.1 of Apache Pig from `http://hive.apache.org/`
- ▸ Test data: download `Nigeria_ACLED_cleaned.tsv` from `http://www.packtpub.com/support` and place the file into HDFS
- ▸ Python 2.6 or greater

How to do it...

The following are the steps to use Python with Hadoop Streaming:

1. Create a shell script named `run_location_regains.sh` that runs the Streaming job. It is important to change the streaming JAR path to match the absolute path of your `hadoop-streaming.jar` file. The path of the `hadoop-streaming.jar` file is different depending on the Hadoop distribution:

```
#!/bin/bash
$HADOOP_HOME/bin/hadoop jar $HADOOP_HOME/contrib/streaming/hadoop-
streaming-0.20.2-cdh3u1.jar \
    -input /input/acled_cleaned/Nigeria_ACLED_cleaned.tsv \
    -output /output/acled_analytic_out \
    -mapper location_regains_mapper.py \
    -reducer location_regains_by_time.py \
    -file location_regains_by_time.py \
```

```
            -file location_regains_mapper.py \
        -jobconf stream.num.map.output.key.fields=2 \
        -jobconf map.output.key.field.separator=\t \
        -jobconf num.key.fields.for.partition=1 \
        -jobconf mapred.reduce.tasks=1
```

2. Create a Python file named `location_regains_mapper.py` and add the following:

```python
#!/usr/bin/python
import sys

for line in sys.stdin:
    (loc, event_date, event_type, actor, lat, lon, src,
fatalities) = line.strip().split('\t');
    (day,month,year) = event_date.split('/')
    if len(day) == 1:
        day = '0' + day
    if len(month) == 1:
        month = '0' + month;
    if len(year) == 2:
        if int(year) > 30 and int(year) < 99:
            year = '19' + year
        else:
            year = '20' + year
    event_date = year + '-' + month + '-' + day
    print '\t'.join([loc, event_date, event_type]);
```

3. Create a Python file named `location_regains_by_time.py` and add the following:

```python
#!/usr/bin/python
import sys

current_loc = "START_OF_APP"
govt_regains=[]
for line in sys.stdin:
    (loc,event_date,event_type) = line.strip('\n').split('\t')
    if loc != current_loc:
        if current_loc != "START_OF_APP":
            print current_loc + '\t' + '\t'.join(govt_regains)
        current_loc = loc
        govt_regains = []
    if event_type.find('regains') != -1:
        govt_regains.append(event_date)
```

4. Run the shell script from the local working directory, which should contain all of the Python scripts that we created previously:

```
./run_location_regains.sh
```

You should see the job start from the command line and finish successfully:

```
INFO streaming.StreamJob: Output: /output/acled_analytic_out
```

How it works...

The shell script sets up the Hadoop Streaming JAR path and passes the necessary arguments to the program. Each argument is explained in detail as follows:

Argument	Description
`-input /input/acled_cleaned/ Nigeria_ACLED_cleaned.tsv \`	The HDFS path to the input data for MapReduce.
`-output /output/acled_analytic_ out \`	The HDFS path for MapReduce to write the job output.
`-mapper location_regains_mapper. py \`	Script to be run as the map function; records passed via `STDIN`/`STDOUT`.
`-reducer location_regains_by_ time.py \`	Script to be run as the reduce function.
`-file location_regains_by_time. py \`	Add a file to the distributed cache. This is required for external scripts.
`-file location_regains_mapper. py \`	Add a file to the distributed cache.
`-jobconf stream.num.map.output. key.fields=2 \`	Tells the streaming tool which field/fields should be treated as the map output key. Our mapper outputs three fields per record. This parameter tells the program to treat the first two as the key. This will leverage the secondary sort feature in MapReduce to sort our rows based on the composite of these two fields.
`-jobconf map.output.key.field. separator=\t \`	Parameter for setting the delimiter token on the key.
`-jobconf num.key.fields.for. partition=1 \`	Guarantees that all of the map output records with the same value in the first field of the key are sent to the same reducer.
`-jobconf mapred.reduce.tasks=1`	Number of JVM tasks to reduce over the output keys.

The Python script used in the map phase gets a `line` corresponding to each record. We call `strip()` to remove any leading/trailing whitespace and then split the line on tabs. The result is an array of variables descriptively named to the row fields they hold.

The `event_date` field in the raw input requires some processing. In order for the framework to sort records in ascending order of dates, we want to take the current form, which is dd/mm/yy and convert it to yyyy-mm-dd. Since some of the events occurred before the year 2000, we need to expand the year variable out to four digits. Single-digit days and months are zero-padded, so that it sorts correctly.

This analytics only requires `location`, `event_date`, and `event_type` to be output to the reduce stage. In the shell script, we specified the first two fields as the output key. Specifying `location` as the first field groups all records with the same location on a common reducer. Specifying `event_date` as the second field allows the MapReduce framework to sort the records by the composite of `location` and `event_date`. The value in each key-value pair is simply of the `event_type` field.

Sample map output:

```
(cityA, 2010-08-09, explosion)
(cityB, 2008-10-10, fire)
(cityA, 2009-07-03, riots)
```

Order reducer shows the records that are sorted on the composite value of `location` and `event_date`

```
(cityA, 2009-07-03, riots)
(cityA, 2010-08-09,explosion)
(cityB, 2008-10-10,fire)
```

Our configuration specifies only one reducer, so in this recipe all of the rows will partition to the same reduce Java Virtual Machine (JVM). If multiple reduce tasks are specified, `cityA` and `cityB` could be processed independently on separate reduce JVMs.

Understanding how the MapReduce framework sorts and handles the output of the `location_regains_mapper.py` file is important to determine how the reduce script works.

We use `location_regains_by_time.py` to iterate over the sorted collection of events per location, and aggregate events that match a particular type.

As the records were partitioned by location, we can assume that each partition will go to its own mapper. Furthermore, because we specified `event_date` as an additional sort column, we can make the assumption that the events corresponding to a given location are sorted by date in the ascending order. Now we are in a position to understand how the script works.

The script must keep a track of when a `loc` input changes from the previous location. Such a change signifies that we are done processing the previous location, since they are all in sorted order. We initialize the `current_loc` flag to START_OF_APP. We also declare an empty array `govt_regains` to hold the dates of events we are interested in.

The program starts by processing each line into variables. If there is a change in `loc` and it is not the beginning of the application, we know to output the current `govt_regains` collection to standard out. The change means that we are done processing the previous location, and can safely write its collection of event dates out of the reducer.

If the incoming `loc` value is the same as `current_loc`, we know that the incoming event still corresponds to the location we are currently processing. We check to see if the event is of the type `regains` to show the government the regained territories in that region. If it matches that type, we add it to the current `govt_regains` collection. Since the incoming records are sorted by `event_date`, we are guaranteed that the records are inserted in `govt_regains` in the ascending order of dates.

The net result is a single part file that is output from the reducer with a list of locations in lexicographically sorted order. To the right-hand side of each location is a tab-separated sorted list of dates matching the occurrences of when the government regained territory in that location.

There's more...

Hadoop Streaming is a very popular component. The following are a few important additions to know:

Using Hadoop Streaming with any language that can read from stdin and write to stdout

You are not limited to just Python when working with Hadoop Streaming. Java classes, shell scripts, ruby scripts, and many other languages are frequently used to transition existing code and functionality into full-fledged MapReduce programs. Any language that can read stdin and write to stdout will work with Hadoop Streaming.

Using the –file parameter to pass additional required files for MapReduce jobs

Similar to normal MapReduce programs, you can pass additional dependencies over the distributed cache to be used in your applications. Simply add additional –file parameters. For example:

```
-file mapper.py \
-file wordlist.txt
```

Using MultipleOutputs in MapReduce to name output files

A common request among MapReduce users is to control output file names to something other than `part-*`. This recipe shows how you can use the `MultipleOutputs` class to emit different key-value pairs to the same named file that you chose.

Getting ready

You will need to download the `ip-to-country.txt` dataset from the Packt website, `http://www.packtpub.com/support`, and place the file in HDFS.

How to do it...

Follow these steps to use `MultipleOutputs`:

1. Create a class named `NamedCountryOutputJob` and configure the MapReduce job:

```
import org.apache.hadoop.conf.Configuration;
import org.apache.hadoop.fs.Path;
import org.apache.hadoop.io.IntWritable;
import org.apache.hadoop.io.LongWritable;
import org.apache.hadoop.io.NullWritable;
import org.apache.hadoop.io.Text;
import org.apache.hadoop.mapreduce.Job;
import org.apache.hadoop.mapreduce.Mapper;
import org.apache.hadoop.mapreduce.Reducer;
import org.apache.hadoop.mapreduce.lib.input.FileInputFormat;
import org.apache.hadoop.mapreduce.lib.input.TextInputFormat;
import org.apache.hadoop.mapreduce.lib.output.FileOutputFormat;
import org.apache.hadoop.mapreduce.lib.output.MultipleOutputs;
import org.apache.hadoop.mapreduce.lib.output.TextOutputFormat;
import org.apache.hadoop.util.Tool;
import org.apache.hadoop.util.ToolRunner;

import java.io.IOException;
import java.util.regex.Pattern;


public class NamedCountryOutputJob implements Tool{
```

```
    private Configuration conf;
    public static final String NAME = "named_output";


    public static void main(String[] args) throws Exception {
        ToolRunner.run(new Configuration(), new
NamedCountryOutputJob(), args);
    }
    public int run(String[] args) throws Exception {
        if(args.length != 2) {
            System.err.println("Usage: named_output <input>
<output>");
            System.exit(1);
        }

        Job job = new Job(conf, "IP count by country to named
files");
        job.setInputFormatClass(TextInputFormat.class);

        job.setMapperClass(IPCountryMapper.class);
        job.setReducerClass(IPCountryReducer.class);

        job.setMapOutputKeyClass(Text.class);
        job.setMapOutputValueClass(IntWritable.class);
        job.setJarByClass(NamedCountryOutputJob.class);

        FileInputFormat.addInputPath(job, new Path(args[0]));
        FileOutputFormat.setOutputPath(job, new Path(args[1]));

        return job.waitForCompletion(true) ? 1 : 0;

    }

    public void setConf(Configuration conf) {
        this.conf = conf;
    }

    public Configuration getConf() {
        return conf;
    }
```

2. Create a mapper to emit the key-value pair `country`, and the number `1`:

```
public static class IPCountryMapper
            extends Mapper<LongWritable, Text, Text, IntWritable>
    {

            private static final int country_pos = 1;
            private static final Pattern pattern = Pattern.
compile("\\t");

            @Override
            protected void map(LongWritable key, Text value,
                              Context context)    throws IOException,
    InterruptedException {
                String country = pattern.split(value.toString())
    [country_pos];
                context.write(new Text(country), new IntWritable(1));
            }
        }
```

3. Create a reducer that sums all of the `country` counts, and writes the output to separate files using `MultipleOutputs`:

```
public static class IPCountryReducer
            extends Reducer<Text, IntWritable, Text, IntWritable>
    {

            private MultipleOutputs output;

            @Override
            protected void setup(Context context
            ) throws IOException, InterruptedException {
                output = new MultipleOutputs(context);
            }


            @Override
            protected void reduce(Text key, Iterable<IntWritable>
    values, Context context) throws IOException, InterruptedException
    {
                int total = 0;
                for(IntWritable value: values) {
                    total += value.get();
                }
                output.write(new Text("Output by MultipleOutputs"),
```

```
                    NullWritable.get(), key.toString());
            output.write(key, new IntWritable(total), key.
    toString());
        }

        @Override
        protected void cleanup(Context context
        ) throws IOException, InterruptedException {
            output.close();
        }
    }
}
```

Once the job completes successfully, you should see named output files under the provided output directory (for example, `Qatar-r-#####`, `Turkey-r-#####`).

How it works...

We first set up our job using the `Tool` interface provided by Hadoop. The `run()` method inside `NamedCountryOutputJob` checks that both input and output HDFS path directories are provided. In addition, both the mapper and reducer classes are set, and we configure the InputFormat to read lines of text.

The mapper class defines a statically initialized position to read the country from each line, as well as the regex pattern to split each line. The mapper will output the country as the key and `1` for every line it appears on.

At the reduce phase, each task JVM runs the `setup()` routine and initializes a `MultipleOutputs` instance named `output`.

Each call to `reduce()` presents a country and a tally of every occurrence of the country appearing in the dataset. We sum the tally into a final count. Before we emit the final count, we will use the output instance to write a header to the file. The key contains the text for the header `Output by MultipleOutputs`, and we null out the value since we don't need it. We specify `key.toString()` to write the header to a custom file named by the current country. On the next line we call `output.write()` again, except this time with the input key as the output key, the final count as the output value, and the `key.toString()` method to specify the same output file as the previous `output.write()` method.

The end result is a named country file containing both the header and the final tallied count for that country.

By using `MultipleOutputs`, we don't have to configure an `OutputFormat` class in our job setup routine. Also, we are not limited to just one concrete type for the reducer output key and value. We were able to output key-value pairs for both `Text/NullWritable` and `Text/IntWritable` to the exact same file.

Creating custom Hadoop Writable and InputFormat to read geographical event data

When reading input, or writing output from a MapReduce application, it is sometimes easier to work with data using an abstract class instead of the primitive Hadoop Writable classes (for example, `Text` and `IntWritable`). This recipe demonstrates how to create a custom Hadoop Writable and InputFormat that can be used by MapReduce applications.

Getting ready

You will need to download the `Nigeria_ACLED_cleaned.tsv` dataset from `http://www.packtpub.com/support` and place the file into HDFS.

How to do it...

Follow these steps to create custom InputFormat and Writable classes:

1. First we will define two custom `WritableComparable` classes. These classes represent the key-value pairs that are passed to the mapper, much as how `TextInputFormat` passes `LongWritable` and `Text` to the mapper.

    Write the key class:

    ```java
    public class GeoKey implements WritableComparable {
        private Text location;
        private FloatWritable latitude;
        private FloatWritable longitude;
        public GeoKey() {
            location = null;
            latitude = null;
            longitude = null;
        }

        public GeoKey(Text location, FloatWritable latitude,
          FloatWritable longitude) {
            this.location = location;
            this.latitude = latitude;
            this.longitude = longitude;
        }

        //...getters and setters
    ```

```
public void readFields(DataInput di) throws IOException {
    if (location == null) {
        location = new Text();
    }
    if (latitude == null) {
        latitude = new FloatWritable();
    }
    if (longitude == null) {
        longitude = new FloatWritable();
    }
    location.readFields(di);
    latitude.readFields(di);
    longitude.readFields(di);
}
public int compareTo(Object o) {
    GeoKey other = (GeoKey)o;
    int cmp = location.compareTo(other.location);
    if (cmp != 0) {
        return cmp;
    }
    cmp = latitude.compareTo(other.latitude);
    if (cmp != 0) {
        return cmp;
    }
    return longitude.compareTo(other.longitude);
}

}
```

2. Now, the value class:

```
public class GeoValue implements WritableComparable {
    private Text eventDate;
    private Text eventType;
    private Text actor;
    private Text source;
    private IntWritable fatalities;

    public GeoValue() {
        eventDate = null;
        eventType = null;
        actor = null;
        source = null;
        fatalities = null;
    }
```

```
//...getters and setters

public void write(DataOutput d) throws IOException {
    eventDate.write(d);
    eventType.write(d);
    actor.write(d);
    source.write(d);
    fatalities.write(d);
}

public void readFields(DataInput di) throws IOException {
    if (eventDate == null) {
        eventDate = new Text();
    }
    if (eventType == null) {
        eventType = new Text();
    }
    if (actor == null) {
        actor = new Text();
    }
    if (source == null) {
        source = new Text();
    }
    if (fatalities == null) {
        fatalities = new IntWritable();
    }
    eventDate.readFields(di);
    eventType.readFields(di);
    actor.readFields(di);
    source.readFields(di);
    fatalities.readFields(di);
}

public int compareTo(Object o) {
    GeoValue other = (GeoValue)o;
    int cmp = eventDate.compareTo(other.eventDate);
    if (cmp != 0) {
        return cmp;
    }
    cmp = eventType.compareTo(other.eventType);
    if (cmp != 0) {
        return cmp;
    }
    cmp = actor.compareTo(other.actor);
```

```
        if (cmp != 0) {
            return cmp;
        }
        cmp = source.compareTo(other.source);
        if (cmp != 0) {
            return cmp;
        }
        return fatalities.compareTo(other.fatalities);
    }

}
```

3. Next, we need to create an InputFormat to serialize the text from our input file and create the `GeoKey` and `GeoValue` instances. This input format extends the Hadoop `FileInputFormat` class and returns our own implementation of a RecordReader:

```
public class GeoInputFormat extends FileInputFormat<GeoKey,
GeoValue> {

    @Override
    public RecordReader<GeoKey, GeoValue>
createRecordReader(InputSplit split, TaskAttemptContext context) {
        return new GeoRecordReader();
    }

    @Override
    protected boolean isSplitable(JobContext context, Path file) {
        CompressionCodec codec =
                new CompressionCodecFactory(context.
getConfiguration()).getCodec(file);
        return codec == null;
    }
}
```

4. Now, create a RecordReader to read from the `Nigeria_ACLED_cleaned.tsv` dataset:

```
public class GeoRecordReader extends RecordReader<GeoKey,
GeoValue> {

    private GeoKey key;
    private GeoValue value;
    private LineRecordReader reader = new LineRecordReader();
    @Override
    public void initialize(InputSplit is, TaskAttemptContext tac)
throws IOException, InterruptedException {
        reader.initialize(is, tac);
```

```
    }

    @Override
    public boolean nextKeyValue() throws IOException,
InterruptedException {

        boolean gotNextKeyValue = reader.nextKeyValue();
        if(gotNextKeyValue) {
            if (key == null) {
                key = new GeoKey();
            }
            if (value == null) {
                value = new GeoValue();
            }
            Text line = reader.getCurrentValue();
            String[] tokens = line.toString().split("\t");
            key.setLocation(new Text(tokens[0]));
            key.setLatitude(new FloatWritable(Float.
parseFloat(tokens[4])));
            key.setLongitude(new FloatWritable(Float.
parseFloat(tokens[5])));

            value.setActor(new Text(tokens[3]));
            value.setEventDate(new Text(tokens[1]));
            value.setEventType(new Text(tokens[2]));
            try {
                value.setFatalities(new IntWritable(Integer.
parseInt(tokens[7])));
            } catch(NumberFormatException ex) {
                value.setFatalities(new IntWritable(0));
            }
            value.setSource(new Text(tokens[6]));
        }
        else {
            key = null;
            value = null;
        }
        return gotNextKeyValue;
    }

    @Override
    public GeoKey getCurrentKey() throws IOException,
InterruptedException {
        return key;
    }
```

```
    @Override
    public GeoValue getCurrentValue() throws IOException,
InterruptedException {
        return value;
    }
    @Override
    public float getProgress() throws IOException,
InterruptedException {
        return reader.getProgress();
    }
    @Override
    public void close() throws IOException {
        reader.close();
    }

}
```

5. Finally, create a simple map-only job to test the InputFormat:

```
public class GeoFilter extends Configured implements Tool {

    public static class GeoFilterMapper extends Mapper<GeoKey,
GeoValue, Text, IntWritable> {
        @Override
        protected void map(GeoKey key, GeoValue value, Context
context) throws IOException, InterruptedException {
            String location = key.getLocation().toString();
            if (location.toLowerCase().equals("aba")) {
                context.write(value.getActor(),
                    value.getFatalities());
            }
        }
    }

    public int run(String[] args) throws Exception {

        Path inputPath = new Path(args[0]);
        Path outputPath = new Path(args[1]);

        Configuration conf = getConf();
        Job geoJob = new Job(conf);
        geoJob.setNumReduceTasks(0);
        geoJob.setJobName("GeoFilter");
        geoJob.setJarByClass(getClass());
        geoJob.setMapperClass(GeoFilterMapper.class);
```

```
geoJob.setMapOutputKeyClass(Text.class);
geoJob.setMapOutputValueClass(IntWritable.class);
geoJob.setInputFormatClass(GeoInputFormat.class);
geoJob.setOutputFormatClass(TextOutputFormat.class);

FileInputFormat.setInputPaths(geoJob, inputPath);
FileOutputFormat.setOutputPath(geoJob, outputPath);

if(geoJob.waitForCompletion(true)) {
    return 0;
}
return 1;
}

public static void main(String[] args) throws Exception {
    int returnCode = ToolRunner.run(new GeoFilter(), args);
    System.exit(returnCode);
}
}
```

How it works...

The first task was to define our own Hadoop key and value representations by implementing the `WritableComparable` interface. The `WritableComparable` interface allows us to create our own abstract types, which can be used as keys or values by the MapReduce framework.

Next, we created an InputFormat that inherits from the `FileInputFormat` class. The Hadoop `FileInputFormat` is the base class for all file-based InputFormats. The InputFormat takes care of managing the input files for a MapReduce job. Since we do not want to change the way in which our input files are split and distributed across the cluster, we only need to override two methods, `createRecordReader()` and `isSplitable()`.

The `isSplitable()` method is used to instruct the `FileInputFormat` class that it is acceptable to split up the input files if there is a codec available in the Hadoop environment to read and split the file. The `createRecordReader()` method is used to create a Hadoop RecordReader that processes individual file splits and generates a key-value pair for the mappers to process.

After the `GeoInputFormat` class was written, we wrote a RecordReader to process the individual input splits and create `GeoKey` and `GeoValue` for the mappers. The `GeoRecordReader` class reused the Hadoop `LineRecordReader` class to read from the input split. When the `LineRecordReader` class completed reading a record from the `Nigeria_ACLED_cleaned.tsv` dataset, we created two objects. These objects are `GeoKey` and `GeoValue`, which are sent to the mapper.

4

Performing Common Tasks Using Hive, Pig, and MapReduce

In this chapter we will cover:

- ▶ Using Hive to map an external table over weblog data in HDFS
- ▶ Using Hive to dynamically create tables from the results of a weblog query
- ▶ Using the Hive string UDFs to concatenate fields in weblog data
- ▶ Using Hive to intersect weblog IPs and determine the country
- ▶ Generating *n*-grams over news archives using MapReduce
- ▶ Using the distributed cache in MapReduce to find lines that contain matching keywords over news archives
- ▶ Using Pig to load a table and perform a SELECT operation with GROUP BY

Introduction

When working with Apache Hive, Pig, and MapReduce, you may find yourself having to perform certain tasks frequently. The recipes in this chapter provide solutions for executing several very common routines.

You will find that these tools let you solve the same problems in numerous different ways. Deciding on the right implementation can be a difficult task. The recipes presented here were designed for coding efficiency and clarity.

Hive and Pig provide a clean abstraction layer between your data flow and meaningful queries, and the complex MapReduce workflows they compile to. You can leverage the power of MapReduce for scalable queries without having to think about the underlying MapReduce semantics. Both tools handle the decomposition and building of your expressions into the proper MapReduce sequences. Hive lets you build analytics and manage data using a declarative, SQL-like dialect known as **HiveQL**. Pig operations are written in Pig Latin and take a more imperative form.

Using Hive to map an external table over weblog data in HDFS

You will often want to create tables over existing data that does not live within the managed Hive warehouse in HDFS. Creating a Hive external table is one of the easiest ways to handle this scenario. Queries from the Hive client will execute as they normally do over internally managed tables.

Getting ready

Make sure you have access to a pseudo-distributed or fully-distributed Hadoop cluster, with Apache Hive 0.7.1 installed on your client machine and on the environment path for the active user account. This recipe depends on having the `weblog_entries` dataset loaded into an HDFS directory at the absolute path `/input/weblog/weblog_records.txt`.

How to do it...

Carry out the following steps to map an external table in HDFS:

1. Open a text editor of your choice, ideally one with SQL syntax highlighting. I have used the Textmate text editor for this recipe.

2. Add the `CREATE TABLE` syntax, as follows:

```
DROP TABLE IF EXISTS weblog_entries;
CREATE EXTERNAL TABLE weblog_entries (
        md5 STRING,
        url STRING,
        request_date STRING,
        request_time STRING,
        ip STRING
)
ROW FORMAT DELIMITED FIELDS TERMINATED BY '\t' LINES TERMINATED BY
'\n'
LOCATION '/input/weblog/';
```

3. Save the script as `weblog_create_external_table.hsql` in the working directory.

4. Run the script from the operating system shell by supplying the `-f` option to the Hive client, as follows:

```
hive -f weblog_create_external_table.hql
```

5. You should see two successful commands issued to the Hive client.

```
OK
Time taken: 2.654 seconds
OK
Time taken: 0.473 seconds
```

How it works...

The existing definition of the table `weblog_entries` is deleted if it already exists. Following this, the script issues a `CREATE` command with the `EXTERNAL` keyword, which tells the Hive Metastore that the data is not managed by the Hive warehouse in HDFS.

The table is defined as having five fields per entry. The MD5 of the URL, the URL itself, the date of the request, the exact time of the request, and the IP address that the request was associated with.

`ROW FORMAT DELIMITED` uses the native Hive **SerDe**, which is Hive's extensible and internal serialization/deserialization mechanism for reading and writing raw data. We explicitly tell the SerDe that a tab character separates each field and a newline character separates each record. The `LOCATION` keyword is required by Hive when creating an external table. It points to the HDFS directory that contains the table data using an absolute path.

There's more...

There are a few handy tips that you need to know when working with external tables.

LOCATION must point to a directory, not a file

As of Hive release 0.7.1, the `LOCATION` keyword requires an absolute path to a directory in HDFS.

Dropping an external table does not delete the data stored in the table

Unlike a managed table in Hive, the `DROP` command only deletes the table entry from the Metastore and not the physical data in HDFS. Other applications that depend on data stored in the supplied HDFS directory will continue to operate normally.

You can add data to the path specified by LOCATION

If new data is inserted into a directory specified in an external table's LOCATION attribute, the data will be visible to any subsequent queries performed on the table.

Using Hive to dynamically create tables from the results of a weblog query

This recipe will outline a shorthand technique for inline table creation when the query is executed. Having to create every table definition up front is impractical and does not scale for large ETL. Being able to dynamically define intermediate tables is tremendously useful for complex analytics with multiple staging points.

In this recipe, we will create a new table that contains three fields from the weblog entry dataset, namely request_date, request_time, and url. In addition to this, we will define a new field called url_length.

Getting ready

Make sure you have access to a pseudo-distributed or fully-distributed Hadoop cluster, with Apache Hive 0.7.1 installed on your client machine and on the environment path for the active user account.

This recipe depends on having the weblog_entries dataset loaded into Hive table named weblog_entries with the following fields mapped to the respective datatypes.

Issue the following command to the Hive client:

```
describe weblog_entries
```

You should see the following response:

```
OK
md5 string
url string
request_date string
request_time string
ip string
```

How to do it...

Carry out the following steps to create an inline table definition using an alias:

1. Open a text editor of your choice, ideally one with SQL syntax highlighting.

2. Add the following inline creation syntax:

```
CREATE TABLE weblog_entries_with_url_length AS
SELECT url, request_date, request_time, length(url) as url_length
FROM weblog_entries;
```

3. Save the script as `weblog_entries_create_table_as.hql` in the active directory.

4. Run the script from the operating system shell by supplying the `-f` option to the Hive client, as follows:

```
hive -f weblog_create_table_as.hql
```

5. To verify that the table was created successfully, issue the following command to the Hive client directly, using the `-e` option:

```
hive -e "describe weblog_entries_with_url_length"
```

6. You should see a table with three `string` fields and a fourth `int` field holding the URL length:

```
OK
url string
request_date string
request_time string
url_length int
```

How it works...

The following statement initially defines a new table by the name `weblog_entries_with_url_length`:

```
CREATE TABLE weblog_entries_with_url_length AS
```

We then define the body of this table as an alias to the result set of a nested `SELECT` statement. In this case, our `SELECT` statement simply grabs the `url`, `request_date`, and `request_time` fields from each entry in the `weblog_entries` table. The field names are copied as field names to our new table `weblog_entires_with_url_length`. We also defined an additional field aliased as `url_length` to be calculated for each selected record. It stores an int value that represents the number of characters in the record's `url` field.

```
SELECT url, request_date, request_time, length(url) as url_length FROM
weblog_entries;
```

In one simple statement, we created a table with a subset of fields from our starting table, as well as a new derived field.

There's more...

The following are a few reminders for when using external tables:

CREATE TABLE AS cannot be used to create external tables

As of Apache Hive 0.7.1, you cannot create external tables using aliases with SELECT statements.

DROP temporary tables

The ease of the CREATE TABLE AS syntax lets Hive users create new tables very quickly, but don't forget to DROP any temporary tables. If you are scripting the CREATE ALIAS for repeated use, the next execution, especially, will fail if there are table name conflicts. Moreover, such intermediate tables will create a warehouse namespace that will quickly become unmanageable.

Using the Hive string UDFs to concatenate fields in weblog data

String concatenation is a very common operation in any development task. It frequently comes up when using Hive for report generation and even simple ETL tasks. This recipe will show a very basic and useful example using one of the Hive string concatenation UDFs.

In this recipe, we will take the separate request_date and request_time fields from the weblog_entries and print a single concatenated column to the console for every record, containing both the request_date and request_time fields separated by an underscore (_).

Getting ready

Make sure you have access to a pseudo-distributed or fully-distributed Hadoop cluster, with Apache Hive 0.7.1 installed on your client machine and on the environment path for the active user account.

This recipe depends on having the weblog_entries dataset loaded into a Hive table named weblog_entries with the following fields mapped to the respective datatypes.

Issue the following command to the Hive client:

```
describe weblog_entries
```

You should see the following response:

```
OK
md5 string
url string
request_date string
request_time string
ip string
```

How to do it...

Carry out the following steps to perform string concatenation in HiveQL:

1. Open a text editor of your choice, ideally one with SQL syntax highlighting.

2. Add the following inline creation syntax:

   ```
   SELECT concat_ws('_', request_date, request_time) FROM weblog_
   entries;
   ```

3. Save the script as `weblog_concat_date_time.hql` in the active directory.

4. Run the script from the operating system shell by supplying the `-f` option to the Hive client. You should see the results of the `SELECT` statement printed out to the console. The following snippet is an example that contains only two sample rows. The full printout will contain all 3000 rows.

   ```
   2012-05-10_21:33:26
   2012-05-10_21:13:10
   ```

How it works...

The script relies on the Hive built-in UDF to concatenate two strings together with a supplied separator token. For each row, it supplies the function with the respective `request_date` and `request_time` values that correspond to that row. The output of the function is a single string containing both the fields separated by an underscore (_). Since the `SELECT` statement consists of only that function, and the function outputs just a single string, we see a single column for all 3000 rows, one printed per line.

There's more...

The following are a few additional notes to help with the `concat_ws()` function:

The UDF concat_ws() function will not automatically cast parameters to String

If you pass non-string datatypes as parameters to `concat_ws()`, you will be greeted with a very descriptive error message:

```
FAILED: Error in semantic analysis: Line 1:21 Argument type mismatch
field1: Argument 2 of function CONCAT_WS must be "string", but "int"
was found.
```

If you wish to encapsulate the auto-casting of your parameters to string, use the regular `concat()` function.

Alias your concatenated field

Like most Hive UDFs, you can alias the output of `concat_ws()`. This comes in handy if you are persisting the results of the concatenation and want a very descriptive column header.

The concat_ws() function supports variable length parameter arguments

When using `concat_ws()`, you must, at the very least, supply the separator character first and one input string parameter to be printed out. However, you are not limited in the number of input string parameters that you can supply to be concatenated and separated.

The following usage is valid:

```
concat_ws('_','test')
```

The following output will be printed to the console:

```
test
```

The following usage of the `concat_ws()` function is also valid:

```
concat_ws('_','hi','there','my','name','is')
```

The following output will be printed to the console:

```
hi_there_my_name_is
```

See also

- The following recipes in *Chapter 6, Big Data Analysis*:

    - *Using Hive date UDFs to transform and sort event dates from geographic event data*

    - *Using Hive to build a per-month report of fatalities over geographic event data*

Using Hive to intersect weblog IPs and determine the country

Hive does not directly support foreign keys. Nevertheless, it is still very common to join records on identically matching keys contained in one or more tables. This recipe will show a very simple inner join over weblog data that links each request record in the `weblog_entries` table to a country, based on the request IP.

For each record contained in the `weblog_entries` table, the query will print the record out with an additional trailing value showing the determined country.

Getting ready

Make sure that you have access to a pseudo-distributed or fully-distributed Hadoop cluster, with Apache Hive 0.7.1 installed on your client machine and on the environment path for the active user account.

This recipe depends on having the `weblog_entries` dataset loaded into a Hive table named `weblog_entries` with the following fields mapped to the respective datatypes.

Issue the following command to the Hive client:

```
describe weblog_entries
```

You should see the following response:

```
OK
md5 string
url string
request_date string
request_time string
ip string
```

Additionally, this recipe requires that the `ip-to-country` dataset be loaded into a Hive table named `ip_to_country` with the following fields mapped to the respective datatypes.

Issue the following command to the Hive client:

```
describe ip_to_country
```

You should see the following response:

```
OK
Ip string
country string
```

How to do it...

Carry out the following steps to perform an inner join in HiveQL:

1. Open a text editor of your choice, ideally one with SQL syntax highlighting.

2. Add the following inline creation syntax:

```
SELECT wle.*, itc.country FROM weblog_entries wle
    JOIN ip_to_country itc ON wle.ip = itc.ip;
```

3. Save the script as `weblog_simple_ip_join.hql` in the active directory.

4. Run the script from the operating system shell by supplying the `-f` option to the Hive client. You should see the results of the `SELECT` statement printed out to the console. The following snippet is a printout containing only two sample rows. The full printout will contain all 3000 rows:

```
11402ba8f780f7fbfb108f213449e1b9   /u.html   2012-05-10   21:19:05
98.90.200.33 United States
7ffb8f8ed136c5fe3a5dd6eedc32eae7   /cx.html   2012-05-10   21:17:05
59.19.27.24   Korea, Republic of
```

How it works...

The statement `SELECT wle.*` tells Hive to print every column for each record contained in the table `weblog_entires`, which is an alias for `wle` in shorthand.

Additionally, the `JOIN` operator tells Hive to perform a lookup in the `ip_to_country` table for each record, and find the specific country that maps to that weblog record's IP address. In other words, our join key is the IP address contained in both the tables.

There's more...

The following are a few more helpful introductory tips for the Hive `JOIN` syntax.

Hive supports multitable joins

A single `SELECT` statement can use multiple instances of the `JOIN <table> ON` syntax to match the conditions contained in multiple tables.

The ON operator for inner joins does not support inequality conditions

As of Hive 0.7.1, `ON` conditions cannot match records based on inequality.

The same query from the recipe will fail once the conditional operator is changed to inequality.

The following is the same query from the recipe, except that we wish to match every record for which the IP *does not* match an IP in the JOIN table:

```
SELECT wle.*, itc.country FROM weblog_entries wle
    JOIN ip_to_country itc ON wle.ip != itc.ip;
```

This query produces the following error:

```
FAILED: Error in semantic analysis: Line 2:30 Both left and right
aliases encountered in JOIN ip
```

See also

This recipe is designed as a quick reference for simple table joins. More advanced Hive joins are covered in depth in the following recipes of *Chapter 5, Advanced Joins*:

- ▶ *Joining data in the Mapper using MapReduce*
- ▶ *Joining data using Apache Pig replicated join*
- ▶ *Join sorted data using Apache Pig merge join*
- ▶ *Using a map-side join in Apache Hive to analyze geographical events*

Generating *n*-grams over news archives using MapReduce

n-gram analysis is one approach for looking at blocks of free text that analyze contiguous words (grams) together in a sequence. This recipe will demonstrate how to use the Java MapReduce API to calculate *n*-grams over news archives. Some of the code listed in this recipe will be useful across a variety of different MapReduce jobs. It includes code for the ToolRunner setup, custom parameter passing via configuration, and automatic output directory removal before job submission.

Getting ready

This recipe assumes you have a basic familiarity with the Hadoop 0.20 MapReduce API and the general concept of *n*-gram calculations. You will need access to the news_archives. zip dataset supplied with this book. Inside the ZIP file, you will find the rural.txt and science.txt files. Place both in a single HDFS directory.

You will need access to a pseudo-distributed or fully-distributed cluster capable of running MapReduce jobs using the newer MapReduce API introduced in Hadoop 0.20.

You will also need to package this code inside a JAR file that is to be executed by the Hadoop JAR launcher from the shell. Only the core Hadoop libraries are required to compile and run this example.

How to do it...

Carry out the following steps to implement *n*-gram in MapReduce:

1. Create a class named `NGram.java` in your JAR file at whatever source package is appropriate.

2. The first step involves creating your concrete `Tool` class for job submission. The methods are implemented as follows:

```
import org.apache.hadoop.conf.Configuration;
import org.apache.hadoop.fs.FileSystem;
import org.apache.hadoop.fs.Path;
import org.apache.hadoop.io.LongWritable;
import org.apache.hadoop.io.NullWritable;
import org.apache.hadoop.io.Text;
import org.apache.hadoop.mapreduce.Job;
import org.apache.hadoop.mapreduce.Mapper;
import org.apache.hadoop.mapreduce.lib.input.FileInputFormat;
import org.apache.hadoop.mapreduce.lib.input.TextInputFormat;
import org.apache.hadoop.mapreduce.lib.output.FileOutputFormat;
import org.apache.hadoop.mapreduce.lib.output.TextOutputFormat;
import org.apache.hadoop.util.Tool;
import org.apache.hadoop.util.ToolRunner;

import java.io.IOException;
import java.util.regex.Pattern;


public class NGramJob implements Tool{

    private Configuration conf;

    public static final String NAME = "ngram";
    private static final String GRAM_LENGTH =      "number_of_
grams";

    public void setConf(Configuration conf) {
        this.conf = conf;
    }

    public Configuration getConf() {
        return conf;
    }
```

```
public static void main(String[] args) throws Exception {
    if(args.length != 3) {
        System.err.println("Usage: ngram <input> <output>
    <number_of_grams>");
        System.exit(1);
    }
    ToolRunner.run(new NGramJob(new Configuration()), args);
}
public NGramJob(Configuration conf) {
    this.conf = conf;
}
```

3. The `run()` method is where we set the input/output formats, mapper class configuration, and key-value class configuration:

```
public int run(String[] args) throws Exception {
    conf.setInt(GRAM_LENGTH, Integer.parseInt(args[2]));

    Job job = new Job(conf, "NGrams");
    job.setInputFormatClass(TextInputFormat.class);
    job.setOutputFormatClass(TextOutputFormat.class);
    job.setMapperClass(NGramJob.NGramMapper.class);
    job.setNumReduceTasks(0);
    job.setOutputKeyClass(Text.class);
    job.setOutputValueClass(NullWritable.class);
    job.setJarByClass(NGramJob.class);

    FileInputFormat.addInputPath(job, new Path(args[0]));
    FileOutputFormat.setOutputPath(job,
removeAndSetOutput(args[1]));

    return job.waitForCompletion(true) ? 1 : 0;
}
```

4. The `removeAndSetOutput()` method is not required, but helps circumvent previously existing directories that have errors at the mentioned path:

```
private Path removeAndSetOutput(String outputDir) throws
IOException {
    FileSystem fs = FileSystem.get(conf);
    Path path = new Path(outputDir);
    fs.delete(path, true);
    return path;
}
```

5. The `map()` function is implemented in the following code snippet by extending
    `mapreduce.Mapper`:

```
public static class NGramMapper extends Mapper<LongWritable,
Text, Text, NullWritable> {

        private int gram_length;
        private Pattern space_pattern = Pattern.compile("[ ]");
        private StringBuilder gramBuilder = new StringBuilder();

        @Override
        protected void setup(Context context) throws IOException,
InterruptedException {
            gram_length = context.getConfiguration().
getInt(NGramJob.GRAM_LENGTH, 0);
        }

        @Override
        protected void map(LongWritable key, Text value,
                           Context context) throws IOException,
InterruptedException {
            String[] tokens = space_pattern.split(value.
toString());
            for (int i = 0; i < tokens.length; i++) {
                String token = tokens[i];
                gramBuilder.setLength(0);
                if(i + gram_length <= tokens.length) {
                    for(int j = i; j < i + gram_length; j++) {
                        gramBuilder.append(tokens[j]);
                        gramBuilder.append(" ");
                    }
                    context.write(new Text(gramBuilder.toString()),
NullWritable.get());
                }
            }
        }

    }
}
```

How it works...

First, we set up our imports and create a public class named NGram that implements the MapReduce Tool interface. The static string NAME is useful, should you decide to configure this job in a Hadoop Driver implementation. The NGram program requires three parameters in exact order, namely the input path in HDFS, the desired output location in HDFS, and the total number of grams to be calculated per token. We pass the ToolRunner with an instance of the NGramJob class, as well as a Configuration object initialized with the aforementioned parameters.

Inside the run() method, we configure the job to accept TextInputFormat and TextOutputFormat to read the input as lines of text, and write lines of text out from the map phase. We are also required to set the Mapper class to the public static inner class NGramMapper. Since this is a map-only job, we set the number of reducers to zero. Then we set the parameterized Writable types for the key-value pairs out of the mapper. It's also very important to call the setJarByClass() method so the TaskTrackers can properly unpack and find the Mapper and Reducer classes. The job uses the static helper methods on FileInputFormat and FileOutputFormat to set the input and output directories respectively. Since the output directory cannot exist, the program first deletes any previously defined HDFS files or directories located at the supplied path. With everything configured properly, the job is now ready for submission to the JobTracker.

The NGramMapper class has a few very important member variables. The variable gram_length is dereferenced from the job configuration, which was set before submission to the user-supplied argument. The variable space_pattern is statically compiled to perform a regex split on space characters. The StringBuilder instance gramBuilder is used to store the space-separated list of grams that correspond to each string token. The mapper receives line numbers as LongWritable instances and the line content as a Text instance. The function immediately splits the line into space-separated tokens. For each token, reset gramBuilder, and if that token's position on the line when summed with gram_length exceeds the total length in characters of the line, ignore it. Otherwise, iterate over and store each following token in gramBuilder until the loop reaches gram_length; then, output the gramBuilder content and cycle the outer loop to the next token. The net result is one or more part files stored in the directory specified by the user-supplied argument, which contains a line-separated list of *n*-grams in the news archives.

Sample output of bigrams (2 grams):

```
AWB has
has been
been banned
banned from
from trading
```

There's more...

The following two sections discuss how to use `NullWritable` objects effectively, and also remind developers to use the HDFS filesystem delete functions with care.

Use caution when invoking FileSystem.delete()

The method `removeAndSetPath()` in this implementation automatically removes the directory string argument without warning. This method is supplied this parameter by the user-supplied output directory argument, which if reversed accidentally with the input argument, would remove the input directory. Although programmatically inserting this kind of behavior into a MapReduce setup routine is very handy, `FileSystem.delete()` should be used with extreme caution.

Use NullWritable to avoid unnecessary serialization overhead

This program makes use of `NullWritable` as the output value type from the mapper. Since the program writes a single gram per line, we can just use the key to emit all our output. If your MapReduce job does not require both the key and the value to be emitted, using `NullWritable` will save the framework the trouble of having to serialize unnecessary objects out to the disk. In many scenarios, it is often cleaner and more readable than using blank placeholder values or static singleton instances for output.

Using the distributed cache in MapReduce to find lines that contain matching keywords over news archives

The distributed cache in MapReduce is almost always required for any complex assignment involving dependent libraries and code. One very common operation is passing cache files for use in each map/reduce task JVM. This recipe will use the MapReduce API and the distributed cache to mark any lines in the news archive dataset that contain one or more keywords denoted in a list. We will use the distributed cache to make each mapper aware of the list location in HDFS.

Getting ready

This recipe assumes you have a basic familiarity with the Hadoop 0.20 MapReduce API. You will need access to the `news_archives.zip` dataset supplied with this book. Inside the ZIP file, you will find `rural.txt` and `science.txt`. Place both in a single HDFS directory. Additionally, inside the ZIP file you will find `news_keywords.txt`. You will need to place this file in an HDFS directory with the absolute path `/cache_files/news_archives.txt`. Feel free to add any additional words to this file, so long as they each appear on a new line.

You will need access to a pseudo-distributed or fully-distributed cluster capable of running MapReduce jobs using the newer MapReduce API introduced in Hadoop 0.20.

You will also need to package this code inside a JAR file that is to be executed by the Hadoop JAR launcher from the shell. Only the core Hadoop libraries are required to compile and run this example.

How to do it...

Carry out the following steps to implement a word-matching MapReduce job:

1. Create a class named `LinesWithMatchingWordsJob.java` in your JAR file at whatever source package is appropriate.

2. The following code will serve as the `Tool` implementation for job submission:

```java
import org.apache.hadoop.conf.Configuration;
import org.apache.hadoop.filecache.DistributedCache;
import org.apache.hadoop.fs.FileSystem;
import org.apache.hadoop.fs.Path;
import org.apache.hadoop.io.LongWritable;
import org.apache.hadoop.io.Text;
import org.apache.hadoop.mapreduce.Job;
import org.apache.hadoop.mapreduce.Mapper;
import org.apache.hadoop.mapreduce.lib.input.FileInputFormat;
import org.apache.hadoop.mapreduce.lib.input.TextInputFormat;
import org.apache.hadoop.mapreduce.lib.output.FileOutputFormat;
import org.apache.hadoop.mapreduce.lib.output.TextOutputFormat;
import org.apache.hadoop.util.Tool;
import org.apache.hadoop.util.ToolRunner;

import java.io.BufferedReader;
import java.io.File;
import java.io.FileReader;
import java.io.IOException;
import java.net.URI;
import java.util.HashSet;
import java.util.Set;
import java.util.regex.Pattern;

public class LinesWithMatchingWordsJob implements Tool {
    private Configuration conf;

    public static final String NAME = "linemarker";

    public void setConf(Configuration conf) {
```

```
        this.conf = conf;
    }

    public Configuration getConf() {
        return conf;
    }

    public static void main(String[] args) throws Exception {
        if(args.length != 2) {
            System.err.println("Usage: linemarker <input>
<output>");
            System.exit(1);
        }
        ToolRunner.run(new LinesWithMatchingWordsJob(    new
Configuration()), args);
    }

    public LinesWithMatchingWordsJob(Configuration conf) {
        this.conf = conf;
    }
```

3. The `run()` method is where we set the input/output formats, mapper class configuration, and key-value class configuration:

```
    public int run(String[] args) throws Exception {

        DistributedCache.addCacheFile(new Path("/cache_files/news_
keywords.txt").toUri(), conf);

        Job job = new Job(conf, "Line Marker");
        job.setInputFormatClass(TextInputFormat.class);
        job.setOutputFormatClass(TextOutputFormat.class);
        job.setMapperClass(LineMarkerMapper.class);
        job.setNumReduceTasks(0);
        job.setOutputKeyClass(LongWritable.class);
        job.setOutputValueClass(Text.class);
        job.setJarByClass(LinesWithMatchingWordsJob.class);

        FileInputFormat.addInputPath(job, new Path(args[0]));
        FileOutputFormat.setOutputPath(job,new Path(args[1]));

        return job.waitForCompletion(true) ? 1 : 0;
    }
```

4. The `map()` function is implemented in the following code snippet by extending `mapreduce.Mapper`:

```
public static class LineMarkerMapper extends
Mapper<LongWritable, Text, LongWritable, Text> {

    private Pattern space_pattern = Pattern.compile("[ ]");
    private Set<String> keywords = new HashSet<String>();
```

5. Inside the `setup()` routine, we must load and write the file to a local disk from the distributed cache:

```
    @Override
    protected void setup(Context context) throws IOException,
InterruptedException {
        URI[] uris =DistributedCache.getCacheFiles(
         context.getConfiguration());
        FileSystem fs =
            FileSystem.get(context.getConfiguration());
        if(uris == null || uris.length == 0) {
            throw new IOException("Error reading file from
                    distributed cache. No URIs found.");
        }
        String localPath = "./keywords.txt";
        fs.copyToLocalFile(new Path(uris[0]), new
                    Path(localPath));
        BufferedReader reader = new BufferedReader(new
                    FileReader(localPath));
        String word = null;
        while((word = reader.readLine()) != null) {
            keywords.add(word);
        }
    }
```

The `map()` function:

```
    @Override
    protected void map(LongWritable key, Text value,
                Context context) throws
                    IOException, InterruptedException {
        String[] tokens =
                    space_pattern.split(value.toString());
        for(String token : tokens) {
            if(keywords.contains(token)) {
                context.write(key, new Text(token));
            }
        }
    }

    }
}
```

How it works...

First, we set up our imports and create a public class `LinesWithMatchingWordsJob`. This class implements the Hadoop `Tool` interface for easy submission using the `ToolRunner`. Before the job is submitted, we first check for the existence of both input and output parameters. Inside the `run()` method, we immediately call the `DistributedCache` static helper method `addCacheFile()` and pass it a hardcoded reference to the HDFS cache file at the absolute path `/cache_files/news_keywords.txt`. This file contains the keywords, separated by newline characters, that we are interested in locating within the news archives corpus. We pass the helper method a URI reference to this path and the `Configuration` instance.

Now we can begin configuring the rest of the job. Since we are working with text, we will use the `TextInputFormat` and `TextOutputFormat` classes to read and write lines as strings. We will also configure the `Mapper` class to use the public static inner class `LineMarkerMapper`. This is a map-only job, so we set the number of reducers to zero. We also configure the output key type to be `LongWritable` for the line numbers and the output value as `Text` for the words, as we locate them. It's also very important to call `setJarByClass()` so that the `TaskTrackers` can properly unpack and find the `Mapper` and `Reducer` classes. The job uses the static helper methods on `FileInputFormat` and `FileOutputFormat` to set the input and output directories respectively. Now we are completely set up and ready to submit the job.

The `Mapper` class has two very important member variables. There is a statically compiled regex pattern used to tokenize each line by spaces, and a wordlist `Set` used to store each distinct word we are interested in searching for.

The `setup()` method in the Mapper is told to pull the complete list of cache file URIs currently in the distributed cache. We first check that the URI array returned a non-null value and that the number of elements is greater than zero. If the array passes these tests, grab the keywords file located in HDFS and write it to the temporary working directory for the task. Save the contents in a local file named `./keywords.txt`. Now we are free to use the standard Java I/O classes to read/write off the local disk. Each line contained in the file denotes a keyword that we can store in the keywords' HashSet. Inside our `map()` function, we first tokenize the line by spaces, and for each token, we see if it's contained in our keyword list. If a match is found, emit the line number it was found on as the key and the token itself as the value.

There's more...

The following are a few additional tips to know when starting out with the distributed cache in MapReduce.

Use the distributed cache to pass JAR dependencies to map/reduce task JVMs

Very frequently, your map and reduce tasks will depend on third-party libraries that take the form of JAR files. If you store these dependencies in HDFS, you can use the static helper method `DistributedCache.addArchiveToClassPath()` to initialize your job with the dependencies and have Hadoop automatically add the JAR files as classpath dependencies for every task JVM in that job.

Distributed cache does not work in local jobrunner mode

If the configuration parameter `mapred.job.tracker` is set to `local`, the `DistributedCache` cannot be used to configure archives or cache files from HDFS.

Using Pig to load a table and perform a SELECT operation with GROUP BY

This recipe will use Pig to group the IP addresses contained in the `ip_to_country` dataset and count the number of IP addresses listed for each country.

Getting ready

Make sure you have access to a pseudo-distributed or fully-distributed Hadoop cluster with Apache Pig 0.9.2 installed on your client machine and on the environment path for the active user account. This recipe depends on having the `ip-to-country` named dataset included in the book loaded into HDFS at the absolute path `/input/weblog_ip/ip_to_country.txt`.

How to do it...

Carry out the following steps to perform a `SELECT` and `GROUP BY` operation in Pig:

1. Open a text editor of your choice, ideally one with SQL syntax highlighting.

2. Add the following inline creation syntax:

```
ip_countries = LOAD '/input/weblog_ip/ip_to_country.txt' AS
(ip: chararray, country:chararray);
country_grpd = GROUP ip_countries BY country;
country_counts = FOREACH country_grpd GENERATE FLATTEN(group),
COUNT(ip_countries) as counts;
STORE country_counts INTO '/output/geo_weblog_entries';
```

3. Save the file as `group_by_country.pig`.

4. In the directory containing the script, run the command line using the Pig client with the `-f` option.

How it works...

The first line creates a Pig relation named `ip_countries` from the tab-delimited records stored in HDFS. The relation specifies two attributes, namely `ip` and `country`, both character arrays. The second line creates the `country_grpd` relation containing a record for each distinct country in the `ip_countries` relation. The third line tells Pig to iterate over the `country_grpd` relation and count the number of records in the `ip_countries` relation that map to the current country. The results of this iteration are persisted to a new relation named `country_counts`, which consists of tuples containing exactly two attributes, namely `group` and `counts`. Store the tuples contained in this relation to the output directory specified by `/output/geo_weblog_entries`.

The output is not sorted in `country` in the ascending or descending order.

You should see in HDFS, under `/output/geo_weblog_entries`, one or more part files containing tab-delimited country listings and their IP address counts.

See also

▶ The following recipes in Chapter 3, *Extracting and Transforming Data*

❑ *Using Apache Pig to filter bot traffic from web server logs*

❑ *Using Apache Pig to sort web server logs data by timestamp*

▶ The *Calculate cosine similarity of Artists in the Audioscrobbler dataset using Pig* recipe in Chapter 6, *Big Data Analysis*

5
Advanced Joins

In this chapter, we will cover:

- ▶ Joining data in the Mapper using MapReduce
- ▶ Joining data using Apache Pig replicated join
- ▶ Joining sorted data using Apache Pig merge join
- ▶ Joining skewed data using Apache Pig skewed join
- ▶ Using a map-side join in Apache Hive to analyze geographical events
- ▶ Using optimized full outer joins in Apache Hive to analyze geographical events
- ▶ Joining data using an external key-value store (Redis)

Introduction

In most processing environments, there will be a need to join multiple datasets to produce some final result. Unfortunately, joins in MapReduce are non-trivial and can be an expensive operation. This chapter will demonstrate different approaches to joining data in Hadoop using a number of tools, including Java MapReduce, Apache Pig, and Apache Hive. In addition, this chapter will demonstrate how to leverage external memory resources using Hadoop MapReduce.

Joining data in the Mapper using MapReduce

Joining data in MapReduce is an expensive operation. Depending on the size of the datasets, you can choose to perform a **map-side** join or a **reduce-side** join. In a map-side join, two or more datasets are joined on a key in the map phase of a MapReduce job. In a reduce-side join, the mapper emits the join key, and the reduce phase is responsible for joining the two datasets. In this recipe we will demonstrate how to perform a map-side replicated join using Pig. We will join a weblog dataset, and a dataset containing a list of distinct IPs and their associated country. As the datasets will be joined in the map-phase, this will be a map-only job.

Getting ready

Download the `apache_nobots_tsv.txt` and `nobots_ip_country_tsv.txt` datasets from `http://www.packtpub.com/support` and place them into HDFS.

How to do it...

Carry out the following steps to join data in the map phase using MapReduce:

1. Set up a map-only MapReduce job that will load the `nobots_ip_country_tsv.txt` dataset into the distributed cache:

```
public class MapSideJoin extends Configured implements Tool {

    public int run(String[] args) throws Exception {

        Path inputPath = new Path(args[0]);
        Path outputPath = new Path(args[1]);

        Configuration conf = getConf();
        DistributedCache.addCacheFile(new
          URI("/user/hadoop/nobots_ip_country_tsv.txt"), conf);
        Job weblogJob = new Job(conf);
        weblogJob.setJobName("MapSideJoin");
        weblogJob.setNumReduceTasks(0);
        weblogJob.setJarByClass(getClass());
        weblogJob.setMapperClass(WeblogMapper.class);
        weblogJob.setMapOutputKeyClass(Text.class);
        weblogJob.setMapOutputValueClass(Text.class);
        weblogJob.setOutputKeyClass(Text.class);
        weblogJob.setOutputValueClass(Text.class);
```

```
      weblogJob.setInputFormatClass(TextInputFormat.class);
      weblogJob.setOutputFormatClass(TextOutputFormat.class);
      FileInputFormat.setInputPaths(weblogJob, inputPath);
      FileOutputFormat.setOutputPath(weblogJob, outputPath);


      if(weblogJob.waitForCompletion(true)) {
        return 0;
      }
      return 1;
    }

    public static void main( String[] args ) throws Exception {
      int returnCode = ToolRunner.run(new MapSideJoin(), args);
       System.exit(returnCode);
    }
  }
}
```

2. Create a mapper to read the `nobots_ip_country_tsv.txt` dataset from the distributed cache, and store the `IP/Country` table into a HashMap.

```
public class WeblogMapper extends Mapper<Object, Text, Text, Text>
{

  public static final String IP_COUNTRY_TABLE_FILENAME =
    "nobots_ip_country_tsv.txt";
  private Map<String, String> ipCountryMap = new
    HashMap<String, String>();

  private Text outputKey = new Text();
  private Text outputValue = new Text();

  @Override
  protected void setup(Context context) throws IOException,
InterruptedException {
      Path[] files = DistributedCache.getLocalCacheFiles(context.
getConfiguration());
      for (Path p : files) {
        if (p.getName().equals(IP_COUNTRY_TABLE_FILENAME)) {
          BufferedReader reader = new BufferedReader(new
FileReader(p.toString()));
          String line = reader.readLine();
          while(line != null) {
            String[] tokens = line.split("\t");
```

```
                         String ip = tokens[0];
                         String country = tokens[1];
                         ipCountryMap.put(ip, country);
                         line = reader.readLine();
                      }
                   }
                }

                if (ipCountryMap.isEmpty()) {
                    throw new IOException("Unable to load IP country table.");
                }
            }

            @Override
            protected void map(Object key, Text value, Context
        context) throws IOException, InterruptedException {
                    String row = value.toString();
                    String[] tokens = row.split("\t");
                    String ip = tokens[0];
                    String country = ipCountryMap.get(ip);
                    outputKey.set(country);
                    outputValue.set(row);
                    context.write(outputKey, outputValue);
            }

        }
```

3. Run the job:

```
$ hadoop jar AdvJoinChapter5-1.0.jar com.packt.ch5.advjoin.
mr.MapSideJoin /user/hadoop/apache_nobots_tsv.txt /user/hadoop/
data_jnd
```

How it works...

In step 1, we called the following static method:

```
DistributedCache.addCacheFile(new URI("/user/hadoop/nobots_ip_country_
tsv.txt"), conf)
```

This method will set the `mapred.cache.files` property in the job configuration. The `mapred.cache.files` property tells the MapReduce framework to distribute the `nobots_ip_country_tsv.txt` file to every node in the cluster that will launch a mapper (and reducer if your job is configured to run reducers).

In step 2, we overrode the `setup()` method of the mapper. The `setup()` method is called by the MapReduce framework only once, prior to any calls to the `map()` method. The `setup()` method is an excellent place to perform any one-time initialization to the mapper class.

To read from the distributed cache, we used the static method `DistributedCache.getLocalCacheFiles(context.getConfiguration())` to get all of the files that have been placed, into the distributed cache. Next, we iterated over every file in the distributed cache, which was only one, and loaded the `nobots_ip_country_tsv.txt` dataset into a HashSet.

Finally, in the `map()` method, we used the HashSet loaded in the `setup()` method to join the `nobots_ip_country_tsv.txt` and the `apache_nobots_tsv.txt` files by emitting the country associated with every IP in the `apache_nobots_tsv.txt` file.

There's more...

The MapReduce framework also supports distributing archive files using the distributed cache. An archive file can be a ZIP file, GZIP file, or even a JAR file. Once the archives have been distributed to the task nodes, they will be decompressed automatically.

To add an archive to the distributed cache, simply use the `addCacheArchive()` static method of the `DistributedCache` class when configuring the MapReduce job:

```
DistributedCache.addCacheArchive(new URI("/user/hadoop/nobots_
ip_country_tsv.zip"), conf);
```

See also

- ▶ *Joining data using Apache Pig replicated join*
- ▶ *Joining sorted data using Apache Pig merge join*
- ▶ *Joining skewed data using Apache Pig skewed join*

Joining data using Apache Pig replicated join

Apache Pig supports a number of advanced joins, including:

- ▶ Reduce-side joins
- ▶ Replicated joins
- ▶ Merge joins
- ▶ Skewed joins

The **reduce-side join** is the default implementation when you use Pig's JOIN operator. Pig also supports map-side joins when you specify the replicated or merge keyword. This recipe will demonstrate how to perform a map-side replicated join using Pig. We will join a weblog dataset, and a dataset containing a list of distinct IPs and their associated countries.

Getting ready

Download the apache_nobots_tsv.txt and nobots_ip_country_tsv.txt datasets from http://www.packtpub.com/support and place them into HDFS. You will also need a recent version of Apache Pig (0.9 or later) installed on the cluster.

How to do it...

Carry out the following steps to perform a replicated join in Apache Pig:

1. Open your favorite text editor and create a file named replicated_join.pig. Create two Pig relations to load the two datasets:

   ```
   nobots_weblogs = LOAD '/user/hadoop/apache_nobots_tsv.txt' AS
   (ip: chararray, timestamp:long, page:chararray, http_status:int,
   payload_size:int, useragent:chararray);
   ip_country_tbl = LOAD '/user/hadoop/nobots_ip_country_tsv.txt' AS
   (ip:chararray, country:chararray);
   ```

2. Join the two datasets using the replicated keyword:

   ```
   weblog_country_jnd = JOIN nobots_weblogs BY ip, ip_country_tbl BY
   ip USING 'replicated';
   ```

3. Format the joined relation and store the result:

```
cleaned = FOREACH weblog_country_jnd GENERATE ip_country_tbl::ip,
country, timestamp, page, http_status, payload_size, useragent;
STORE cleaned  INTO '/user/hadoop/weblog_country_jnd_replicated';
```

4. Run the job:

```
$ pig -f replicated_join.pig
```

How it works...

In step 1, we defined two relations: `nobots_weblogs` and `ip_country_tbl`, to refer to the two input datasets. Next, we joined the two datasets on the `ip` field using Pig's replicated join. Pig will load the right-most relation, `ip_country_tbl`, into memory and will join the data with the `nobots_weblogs` relationship. It is important that the right-most relations be small enough to fit into a mapper's memory. Pig will not warn you if the dataset is too large, the job will just fail with an out of memory exception.

Finally, in step 3, we formatted the joined relation into a new relation named `cleaned`. There is one field that looks odd in the FOREACH statement, and that field is `ip_country_tbl::ip`. We had to use the `::` operator to define which column we wanted to store in the `cleaned` relation, since the joined relation contains two fields named `ip`. We could have easily chosen to use `nobots_weblogs::ip` instead; it makes no difference in this example.

There's more...

The replicated join can be used on more than one relation. For example, we can modify the previous recipe to use a replicated join to perform an inner join on three relations:

```
weblog_country_jnd = JOIN nobots_weblogs BY ip, ip_country_tbl BY ip,
another_relation BY ip USING 'replicated';
```

Again, the right-most datasets must fit into the main memory. In this case, both `ip_country_tbl` and `another_relation` must fit into the memory of a mapper.

See also

▸ *Joining sorted data using Apache Pig merge join*
▸ *Joining skewed data using Apache Pig skewed join*

Joining sorted data using Apache Pig merge join

Like the replicated join described in the previous recipe, the Apache Pig's merge join is another map-side join technique. However, the major difference between the two implementations is that the merge join does not place any data into main memory. This recipe will demonstrate how to use Pig's merge join to join two datasets.

Getting ready

Download the `apache_nobots_tsv.txt` and `nobots_ip_country_tsv.txt` datasets from `http://www.packtpub.com/support` and place them into the folder that you are working on. You will also need a recent version of Apache Pig (0.9 or later) installed on the cluster.

In order to use the merge join functionality in Pig, the two datasets need to be sorted on the join key. To sort the two datasets, run the following commands using Unix sort:

```
$ sort -k1 apache_nobots_tsv.txt > sorted_apache_nobots_tsv.txt
$ sort -k1 nobots_ip_country_tsv.txt > sorted_nobots_ip_country_tsv.txt
```

Place the two new sorted files into HDFS:

```
$ hadoop fs -put sorted_apache_nobots_tsv.txt /user/hadoop
$ hadoop fs -put sorted_nobots_ip_country_tsv.txt /user/hadoop
```

How to do it...

Carry out the following steps to perform a merge join in Apache Pig:

1. Open a text editor and create a file named `merge_join.pig`. Create two Pig relations to load the two datasets:

   ```
   nobots_weblogs = LOAD '/user/hadoop/sorted_apache_nobots_tsv.
   txt' AS (ip: chararray, timestamp:long, page:chararray, http_
   status:int, payload_size:int, useragent:chararray);
   ip_country_tbl = LOAD '/user/hadoop/sorted_nobots_ip_country_tsv.
   txt' AS (ip:chararray, country:chararray);
   ```

2. Join the two datasets using the `merge` keyword:

   ```
   weblog_country_jnd = JOIN nobots_weblogs BY ip, ip_country_tbl BY
   ip USING 'merge';
   ```

3. Format the joined relationship and store the result:

```
cleaned = FOREACH weblog_country_jnd GENERATE ip_country_tbl::ip,
country, timestamp, page, http_status, payload_size, useragent;
STORE cleaned INTO '/user/jowens/weblog_country_jnd_merge';
```

4. Run the job:

```
$ pig -f merge_join.pig
```

How it works...

In step 1, we defined two relations: `nobots_weblogs` and `ip_country_tbl`, to refer to the two datasets.

In step 2, we joined the two datasets on the `ip` field using Pig's merge join. Pig will launch two MapReduce jobs to perform the merge join. First, Pig will send the data associated with the `nobots_weblogs` relation to all of the mappers, and sample the `ip_country_tbl` data to build an index. It is important to place the larger of the two relations as the left-hand side input to the JOIN statement, as we did with the `nobots_weblogs` relation. Once Pig has built the index, it launches a second map-only job, which reads the left-hand side relationship, and the index created in the first MapReduce job to join the two relations.

There's more...

It is important to note that Pig's merge join requires the input data to be sorted in ascending order across all input files. In addition, all of the data must be sorted in an ascending order by filename. For example, if the `nobots_weblogs` relation contains three distinct IPs across two input files, the following IPs could be distributed in this fashion:

- Rows containing the IP 111.0.0.0 in the file named part-00000
- Rows containing the IP 112.0.0.0 must occur after 111.0.0.0 in the file named part-00000
- Rows containing the IP 222.0.0.0 will be placed into a file named part-00001

This example shows the possible total ordering of IPs across a number of files ordered by name. Filenames need to support ascending order because this is the order in which Pig will attempt to read each file to access the sorted data.

See also

- *Joining skewed data using Apache Pig skewed join*

Joining skewed data using Apache Pig skewed join

Data skew is a serious problem in a distributed processing environment, and occurs when the data is not evenly divided among the emitted key tuples from the map phase. This can lead to inconsistent processing times. In the MapReduce framework, data skew can cause some mappers/reducers to take significantly more time to perform a task as compared to other mappers/reducers in the job.

Apache Pig has the skewed join to help alleviate the data skew issue with joins. This recipe will demonstrate how to join a skewed dataset, with a small table.

Getting ready

Download the `apache_nobots_tsv.txt` and `nobots_ip_country_tsv.txt` datasets from `http://www.packtpub.com/support` and place them in the folder which you are currently working on. You will also need a recent version of Apache Pig (0.9 or later) installed on the cluster.

To skew the `apache_nobots_tsv.txt` file, create the following shell script to append the same row a few thousand times to a new file named `skewed_apache_nobots_tsv.txt`:

```
#!/bin/bash

cat apache_nobots_tsv.txt > skewed_apache_nobots_tsv.txt
for i in {1..5000}
do
   head -n1 apache_nobots_tsv.txt >> skewed_apache_nobots_tsv.txt
done
```

The IP address `221.220.8.0` will appear significantly higher number of times in the `skewed_apache_nobots_tsv.txt` file than any other IP.

Place the `skewed_apache_nobots_tsv.txt` and `nobots_ip_country_tsv.txt` files into HDFS:

```
$hadoop fs -put skewed_apache_nobots_tsv.txt /user/hadoop/
$hadoop fs -put nobots_ip_country_tsv.txt /user/hadoop/
```

How to do it...

Follow the steps to perform a skewed join in Apache Pig:

1. Open a text editor and create a file named `skewed_join.pig`. Create two relations to load the two datasets:

   ```
   nobots_weblogs = LOAD '/user/hadoop/skewed_apache_nobots_tsv.
   txt' AS (ip: chararray, timestamp:long, page:chararray, http_
   status:int, payload_size:int, useragent:chararray);
   ip_country_tbl = LOAD '/user/hadoop/nobots_ip_country_tsv.txt' AS
   (ip:chararray, country:chararray);
   ```

2. Join the two datasets using the `skewed` keyword:

   ```
   weblog_country_jnd = JOIN nobots_weblogs BY ip, ip_country_tbl BY
   ip USING 'skewed';
   ```

3. Format the joined relationship and store the result:

   ```
   cleaned = FOREACH weblog_country_jnd GENERATE ip_country_tbl::ip,
   country, timestamp, page, http_status, payload_size, useragent;
   STORE cleaned INTO '/user/hadoop/weblog_country_jnd_skewed';
   ```

4. Run the job:

   ```
   $ pig -f skewed_join.pig
   ```

How it works...

In step 1, we defined two relations: `nobots_weblogs` and `ip_country_tbl`, to refer to the two datasets.

In step 2, we joined the two datasets on the `ip` field using Pig's skewed join. Pig will launch two MapReduce jobs to perform the skewed join. The first MapReduce job will sample the `nobots_weblogs.txt` (the skewed data) dataset. The second MapReduce job will perform a reduce-side join. Pig will determine how the data is distributed to the reducers based on the sampling from the first map reduce job. If there is skew present in the dataset, Pig will attempt to optimize the data distribution to the reducers.

Using a map-side join in Apache Hive to analyze geographical events

When joining two tables in Apache Hive, one table might be significantly smaller than the other. In such cases, Hive can push a hash table representing the smaller table over the distributed cache and join the tables entirely map-side, which can lead to better parallelism and job throughput. In this recipe, we will use a map-side join to attach any significant holiday information that may have occurred on a particular geographic event.

Getting ready

Ensure that Apache Hive 0.7.1 is installed on your client machine and on the environment path for the active user account.

This recipe depends on having the `Nigera_ACLED_cleaned.tsv` dataset loaded into a Hive table with the name `acled_nigeria_cleaned` and with the following fields mapped to the respective datatypes. The `Nigera_ACLED_cleaned.tsv` dataset can be downloaded from `http://www.packtpub.com/support`.

Issue the following command to the Hive client:

```
describe acled_nigeria_cleaned
```

You should see the following response:

```
OK
loc    string
event_date    string
event_type    string
actor    string
latitude    double
longitude    double
source    string
fatalities    int
```

This recipe also requires having `nigeria-holidays.tsv` loaded into a Hive table with the name `nigeria_holidays` and the following fields mapped to the respective datatypes.

Issue the following command to the Hive client:

```
describe nigeria_holidays
```

You should see the following response:

```
OK
yearly_date    string
description    string
```

How to do it...

Carry out the following steps to perform a map-side join in Apache Hive:

1. Open a text editor and create a file named `map-join-acled-holidays.sql`.

2. Add the inline creation and transformation syntax:

    ```
    SELECT /*+ MAPJOIN(nh)*/ acled.event_date, acled.event_type,
    nh.description
        FROM acled_nigeria_cleaned acled
        JOIN nigeria_holidays nh
            ON (substr(acled.event_date, 6) = nh.yearly_date);
    ```

3. Run the `map-join-acled-holidays.sql` script from the operating system shell by supplying the `-f` option to the Hive client. You will know the map-side join is working if you see this message in the output trace:

    ```
    Mapred Local Task Succeeded. Convert the Join into MapJoin
    ```

    The generated MapReduce job should not have any reduce tasks.

4. You should see the following five rows appear first in the output console:

    ```
    2002-01-01  Riots/Protests  New Years Day
    2001-06-12  Battle-No change of territory  Lagos State only; in
    memory of failed 1993 election
    2002-05-29  Violence against civilians  Democracy Day
    2010-10-01  Riots/Protests  Independence Day
    2010-10-01  Violence against civilians  Independence Day
    ```

How it works...

The script inner joins the month-day portion of each record in the `event_date` column in `acled_nigeria_cleaned` to the `yearly_date` column in `nigeria_holidays`. `substr(event_date, 6)` will omit the year portion from each record in the `event_date` column by starting from the position of the sixth character. The inline hint to `/*+ MAPJOIN(nh) */` lets you manually define which table alias to load as the small table to each mapper. The `nigeria_holidays` table is very small and made the most sense to load as a hash table. Each map process in the join can operate over rows from `acled_nigeria_cleaned` with its own copy of the `nigeria_holidays` hash table. The `MAPJOIN` operation handles creating the hash table and distributing it to each map task.

We would like to see the values of the `event_date` and `event_type` columns, and a description of the holiday, if any, the event occurred on.

There's more...

Map-side joins can be tricky to configure and use properly. Here are a few pointers.

Auto-convert to map-side join whenever possible

Set the property `hive.auto.convert.join` to `true` in your Hive config and Hive will automatically try to convert the join to a map-side join, as long as the table fits below a certain size threshold. You can configure the maximum size with the property `hive.smalltable.filesize`. This will tell Hive what file size (or below) constitutes a small table. It's written in bytes expressed as a long (for example, 25000000L = 25M).

Also consider setting `hive.hashtable.max.memory.usage`, which tells the map task to terminate if it requires more than the configured memory percentage.

Map-join behavior

If you omit `/*+ MAPJOIN() */` and rely on auto-convert, it can be difficult to follow what Hive is doing to optimize the join. Following are some tips:

- `TableFoo LEFT OUTER JOIN TableBar`: Try to convert `TableBar` to a hash table

- `TableFoo RIGHT OUTER JOIN TABLE B`: Try to convert `TableFoo` to a hash table

- `TableFoo FULL OUTER JOIN TableBar`: Framework cannot map join full outer joins

▶ *Using optimized full outer joins in Apache Hive to analyze geographical events*

Using optimized full outer joins in Apache Hive to analyze geographical events

This recipe will take a list of Nigerian VIPs and join any Nigerian ACLED events that occurred on any VIP's birthday. We are not only interested in viewing events that did or did not occur on a famous person's birthday, but also in the people who are not linked to any event. To accomplish this analytics in a single query, a full outer join makes the most sense. We would also like to store the results in a table.

Getting ready

Ensure that Apache Hive 0.7.1 is installed on your client machine and on the environment path for the active user account.

This recipe depends on having the `Nigera_ACLED_cleaned.tsv` dataset loaded into a Hive table with the name `acled_nigeria_cleaned` and with the following fields mapped to the respective datatypes. The `Nigera_ACLED_cleaned.tsv` dataset can be downloaded from `http://www.packtpub.com/support`.

Issue the following command to the Hive client:

```
describe acled_nigeria_cleaned
```

You should see the following response:

```
OK
loc string
event_date   string
event_type string
actor   string
latitude   double
longitude   double
source   string
fatalities   int
```

This recipe also requires having `nigeria-vip-birthdays.tsv` loaded into a Hive table with the name `nigeria_vips` and with the following fields mapped to the respective datatypes. The `nigeria-vip-birthdays.tsv` dataset can be downloaded from `http://www.packtpub.com/support`.

Issue the following command to the Hive client:

```
describe nigeria_vips
```

You should see the following response:

```
OK
name    string
birthday string
description string
```

How to do it...

Follow the steps to perform a full outer join in Hive:

1. Open a text editor and create a file named `full_outer_join_acled_vips.sql`.

2. Add the inline creation and transformation syntax:

```
DROP TABLE IF EXISTS acled_nigeria_event_people_links;
CREATE TABLE acled_nigeria_event_people_links AS
SELECT acled.event_date, acled.event_type, vips.name, vips.
description as pers_desc, vips.birthday
    FROM nigeria_vips vips
    FULL OUTER JOIN acled_nigeria_cleaned acled
        ON (substr(acled.event_date,6) = substr(vips.birthday,
6));
```

3. Run the `full_outer_join_acled_vips.sql` script from the operating system shell by supplying the `-f` option to the Hive client.

4. Once the script successfully finishes, it should signal 2931 records loaded into the table `acled_nigeria_event_people_links`.

5. Issue the following query to the Hive shell:

```
SELECT * FROM acled_nigeria_event_people_links WHERE event_date IS
NOT NULL AND birthday IS NOT NULL limit 2";
```

6. You should see the following output:

```
OK
2008-01-01  Battle-No change of territory  Jaja    Wachuku "First
speaker of the Nigerian House of Representatives"  1918-01-01


2002-01-01  Riots/Protests  Jaja Wachuku  "First speaker of the
Nigerian House of Representatives"  1918-01-01
```

How it works...

First, we drop any tables previously created by the name `acled_nigeria_event_people_links`. We use an inline `CREATE TABLE AS` statement to shortcut having to explicitly define the table.

The full outer join will match rows from `acled_nigeria_cleaned` to rows from `nigeria_vips`, where the substring of the records in the `event_date` column, starting at the sixth character position, is equal to a VIP's birthday. We use the `substr(event_date, 6)` method to eliminate the year portion of the records in the `event_date` column as a comparison factor.

The columns our receiving table will contain from the `SELECT` statement are `acled.event_date`, `acled.event_type`, `vips.name`, `vips.description as pers_desc`, and `vips.birthday`. The `vips.description` column gets the alias `pers_desc` to make the column label a little more meaningful. For event records with no matching birthdays, the columns `vips.name`, `vips.description`, and `pers_desc` will be `NULL`. For people with no matching events, the columns `acled.event_date` and `acled.event_type` will be `NULL`.

The decision to include `nigeria_vips` in the `FROM` and `JOIN` clauses on `acled_nigeria_cleaned` was made to optimize the reducer throughput. Since we are performing a Hive common join and not a map-side join, the actual table joining will occur reduce-side. Hive will attempt to buffer the rows from the left-most table and then stream the rows from the right-most table. The table `nigeria_vips` is much smaller than `acled_nigeria_cleaned`, thus we can alleviate the reducer memory footprint by designing the syntax of our query to stream the rows of `acled_nigeria_cleaned` and buffer those in `nigeria_vips`.

As it turns out for this particular VIP list, there were no birthdays for which there was no event listed in `acled_nigeria_cleaned`; therefore, the outer join produces no rows for people whose birthdays did not match an event. Moreover, no two people in our list have the same birthday; therefore, the outer join does not replicate the same event into multiple rows for each VIP birthday joined. The resulting table contains 2931 rows, which is exactly the same as the number of rows in `acled_nigeria_cleaned`.

There's more...

There are other things you can do to improve the performance of the join operations in Hive.

Common join versus map-side join

The Hive documentation will use the term "common join" to refer to a join operation where one or more reducers are required to physically join the table rows. Map-side joins, as the name would suggest, perform the join across parallel map tasks and eliminate the need for the reduce phase.

STREAMTABLE hint

You can dictate which tables to stream during the reduce phase by using `/*+ STREAMTABLE(tablename) */`.

Table ordering in the query matters

The left-to-right ordering of join table declarations in your queries, especially in a multi-table join, is very important. Hive will attempt to buffer the rows from the left-hand side table and stream the results of the right-hand side. In a multi-table join, several map/reduce jobs may occur, but the same semantics apply. The result of the first join will be buffered, while the rows of the next right-most table will be streamed. Use this knowledge to order your table joins wisely.

Joining data using an external key-value store (Redis)

Key-value stores are an efficient tool for storing large datasets. In MapReduce, we can use key-value stores to house large datasets that might not fit into the memory of a mapper or mappers (remember that multiple mappers can run on the same slave node), but can fit into the main memory of the server.

In this recipe, we will demonstrate how to use **Redis** to perform a map-side join using MapReduce.

Getting ready

First, download and install Redis. This book used Redis version 2.4.15. A quick start guide is available on the Redis website, `http://redis.io/topics/quickstart`. Once you have compiled and installed the Redis server, start the server by issuing the following command:

```
$ redis-server
```

Verify that the Redis server is working properly by using `redis-cli`:

`$ redis-cli ping`

Redis should respond with the message "PONG" if everything has been set up properly.

Next, you will need to download and compile Jedis from `https://github.com/xetorthio/jedis`. Jedis is a Redis Java client that we will use in our MapReduce application to communicate with Redis. This book used Jedis version 2.1.0.

Finally, download the `apache_nobots_tsv.txt` and `nobots_ip_country_tsv.txt` datasets from `http://www.packtpub.com/support`. Place the `apache_nobots_tsv.txt` file into HDFS, and leave the `nobots_ip_country_tsv.txt` file in the folder that you are working on.

How to do it...

Follow these steps to join data in MapReduce using Redis:

1. Create a Java method to read the `nobots_ip_country_tsv.txt` file from the folder that you are working on, and load its contents to Redis using the Jedis client:

```java
private void loadRedis(String ipCountryTable) throws IOException {
FileReader freader = new FileReader(ipCountryTable);
        BufferedReader breader = new BufferedReader(freader);
        jedis = new Jedis("localhost");
        jedis.select(0);
        jedis.flushDB();
        String line = breader.readLine();
        while(line != null) {
            String[] tokens = line.split("\t");
            String ip = tokens[0];
            String country = tokens[1];
            jedis.set(ip, country);
            line = breader.readLine();
        }
        System.err.println("db size = " + jedis.dbSize());
    }
```

2. Next, set up a map-only MapReduce job. The following code snippet is the final version of the class to create a map-only MapReduce job. It contains the `loadRedis()` method we created in step 1:

```java
public class MapSideJoinRedis extends Configured implements Tool {

    private Jedis jedis = null;

    private void loadRedis(String ipCountryTable) throws
        IOException {

        FileReader freader = new FileReader(ipCountryTable);
        BufferedReader breader = new BufferedReader(freader);
        jedis = new Jedis("localhost");
        jedis.select(0);
        jedis.flushDB();
        String line = breader.readLine();
        while(line != null) {
            String[] tokens = line.split("\t");
            String ip = tokens[0];
            String country = tokens[1];
            jedis.set(ip, country);
            line = breader.readLine();
        }
        System.err.println("db size = " + jedis.dbSize());
    }

    public int run(String[] args) throws Exception {

        Path inputPath = new Path(args[0]);
        String ipCountryTable = args[1];
        Path outputPath = new Path(args[2]);

        loadRedis(ipCountryTable);

        Configuration conf = getConf();
        Job weblogJob = new Job(conf);
        weblogJob.setJobName("MapSideJoinRedis");
        weblogJob.setNumReduceTasks(0);
        weblogJob.setJarByClass(getClass());
        weblogJob.setMapperClass(WeblogMapper.class);
        weblogJob.setMapOutputKeyClass(Text.class);
        weblogJob.setMapOutputValueClass(Text.class);
```

```
        weblogJob.setOutputKeyClass(Text.class);
        weblogJob.setOutputValueClass(Text.class);
        weblogJob.setInputFormatClass(TextInputFormat.class);
        weblogJob.setOutputFormatClass(TextOutputFormat.class);
        FileInputFormat.setInputPaths(weblogJob, inputPath);
        FileOutputFormat.setOutputPath(weblogJob, outputPath);


        if(weblogJob.waitForCompletion(true)) {
          return 0;
        }
        return 1;
      }

    public static void main(String[] args) throws Exception {
        int returnCode = ToolRunner.run(new
                           MapSideJoinRedis(), args);
        System.exit(returnCode);
    }
  }
```

3. Create a mapper that will join the apache_nobots_tsv.txt dataset with the nobots_ip_country_tsv.txt dataset that has been loaded to Redis:

```
public class WeblogMapper extends Mapper<Object, Text, Text, Text>
{

    private Map<String, String> ipCountryMap = new
      HashMap<String, String>();
    private Jedis jedis = null;
    private Text outputKey = new Text();
    private Text outputValue = new Text();

    private String getCountry(String ip) {
        String country = ipCountryMap.get(ip);
        if (country == null) {
            if (jedis == null) {
                jedis = new Jedis("localhost");
                jedis.select(0);
            }
            country = jedis.get(ip);
            ipCountryMap.put(ip, country);
        }
```

```
                return country;
        }


        @Override
        protected void map(Object key, Text value, Context
            context) throws IOException, InterruptedException {
                String row = value.toString();
                String[] tokens = row.split("\t");
                String ip = tokens[0];
                String country = getCountry(ip);
                outputKey.set(country);
                outputValue.set(row);
                context.write(outputKey, outputValue);
        }

    }
```

4. Finally, launch the MapReduce job:

```
$ hadoop jar AdvJoinChapter5-1.0-SNAPSHOT.jar com.packt.ch5.
advjoin.redis.MapSideJoinRedis /user/hadoop/apache_nobots_tsv.txt
./nobots_ip_country_tsv.txt /user/hadoop/data_jnd
```

How it works...

In steps 1 and 2, we created a class to set up a map-only job. This class looks very familiar to other map-only jobs we've created in past recipes, except for the `loadRedis()` method.

The `loadRedis()` method first connects to the local Redis instance using the Jedis constructor. Next, we used the `select()` method to choose which Redis database we wanted to use. A single Redis instance can contain a number of databases, which are identified using a numeric index. Once we get connected to the desired database, we call the method `flushDB()`, which deletes everything currently stored in the current database. Finally, we read the `nobots_ip_country_tsv.txt` file from the folder in which you are currently working, and load the Redis instance with the key-value pair `ip/country` by using the `set()` method.

There's more...

This recipe used a very simple string data structure to store the `ip/country` key-value pairs. Redis supports many other data structures, including hashes, lists, and sorted sets. In addition, Redis has support for transactions, and a publish/subscribe mechanism. Visit the Redis website `http://redis.io/`, to review all of this functionality in depth.

6
Big Data Analysis

In this chapter, we will cover:

- ▶ Counting distinct IPs in weblog data using MapReduce and Combiners
- ▶ Using Hive date UDFs to transform and sort event dates from geographic event data
- ▶ Using Hive to build a per-month report of fatalities over geographic event data
- ▶ Implementing a custom UDF in Hive to help validate source reliability over geographic event data
- ▶ Marking the longest period of non-violence using Hive MAP/REDUCE operators and Python
- ▶ Calculating the cosine similarity of Artists in the Audioscrobbler dataset using Pig
- ▶ Trim outliers from the Audioscrobbler dataset using Pig and datafu

Introduction

Learning to apply Apache Hive, Pig, and MapReduce to solve the specific problems you are faced with can be difficult. The recipes in this chapter present a few big data problems and provide solutions that show how to tackle them. You will notice that the questions we ask of the data are not incredibly complicated, but you will require a different approach when dealing with a large volume of data. Even though the sample datasets in the recipes are small, you will find that the code is still very applicable to bigger problem spaces distributed over large Hadoop clusters.

The analytic questions in this chapter are designed to highlight many of the more powerful features of the various tools. You will find many of these features and operators useful as you begin solving your own problems.

Counting distinct IPs in weblog data using MapReduce and Combiners

This recipe will walk you through creating a MapReduce program to count distinct IPs in weblog data. We will demonstrate the application of a combiner to optimize data transfer overhead between the map and reduce stages. The code is implemented in a generic fashion and can be used to count distinct values in any tab-delimited dataset.

Getting ready

This recipe assumes that you have a basic familiarity with the Hadoop 0.20 MapReduce API. You will need access to the `weblog_entries` dataset supplied with this book and stored in an HDFS folder at the path `/input/weblog`.

You will need access to a pseudo-distributed or fully-distributed cluster capable of running MapReduce jobs using the newer MapReduce API introduced in Hadoop 0.20.

You will also need to package this code inside a JAR file to be executed by the Hadoop JAR launcher from the shell. Only the core Hadoop libraries are required to compile and run this example.

How to do it...

Perform the following steps to count distinct IPs using MapReduce:

1. Open a text editor/IDE of your choice, preferably one with Java syntax highlighting.

2. Create a class named `DistinctCounterJob.java` in your JAR file at whatever source package is appropriate.

3. The following code will serve as the Tool implementation for job submission:

```
import org.apache.hadoop.conf.Configuration;
import org.apache.hadoop.fs.Path;
import org.apache.hadoop.io.IntWritable;
import org.apache.hadoop.io.LongWritable;
import org.apache.hadoop.io.Text;
import org.apache.hadoop.mapreduce.Job;
import org.apache.hadoop.mapreduce.Mapper;
import org.apache.hadoop.mapreduce.Reducer;
import org.apache.hadoop.mapreduce.lib.input.FileInputFormat;
import org.apache.hadoop.mapreduce.lib.input.TextInputFormat;
import org.apache.hadoop.mapreduce.lib.output.FileOutputFormat;
import org.apache.hadoop.mapreduce.lib.output.TextOutputFormat;
import org.apache.hadoop.util.Tool;
import org.apache.hadoop.util.ToolRunner;
```

```
import java.io.IOException;
import java.util.regex.Pattern;


public class DistinctCounterJob implements Tool {

    private Configuration conf;
    public static final String NAME = "distinct_counter";
    public static final String COL_POS = "col_pos";


    public static void main(String[] args) throws Exception {
        ToolRunner.run(new Configuration(),    new
DistinctCounterJob(), args);
    }
```

4. The `run()` method is where we set the input/output formats, mapper class configuration, combiner class, and key/value class configuration:

```
    public int run(String[] args) throws Exception {
        if(args.length != 3) {
            System.err.println("Usage: distinct_counter <input>
<output> <element_position>");
            System.exit(1);
        }
        conf.setInt(COL_POS, Integer.parseInt(args[2]));

        Job job = new Job(conf, "Count distinct elements at
position");
        job.setInputFormatClass(TextInputFormat.class);
        job.setOutputFormatClass(TextOutputFormat.class);

        job.setMapperClass(DistinctMapper.class);
        job.setReducerClass(DistinctReducer.class);
        job.setCombinerClass(DistinctReducer.class);

        job.setMapOutputKeyClass(Text.class);
        job.setMapOutputValueClass(IntWritable.class);
        job.setJarByClass(DistinctCounterJob.class);

        FileInputFormat.addInputPath(job, new Path(args[0]));
        FileOutputFormat.setOutputPath(job, new Path(args[1]));

        return job.waitForCompletion(true) ? 1 : 0;

    }
```

```
        public void setConf(Configuration conf) {
            this.conf = conf;
        }

        public Configuration getConf() {
            return conf;
        }
    }
```

5. The `map()` function is implemented in the following code by extending `mapreduce.Mapper`:

```
    public static class DistinctMapper
            extends Mapper<LongWritable, Text, Text, IntWritable>
    {

        private static int col_pos;
        private static final Pattern pattern = Pattern.
compile("\\t");
        private Text outKey = new Text();
        private static final IntWritable outValue = new
IntWritable(1);

        @Override
        protected void setup(Context context
        ) throws IOException, InterruptedException {
            col_pos = context.getConfiguration().
getInt(DistinctCounterJob.COL_POS, 0);
        }

        @Override
        protected void map(LongWritable key, Text value,
                            Context context) throws IOException,
InterruptedException {
            String field = pattern.split(value.toString())[col_
pos];
            outKey.set(field);
            context.write(outKey, outValue);
        }
    }
```

6. The `reduce()` function is implemented in the following code by extending `mapreduce.Reducer`:

```
public static class DistinctReducer
        extends Reducer<Text, IntWritable, Text, IntWritable>
{

        private IntWritable count = new IntWritable();

        @Override
        protected void reduce(Text key, Iterable<IntWritable>
values, Context context
        ) throws IOException, InterruptedException {
            int total = 0;
            for(IntWritable value: values) {
                total += value.get();
            }
            count.set(total);
            context.write(key, count);
        }
}
```

7. The following command shows the sample usage against weblog data with column position number 4, which is the IP column:

```
hadoop jar myJobs.jar distinct_counter /input/weblog/ /output/
weblog_distinct_counter 4
```

How it works...

First we set up `DistinctCounterJob` to implement a Tool interface for remote submission. The static constant `NAME` is of potential use in the Hadoop `Driver` class, which supports the launching of different jobs from the same JAR file. The static constant `COL_POS` is initialized to the third required argument from the command line `<element_position>`. This value is set within the job configuration, and should match the position of the column you wish to count for each distinct entry. Supplying 4 will match the IP column for the weblog data.

Since we are reading and writing text, we can use the supplied `TextInputFormat` and `TextOutputFormat` classes. We will set the `Mapper` and `Reduce` classes to match our `DistinctMapper` and `DistinctReducer` implemented classes respectively. We also supply `DistinctReducer` as a combiner class. This decision is explained in more detail as follows:

It's also very important to call `setJarByClass()` so that the `TaskTrackers` can properly unpack and find the `Mapper` and `Reducer` classes. The job uses the static helper methods on `FileInputFormat` and `FileOutputFormat` to set the input and output directories respectively. Now we're set up and ready to submit the job.

The `Mapper` class sets up a few member variables as follows:

- `col_pos`: This is initialized to a value supplied in the configuration. It allows users to change which column to parse and apply the count distinct operation on.
- `pattern`: This defines the column's split point for each row based on tabs.
- `outKey`: This is a class member that holds output values. This avoids having to create a new instance for each output that is written.
- `outValue`: This is an integer representing one occurrence of the given key. It is similar to the WordCount example.

The `map()` function splits each incoming line's value and extracts the string located at `col_pos`. We reset the internal value for `outKey` to the string found on that line's position. For our example, this will be the IP value for the row. We emit the value of the newly reset `outKey` variable along with the value of `outValue` to mark one occurrence of that given IP address.

Without the assistance of the combiner, this would present the reducer with an iterable collection of 1s to be counted.

The following is an example of a reducer {key, value:[]} without a combiner:

{10.10.1.1, [1,1,1,1,1,1]} = six occurrences of the IP "10.10.1.1".

The implementation of the `reduce()` method will sum the integers and arrive at the correct total, but there's nothing that requires the integer values to be limited to the number 1. We can use a combiner to process the intermediate key-value pairs as they are output from each mapper and help improve the data throughput in the shuffle phase. Since the combiner is applied against the local map output, we may see a performance improvement as the amount of data we need to transfer for an intermediate key/value can be reduced considerably.

Instead of seeing {10.10.1.1, [1,1,1,1,1,1]}, the combiner can add the 1s and replace the value of the intermediate value for that key to {10.10.1.1, [6]}. The reducer can then sum the various combined values for the intermediate key and arrive at the same correct total. This is possible because addition is both a commutative and associative operation. In other words:

- **Commutative**: The order in which we process the addition operation against the values has no effect on the final result. For example, $1 + 2 + 3 = 3 + 1 + 2$.
- **Associative**: The order in which we apply the addition operation has no effect on the final result. For example, $(1 + 2) + 3 = 1 + (2 + 3)$.

For counting the occurrences of distinct IPs, we can use the same code in our reducer as a combiner for output in the map phase.

When applied to our problem, the normal output with no combiner from two separate independently running map tasks might look like the following where {key: value[]} is equal to the intermediate key-value collection:

▶ Map Task A = {10.10.1.1, [1,1,1]} = three occurrences

▶ Map Task B = {10.10.1.1, [1,1,1,1,1,1]} = six occurrences

Without the aid of a combiner, this will be merged in the shuffle phase and presented to a single reducer as the following key-value collection:

▶ {10.10.1.1, [1,1,1,1,1,1,1,1,1]} = nine total occurrences

Now let's revisit what would happen when using a Combiner against the exact same sample output:

Map Task A = {10.10.1.1, [1,1,1]} = three occurrences

▶ Combiner = {10.10,1,1, [3] = still three occurrences, but reduced for this mapper.

Map Task B = {10.10.1.1, [1,1,1,1,1,1] = six occurrences

▶ Combiner = {10.10.1.1, [6] = still six occurrences

Now the reducer will see the following for that key-value collection:

▶ {10.10.1.1, [3,6]} = nine total occurrences

We arrived at the same total count for that IP address, but we used a combiner to limit the amount of network I/O during the MapReduce shuffle phase by pre-reducing the intermediate key-value output from each mapper.

There's more...

The combiner can be confusing to newcomers. Here are some useful tips:

The Combiner does not always have to be the same class as your Reducer

The previous recipe and the default WordCount example show the `Combiner` class being initialized to the same implementation as the `Reducer` class. This is not enforced by the API, but ends up being common for many types of distributed aggregate operations such as `sum()`, `min()`, and `max()`. One basic example might be the `min()` operation of the `Reducer` class that specifically formats output in a certain way for readability. This will take a slightly different form from that of the `min()` operator of the `Combiner` class, which does not care about the specific output formatting.

Combiners are not guaranteed to run

Whether or not the framework invokes your combiner during execution depends on the intermediate spill file size from each map output, and is not guaranteed to run for every intermediate key. Your job should not depend on the combiner for correct results, it should be used only for optimization.

You can control the spill file threshold when MapReduce tries to combine intermediate values with the configuration property `min.num.spills.for.combine`.

Using Hive date UDFs to transform and sort event dates from geographic event data

This recipe will illustrate the efficient use of the Hive date UDFs to list the 20 most recent events and the number of days between the event date and the current system date.

Getting ready

Make sure you have access to a pseudo-distributed or fully-distributed Hadoop cluster with Apache Hive 0.7.1 installed on your client machine and on the environment path for the active user account.

This recipe depends on having the `Nigera_ACLED_cleaned.tsv` dataset loaded into a Hive table named `acled_nigeria_cleaned` with the fields mapped to the respective datatypes.

Issue the following command to the Hive client to see the mentioned fields:

```
describe acled_nigeria_cleaned
```

You should see the following response:

```
OK
Loc     string
event_date      string
event_type      string
actor   string
latitude        double
longitude       double
source  string
fatalities      int
```

How to do it...

Perform the following steps to utilize Hive UDFs for sorting and transformation:

1. Open a text editor of your choice, ideally one with SQL syntax highlighting.

2. Add the inline creation and transform syntax:

```
SELECT event_type,event_date,days_since FROM (
    SELECT event_type,event_date,
            datediff(to_date(from_unixtime(unix_timestamp())),
                to_date(from_unixtime(
                        unix_timestamp(event_date,
                        'yyyy-MM-dd')))) AS days_since
    FROM acled_nigeria_cleaned) date_differences
    ORDER BY event_date DESC LIMIT 20;
```

3. Save the file as `top_20_recent_events.sql` in the active folder.

4. Run the script from the operating system shell by supplying the `-f` option to the Hive client. You should see the following five rows appear first in the output console:

```
OK
Battle-No change of territory   2011-12-31     190
Violence against civilians   2011-12-27     194
Violence against civilians   2011-12-25     196
Violence against civilians   2011-12-25     196
Violence against civilians   2011-12-25     196
```

How it works...

Let's start with the nested `SELECT` subqueries. We select three fields from our Hive table `acled_nigeria_cleaned`: `event_type`, `event_date`, and the result of calling the UDF `datediff()`, which takes as arguments an end date and a start date. Both are expected in the form yyyy-MM-dd. The first argument to `datediff()` is the end date, with which we want to represent the current system date. Calling `unix_timestamp()` with no arguments will return the current system time in milliseconds. We send that return value to `from_unixtimestamp()` to get a formatted timestamp representing the current system date in the default Java 1.6 format (yyyy-MM-dd HH:mm:ss). We only care about the date portion, so calling `to_date()` with the output of this function strips the HH:mm:ss. The result is the current date in the yyyy-MM-dd form.

The second argument to `datediff()` is the start date, which for our query is the `event_date`. The series of function calls operate in almost the exact same manner as our previous argument, except that when we call `unix_timestamp()`, we must tell the function that our argument is in the `SimpleDateFormat` format that is yyyy-MM-dd. Now we have both `start_date` and `end_date` arguments in the yyyy-MM-dd format and can perform the `datediff()` operation for the given row. We alias the output column of `datediff()` as `days_since` for each row.

The outer `SELECT` statement takes these three columns per row and sorts the entire output by `event_date` in descending order to get reverse chronological ordering. We arbitrarily limit the output to only the first 20.

The net result is the 20 most recent events with the number of days that have passed since that event occurred.

There's more...

The date UDFs can help tremendously in performing string date comparisons. Here are some additional pointers:

Date format strings follow Java SimpleDateFormat guidelines

Check out the Javadocs for `SimpleDateFormat` to learn how your custom date strings can be used with the date transform UDFs.

Default date and time formats

- Many of the UDFs operate under a default format assumption.
- For UDFs requiring only date, your column values must be in the form yyyy-MM-dd.
- For UDFs that require date and time, your column values must be in the form yyyy-MM-dd HH:mm:ss.

See also

- *Using Hive to build a per-month report of fatalities over geographic event data*

Using Hive to build a per-month report of fatalities over geographic event data

This recipe will show a very simple analytic that uses Hive to count fatalities for every month appearing in the dataset and print the results to the console.

Getting ready

Make sure you have access to a pseudo-distributed or fully-distributed Hadoop cluster with Apache Hive 0.7.1 installed on your client machine and on the environment path for the active user account.

This recipe depends on having the `Nigera_ACLED_cleaned.tsv` dataset loaded into a Hive table named `acled_nigeria_cleaned` with the following fields mapped to the respective datatypes.

Issue the following command to the Hive client:

```
describe acled_nigeria_cleaned
```

You should see the following response:

```
OK
loc    string
event_date    string
event_type    string
actor    string
latitude    double
longitude    double
source    string
fatalities    int
```

How to do it...

Follow the steps to use Hive for report generation:

1. Open a text editor of your choice, ideally one with SQL syntax highlighting.

2. Add the inline creation and transformation syntax:

```
SELECT from_unixtime(unix_timestamp(event_date, 'yyyy-MM-dd'),
'yyyy-MMM'),
    COALESCE(CAST(sum(fatalities) AS STRING), 'Unknown')
    FROM acled_nigeria_cleaned
    GROUP BY from_unixtime(unix_timestamp(event_date, 'yyyy-MM-
dd'),'yyyy-MMM');
```

3. Save the file as `monthly_violence_totals.sql` in the active folder.

4. Run the script from the operating system shell by supplying the `-f` option to the Hive client. You should see the following three rows appear first in the output console. Note that the output is sorted lexicographically, and not on the order of dates.

```
OK
1997-Apr   115
1997-Aug   4
1997-Dec   26
```

How it works...

The `SELECT` statement uses `unix_timestamp()` and `from_unixtime()` to reformat the `event_date` for each row as just a year-month concatenated field. This is also in the `GROUP BY` expression for totaling fatalities using `sum()`.

The `coalesce()` method returns the first non-null argument passed to it. We pass as the first argument, the value of fatalities summed for that given year-month, cast as a string. If that value is `NULL` for any reason, return the constant `Unknown`. Otherwise return the string representing the total fatalities counted for that year-month combination. Print everything to the console over `stdout`.

There's more...

The following are some additional helpful tips related to the code in this recipe:

The coalesce() method can take variable length arguments.

As mentioned in the Hive documentation, `coalesce()` supports one or more arguments. The first non-null argument will be returned. This can be useful for evaluating several different expressions for a given column before deciding the right one to choose.

The `coalesce()` will return `NULL` if no argument is non-null. It's not uncommon to provide a type literal to return if all other arguments are `NULL`.

Date reformatting code template

Having to reformat dates stored in your raw data is very common. Proper use of `from_unixtime()` and `unix_timestamp()` can make your life much easier.

Remember this general code template for concise date format transformation in Hive:

```
from_unixtime(unix_timestamp(<col>,<in-format>),<out-format>);
```

See also

▶ *Using Hive date UDFs to transform and sort event dates from geographic event data*

Implementing a custom UDF in Hive to help validate source reliability over geographic event data

There are many operations you will want to repeat across various data sources and tables in Hive. For this scenario, it makes sense to write your own user-defined function (UDF). You can write your own subroutine in Java for use on any Writable input fields and to invoke your function from Hive scripts whenever necessary. This recipe will walk you through the process of creating a very simple UDF that takes a source and returns `yes` or `no` for whether that source is reliable.

Getting ready

Make sure you have access to a pseudo-distributed or fully-distributed Hadoop cluster with Apache Hive 0.7.1 installed on your client machine and on the environment path for the active user account.

This recipe depends on having the `Nigera_ACLED_cleaned.tsv` dataset loaded into a Hive table with the name `acled_nigeria_cleaned` with the following fields mapped to the respective datatypes.

Issue the following command to the Hive client:

```
describe acled_nigeria_cleaned;
```

You should see the following response:

```
OK
loc    string
```

```
event_date   string

event_type   string

actor   string

latitude   double

longitude   double

source string

fatalities   int
```

Additionally, you will need to place the following recipe's code into a source package for bundling within a JAR file of your choice. This recipe will use `<myUDFs.jar>` as a reference point for your custom JAR file and `<fully_qualified_path_to_TrustSourceUDF>` as a reference point for the Java package your class exists within. An example of a fully qualified path for a pattern would be `java.util.regex.Pattern`.

In addition to the core Hadoop libraries, your project will need to have `hive-exec` and `hive-common` JAR dependencies on the classpath for this to compile.

How to do it...

Perform the following steps to implement a custom Hive UDF:

1. Open a text editor/IDE of your choice, preferably one with Java syntax highlighting.

2. Create `TrustSourceUDF.java` at the desired source package. Your class should exist at some package `<fully_qualified_path>.TrustSourceUDF.class`.

3. Enter the following source as the implementation for the `TrustSourceUDF` class:

```
import org.apache.hadoop.hive.ql.exec.UDF;
import org.apache.hadoop.io.Text;
import java.lang.String;import java.util.HashSet;
import java.util.Set;


public class TrustSourceUDF extends UDF {

    private static Set<String> untrustworthySources = new
HashSet<String>();
    private Text result = new Text();

    static {
    untrustworthySources.add("");
    untrustworthySources.add("\"\"\"
    http://www.afriquenligne.fr/3-soldiers\"");
    untrustworthySources.add("Africa News Service");
```

```
        untrustworthySources.add("Asharq Alawsat");
        untrustworthySources.add("News Agency of Nigeria (NAN)");
        untrustworthySources.add("This Day (Nigeria)");
    }

    @Override
    public Text evaluate(Text source) {

        if (untrustworthySources.contains(source.toString())) {
            result.set("no");
        } else {
            result.set("yes");
        }
        return result;

    }
}
```

4. Build the containing JAR `<myUDFs.jar>` and test your UDF through the Hive client. Open a Hive client session through the command shell. Hive should already be on the local user environment path. Invoke the Hive shell with the following command:

   ```
   hive
   ```

5. Add the JAR file to the Hive session's classpath:

   ```
   add jar /path/to/<myUDFs.jar>;
   ```

   You will know that the preceding operation succeeded if you see the following messages indicating that the JAR has been added to the classpath and the distributed cache:

   ```
   Added /path/to/<myUDFs.jar> to class path
   Added resource: /path/to/<myUDFs.jar>
   ```

6. Create the function definition `trust_source` as an alias to `TrustSourceUDF` at whatever source package you specified in your JAR:

   ```
   create temporary function trust_source as '<fully_qualified_path_
   to_TrustSourceUDF>';
   ```

   You should see the shell prompt you that the command executed successfully. If you see the following error, it usually indicates your class was not found on the classpath:

   ```
   FAILED: Execution Error, return code 1 from org.apache.hadoop.
   hive.ql.exec.FunctionTask
   ```

7. Test the function with the following query. You should see mostly **yes** printed on each line of the console, with a few no's here and there:

   ```
   select trust_source(source) from acled_nigeria_cleaned;
   ```

How it works...

The class `TrustSourceUDF` extends UDF. No methods are required for implementation; however, in order for the class to function at Hive runtime as a UDF, your subclass must override `evaluate()`. You can have one or more overloaded `evaluate()` methods with different arguments. Ours only needs to take in a `source` value to check.

During class initialization, we set up a static instance of the `java.util.Set` class named `untrustworthySources`. Within a static initialization block, we set up a few sources by their names to be flagged as unreliable.

 The entries here are purely arbitrary and should not be considered reliable or unreliable outside of this recipe.

We flag an empty source as unreliable.

When the function is invoked, it expects a single `Text` instance to be checked against the sources we've flagged as unreliable. Return `yes` or `no` depending on whether the given source appears in the set of unreliable sources or not. We set up the private `Text` instance to be re-used every time the function is called.

Once the JAR file containing the class is added to the classpath, and we set up our temporary function definition, we can now use the UDF across many different queries.

There's more...

User-defined functions are a very powerful feature within Hive. The following sections list a bit more information regarding them:

Check out the existing UDFs

The Hive documentation has a great explanation of the built-in UDFs bundled with the language. A great write up is available at `https://cwiki.apache.org/confluence/display/Hive/LanguageManual+UDF#LanguageManualUDF-BuiltinAggregateFunctions%28UDAF%29`.

To see which functions are available in your specific version of Hive, issue the following command in the Hive shell.

```
show functions;
```

Once you pinpoint a function that looks interesting, learn more information about it from the Hive wiki or directly from the Hive shell by executing the following command:

```
describe function <func>;
```

User-defined table and aggregate functions

Hive UDFs do not need to have a one-to-one interaction for input and output. The API allows the generation of many outputs from one input (GenericUDTF) as well as custom aggregate functions that take a list of input rows and output a single value (UDAF).

Export HIVE_AUX_JARS_PATH in your environment

Adding JAR files dynamically to the classpath is useful for testing and debugging, but can be cumbersome if you have many libraries you repeatedly wish to use. The Hive command line interpreter will automatically look for the existence of `HIVE_AUX_JARS_PATH` in the executing user's environment. Use this environment variable to set additional JAR paths that will always get loaded in the classpath of new Hive sessions for that client machine.

See also

  ▸ *Using Hive date UDFs to transform and sort event dates from geographic event data*

  ▸ *Using Hive to build a per-month report of fatalities over geographic event data*

Marking the longest period of non-violence using Hive MAP/REDUCE operators and Python

The Hive query language provides facilities to control the MapReduce dataflow and inject your own custom map, and to reduce scripts at each stage. When used properly, this is a very powerful technique for writing concise MapReduce programs using minimal syntax.

This recipe will show a complete example of how to write custom MapReduce control flow using different operators in Hive. The analytic will specifically look for the longest gap in events for each location to get an idea of how frequently violence occurs in that location.

Getting ready

Make sure you have access to a pseudo-distributed or fully-distributed Hadoop cluster with Apache Hive 0.7.1 installed on your client machine and on the environment path for the active user account.

Your cluster will also need Python 2.7 or greater installed on each node and available on the environment path for the Hadoop user. The script shown in this recipe assumes an installation at `/usr/bin/env python`. If this does not match your installation, change the script accordingly.

This recipe depends on having the `Nigeria_ACLED_cleaned.tsv` dataset loaded into a Hive table named `acled_nigeria_cleaned` with the following fields mapped to the respective datatypes.

Issue the following command to the Hive client:

```
describe acled_nigeria_cleaned;
```

You should see the following response:

```
OK
loc   string
event_date   string
event_type   string
actor   string
latitude   double
longitude   double
source   string
fatalities   int
```

How to do it...

Perform the following steps to mark the longest period of non-violence using Hive:

1. Open a text editor of your choice, ideally one with SQL and Python syntax highlighting.

2. Add the following inline creation and transform syntax:

```
SET mapred.child.java.opts=-Xmx512M;

DROP TABLE IF EXISTS longest_event_delta_per_loc;
CREATE TABLE longest_event_delta_per_loc (
    loc STRING,
    start_date STRING,
    end_date STRING,
    days INT
);

ADD FILE calc_longest_nonviolent_period.py;
FROM (
        SELECT loc, event_date, event_type
        FROM acled_nigeria_cleaned
        DISTRIBUTE BY loc SORT BY loc, event_date
    ) mapout
INSERT OVERWRITE TABLE longest_event_delta_per_loc
REDUCE mapout.loc, mapout.event_date, mapout.event_type
USING 'python calc_longest_nonviolent_period.py'
AS loc, start_date, end_date, days;
```

3. Save the file in the local working folder as `longest_nonviolent_periods_per_location.sql`.

4. Create a new file in your text editor with the name `calc_longest_nonviolent_period.py` and save it in the same working folder as `longest_nonviolent_periods_per_location.sql`.

5. Add the Python syntax. Python is sensitive to indentation. Keep that in mind if you are cutting and pasting this code:

```python
#!/usr/bin/python
import sys
from datetime import datetime, timedelta

current_loc = "START_OF_APP"
(prev_date, start_date, end_date, start_time_obj, end_time_obj,
current_diff)=('', '', '', None, None, timedelta.min)
for line in sys.stdin:
  (loc,event_date,event_type) = line.strip('\n').split('\t')
  if loc != current_loc and current_loc != "START_OF_APP":
    if end_date != '':
      print '\t'.join([current_loc,start_date,event_
date,str(current_diff.days)])
          (prev_date, start_date, end_date, start_time_obj, end_
time_obj,current_diff)=('', '', '', None, None, timedelta.min)
    end_time_obj = datetime.strptime(event_date,'%Y-%m-%d')
  current_loc = loc
  if start_time_obj is not None: # implies > 2 events
    diff = end_time_obj - start_time_obj
    if diff > current_diff:
      current_diff = diff # set the current max time delta
      start_date = prev_date
      end_date = event_date
  prev_date = event_date
  start_time_obj = end_time_obj
```

6. Run the script from the operating system's shell by supplying the –f option to the Hive client:

```
hive -f longest_nonviolent_periods_per_location.sql
```

7. Issue the following query directly to the Hive shell. You should see rows printed to the console in no particular order:

```
hive -e "select * from longest_event_delta_per_loc;"
```

How it works...

Let's start with the Hive script we created. The first line is simply to force a certain JVM heap size in our execution. You can set this to whatever is appropriate for your cluster. For the ACLED Nigeria dataset, 512 MB is more than enough.

Then we create our table definition for the output, dropping any existing tables with a matching name `longest_event_delta_per_loc`. The table requires four fields per record: `loc` for the location, `start_date` to hold the value of the `event_date` field of the lower bound, `end_date` to hold the value of `event_date` field of the upper bound, and `days` to show the total number of days elapsed between the events.

We then add the file `calc_longest_nonviolent_period.py` to the distributed cache for use across the different reducer JVMs. This will be used as our reduce script, but first we must organize the map output. The inner `SELECT` statement grabs `loc`, `event_date`, and `event_type` from the `acled_nigeria_cleaned` table in Hive. The `DISTRIBUTE BY loc` statement tells Hive to guarantee that all rows with matching values for `loc` go to the same reducer. `SORT BY loc, event_date` tells Hive to sort the data as it arrives to each reducer by the combination of `loc` and `event_date`. Now the same reducer can process every row corresponding to each location locally, and in the sorted order of `event_date`.

We alias the output of this `SELECT` statement to `mapout` and use the shorthand `REDUCE` operator to process each row from `mapout`. The `USING` clause lets us supply a custom Python script to read each record as it comes over `stdin`. The `AS` operator lets us map the delimited fields that are output by the script over `stdout` to pipe into the fields of the receiving table.

The Python script `calc_longest_nonviolent_period.py` will be used by the reduce stage to compute the longest time gap between the events for each location. Since we have guaranteed that all records with a common `loc` value are at the same reducer and that those records are in the date-sorted order for each location, we are now in a position to understand how the Python script works.

In the Python script `calc_longest_nonviolent_period.py`, we start with `#!/usr/bin/python` as a hint to the shell on how to execute the script. We need to import `sys` to use the `stdin` and `stdout` operations. We also need the `datetime` and `timedelta` class definitions from the `datetime` package.

The script operates very procedurally and can be a bit difficult to follow. First we declare `current_loc` and initialize its value to `START_OF_APP` as a flag to the print out conditional. We then set up several different variables to hold different placeholder values to be used on a per-location basis by the `for` loop.

- ▶ `prev_date`: This holds the last observed `event_date` for the `loc` value. It is blank if it's the start of the app, or holds a new location value.

- ▶ `start_date`: This holds the lower bound for the longest currently observed time delta between events for that value of `loc`.

- ► `end_date`: This holds the upper bound for the longest currently observed time elapsed between events for the value of `current_loc`.

- ► `start_time_obj`: This holds the most recently iterated `datetime` object, or `None` if it's the start of the app, or holds a new location value.

- ► `end_time_obj`: This holds the current `event_date datetime` object, or `None` if it's the start of the app, or holds a new location value.

- ► `current_diff`: This holds the time delta for the current longest observed time elapsed between events for the `current_loc`, or the lowest possible time delta if it's the start of the app, or a new location value.

The `for` loop reads rows over `stdin` that have already been sorted by the combination of `loc` and `event_date`. We parse each row into variables representing the column values by first stripping any additional newlines and splitting the line on tab characters.

The first conditional is skipped as `current_loc` is equal to START OF APP. We have only begun processing the first row across all locations on that reducer, and have nothing to output yet. Should we have a value for `loc` that is different from the value of `current_loc`, and we are not at the start of the application, then that is a signal that we are done processing the rows for `current_loc`, and can safely output the longest time delta for events in that location. Should `end_date` still be set to an empty string, then that indicates we only saw one event for that location. In this scenario, we do not output anything for that location. Finally, we reset the six placeholder variables previously explained, so that we may accurately process the records for the next location.

Following the conditional, we immediately set the value of `current_loc` that we are processing equal to `loc`, to avoid unnecessary entry of the mentioned conditional on the next iteration when we have not yet transitioned locations. We set `end_time_obj` to the value of `event_date` for the current row. If `start_time_obj` is set to `None`, then that means we are on the first row for that location and cannot yet do a time delta comparison. Whether or not `start_time_obj` is set to `None`, at the end of the loop we set `prev_date` equal to `event_date` and `start_time_obj` equal to `end_time_obj` of the current iteration. By doing so, on the next iteration, `start_time_obj` will hold the `event_date` of the previous record, while `end_time_obj` will hold the `event_date` of the current record.

When `start_time_obj` is no longer set to `None` after the first iteration for a given location, we can begin doing `diff` comparisons on these two `datetime` objects. Subtracting `start_time_obj` from `end_time_obj` yields a time delta object, which if larger than the `current_diff` value, gets set as the value for `current_diff`. In doing so, we capture the longest elapsed time period for that location between events. We also set the values of `start_date` and `end_date` for easy output later, once we are done processing this location. As mentioned earlier, whether or not we reset `current_diff`, we then change `prev_date` to point to `event_date` and `start_time_obj` equal to the current `end_time_obj`.

The next time the loop encounters the condition where `loc` is not equal to `current_loc`, we output the currently held longest time difference between events, before we move onto the next event. Each print to `stdout` writes a row into the receiving Hive table that holds each location held by `current_loc`, the `lower_bound` `event_date` string held by `start_date`, the upper bound `event_date` string held by `end_date`, and the total number of days elapsed between those two dates held by `current_diff.days`.

There's more...

Here are a few additional notes on some of the operations touched upon in this recipe:.

SORT BY versus DISTRIBUTE BY versus CLUSTER BY versus ORDER BY

These four operator variants always cause confusion to Hive beginners. Here's a quick comparison so you'll know which one is appropriate for your use case:

- ▶ `DISTRIBUTE BY`: Rows with matching column values will partition to the same reducer. When used alone, it does not guarantee sorted input to the reducer.

- ▶ `SORT BY`: This dictates which columns to sort by when ordering reducer input records.

- ▶ `CLUSTER BY`: This is a shorthand operator to perform both `SORT BY` and `DISTRIBUTE BY` operations on a group of columns.

- ▶ `ORDER BY`: This is similar to the traditional SQL operator. Sorted order is maintained across all of the output from every reducer. Use this with caution as it can force all of the output records to a single reducer to perform the sorting. Usage with `LIMIT` is strongly recommended.

MAP and REDUCE keywords are shorthand for SELECT TRANSFORM

The Hive keywords `MAP` and `REDUCE` are shorthand notations for `SELECT TRANSFORM`, and do not force the query execution to jump around stages. You can use any one of the three and achieve the same functional results. They are simply for query readability purposes.

See also

- ▶ The *Using Hive and Python to clean and transform geographical event data* in recipe *Chapter 3, Extracting and Transforming Data*

Calculating the cosine similarity of artists in the Audioscrobbler dataset using Pig

Cosine similarity is used to measure the similarity of two vectors. In this recipe, it will be used to find the similarity of artists based on the number of times Audioscrobbler users have added each user to their playlist. The idea is to show how often users play both artist 1 and artist 2.

Getting ready

Download the `Audioscrobbler` dataset from `http://www.packtpub.com/support`.

How to do it...

Perform the following steps to calculate cosine similarity using Pig:

1. Copy the `artist_data.txt` and `user_artist_data.txt` files into HDFS:

   ```
   hadoop fs –put artist_data.txt user_artist_data.txt /data/
   audioscrobbler/
   ```

2. Load the data into Pig:

   ```
   plays = load '/data/audioscrobbler/user_artist_data.txt'
           using PigStorage(' ') as (user_id:long, artist_id:long,
   playcount:long);

   artist = load '/data/audioscrobbler/artist_data.txt' as (artist_
   id:long, artist_name:chararray);
   ```

3. Sample the `user_artist_data.txt` file:

   ```
   plays = sample plays .01;
   ```

4. Normalize the play counts to `100`:

   ```
   user_total_grp = group plays by user_id;

   user_total = foreach user_total_grp generate group as user_id,
   SUM(plays.playcount) as totalplays;

   plays_user_total = join plays by user_id, user_total by user_id
   using 'replicated';

   norm_plays = foreach plays_user_total generate user_total::user_id
   as user_id, artist_id, ((double)playcount/(double)totalplays) *
   100.0 as norm_play_cnt;
   ```

5. Get artist pairs for each user:

```
norm_plays2 = foreach norm_plays generate *;

play_pairs = join norm_plays by user_id, norm_plays2 by user_id
using 'replicated';

play_pairs = filter play_pairs by norm_plays::plays::artist_id !=
norm_plays2::plays::artist_id;
```

6. Calculate cosine similarity:

```
cos_sim_step1 = foreach play_pairs generate ((double)norm_
plays::norm_play_cnt) * (double)norm_plays2::norm_play_cnt) as
dot_product_step1, ((double)norm_plays::norm_play_cnt *(double)
norm_plays::norm_play_cnt) as play1_sq;
((double)norm_plays2::norm_play_cnt *(double) norm_plays2::norm_
play_cnt) as play2_sq;

cos_sim_grp = group cos_sim_step1 by (norm_plays::plays::artist_
id, norm_plays2::plays::artist_id);

cos_sim_step2 = foreach cos_sim_grp generate flatten(group),
COUNT(cos_sim_step1.dot_prodct_step1) as cnt, SUM(cos_sim_step1.
dot_product_step1) as dot_product, SUM(cos_sim_step1.norm_
plays::norm_play_cnt) as tot_play_sq, SUM(cos_sim_step1.norm_
plays2::norm_play_cnt) as tot_play_sq2;

cos_sim = foreach cos_sim_step2 generate group::norm_
plays::plays::artist_id as artist_id1, group::norm_plays2::plays_
artist_id as artist_id2, dot_product / (tot_play_sq1 * tot_play_
sq2) as cosine_similarity;
```

7. Get the artist's name:

```
art1 = join cos_sim by artist_id1, artist by artist_id using
'replicated';
art2 = join art1 by artist_id2, artist by artist_id using
'replicated';
art3 = foreach art2 generate artist_id1, art1::artist::artist_name
as artist_name1, artist_id2, artist::artist_name as artist_name2,
cosin_similarity;
```

8. To output the top 25 records:

```
top = order art3 by cosine_similarity DESC;
top_25 = limit top 25;
dump top25;
```

The output would be:

```
(1000157,AC/DC,3418,Hole,0.9115799166673817)
(829,Nas,1002216,The Darkness,0.9110152004952198)
(1022845,Jessica Simpson,1002325,Mandy Moore,0.9097097460071537)
(53,Wu-Tang Clan,78,Sublime,0.9096468367168238)
(1001180,Godsmack,1234871,Devildriver,0.9093019011575069)
(1001594,Adema,1007903,Maroon 5,0.909297052154195)
(689,Bette Midler,1003904,Better Than Ezra,0.9089467492461345)
(949,Ben Folds Five,2745,Ladytron,0.908736095810886)
(1000388,Ben Folds,930,Eminem,0.9085664586931873)
(1013654,Who Da Funk,5672,Nancy Sinatra,0.9084521262343653)
(1005386,Stabbing Westward,30,Jane's Addiction,0.9075360259222892)
(1252,Travis,1275996,R.E.M.,0.9071980963712077)
(100,Phoenix,1278,Ryan Adams,0.9071754511713067)
(2247,Four Tet,1009898,A Silver Mt. Zion,0.9069623744896833)
(1037970,Kanye West,1000991,Alison Krauss,0.9058717234023009)
(352,Beck,5672,Nancy Sinatra,0.9056851798338253)
(831,Nine Inch Nails,1251,Morcheeba,0.9051453756031981)
(1007004,Journey,1005479,Mr. Mister,0.9041311825160151)
(1002470,Elton John,1000416,Ramones,0.9040551837635081)
(1200,Faith No More,1007903,Maroon 5,0.9038274644717641)
(1002850,Glassjaw,1016435,Senses Fail,0.9034604126636377)
(1004294,Thursday,2439,HiM,0.902728300518356)
(1003259,ABBA,1057704,Readymade,0.9026955950032872)
(1001590,Hybrid,791,Beenie Man,0.9020872203833108)
(1501,Wolfgang Amadeus Mozart,4569,Simon &
Garfunkel,0.9018860912385024)
```

How it works...

The `load` statements tell Pig about the format and datatypes of the data being loaded. Pig loads data lazily. This means that the `load` statements at the beginning of this script will not do any work until another statement is entered that asks for output.

The `user_artist_data.txt` file is sampled so that a replicated join can be used when it is joined with itself. This significantly reduces the processing time at the cost of accuracy. The sample value of `.01` is used, meaning that roughly one in hundred rows of data will be loaded.

A user selecting to play an artist is treated as a vote for that artist. The play counts are normalized to `100`. This ensures that each user is given the same number of votes.

A self join of the `user_artist_data.txt` file by `user_id` will generate all pairs of artists that users have added to their playlist. The filter removes duplicates caused by the self join.

The next few statements calculate the cosine similarity. For each pair of artists that users have added to their playlist, multiply the number of plays for artist 1 by the number of plays for artist 2. Then output the number of plays for artist 1 and the number of plays for artist 2. Group the previous result by each pair of artists. Sum the multiplication of the number of plays for artist 1 by the number of plays by artist 2 for each user generated previously as the dot product. Sum the number of plays for artist 1 by all users. Sum the number of plays for artist 2 by all users. The cosine similarly is the dot product over the total plays for artist 1 multiplied by the total plays for artist two. The idea is to show how often users play both artist 1 and artist 2.

Trim Outliers from the Audioscrobbler dataset using Pig and datafu

Datafu is a Pig UDF library open sourced by the SNA team at LinkedIn. It contains many useful functions. This recipe will use **play counts** from the `Audioscrobbler` dataset and the **Quantile** UDF from datafu to identify and remove outliers.

Getting ready

- Download Version 0.0.4 of datafu from `https://github.com/linkedin/datafu/downloads`.

- Uncompress and untar the files. Add the `datafu-0.0.4/dist/ datafu-0.0.4.jar` file to a location accessible by Pig.

- Download the `Audioscrobbler` dataset from `http://www.packtpub.com/support`.

How to do it...

1. Register the datafu JAR file and construct the `Quantile` UDF:
```
register /path/to/datafu-0.0.4.jar;
define Quantile datafu.pig.stats.Quantile('.90');
```

2. Load the `user_artist_data.txt` file:
```
plays = load '/data/audioscrobbler.txt'using PigStorage(' ') as
(user_id:long, artist_id:long, playcount:long);
```

3. Group all of the data:

```
plays_grp = group plays ALL;
```

4. Generate the ninetieth percentile value to be used as the outlier's max:

```
out_max = foreach plays_grp{
        ord = order plays by playcount;
        generate Quantile(ord.playcount) as ninetieth ;
        }
```

5. Trim outliers to the ninetieth percentile value:

```
trim_outliers = foreach plays generate user_id, artist_id,
(playcount>out_max.ninetieth ? out_max.ninetieth : playcount);
```

6. Store the `user_artist_data.txt` file with outliers trimmed:

```
store trim_outliers into '/data/audioscrobble/outliers_trimmed.
bcp';
```

How it works...

This recipe takes advantage of the datafu library open sourced by LinkedIn. Once a JAR file is registered, all of its UDFs are available to the Pig script. The `define` command calls the constructor of the `datafu.pig.stats.Quantile` UDF passing it a value of `.90`. The constructor of the `Quantile` UDF will then create an instance that will produce the ninetieth percentile of the input vector it is passed. The `define` also aliases `Quantile` as shorthand for referencing this UDF.

The user artist data is loaded into a relation named `plays`. This data is then grouped by `ALL`. The `ALL` group is a special kind of group that creates a single bag containing all of the input.

The `Quantile` UDF requires that the data it has passed be sorted first. The data is sorted by play count, and the sorted play count's vector is passed to the `Quantile` UDF. The sorted play count simplifies the job of the `Quantile` UDF. It now picks the value at the ninetieth percentile position and returns it.

This value is then compared against each of the play counts in the user artist file. If the play count is greater, it is trimmed down to the value returned by the `Quantile` UDF, otherwise the value remains as it is.

The updated user artist file with outliers trimmed is then stored back in HDFS to be used for further processing.

There's more...

The datafu library also includes a `StreamingQuantile` UDF. This UDF is similar to the `Quantile` UDF except that it does not require the data to be sorted before it is used. This will greatly increase the performance of this operation. However, it does come at a cost. The `StreamingQuantile` UDF only provides an estimation of the values.

```
define Quantile datafu.pig.stats.StreamingQuantile('.90');
```

7
Advanced Big Data Analysis

In this chapter, we will cover:

- ▶ PageRank with Apache Giraph
- ▶ Single-source shortest-path with Apache Giraph
- ▶ Using Apache Giraph to perform a distributed breadth-first search
- ▶ Collaborative filtering with Apache Mahout
- ▶ Clustering with Apache Mahout
- ▶ Sentiment classification with Apache Mahout

Introduction

Graph and machine learning problems are hard to solve using the MapReduce framework. Most of these problems require iterative steps and/or knowledge of complex algorithms, which can be cumbersome to implement in MapReduce. Luckily, there are two frameworks available to help with graph and machine learning problems in the Hadoop environment. Apache **Giraph** is a graph-processing framework designed to run large-scale algorithms. Apache **Mahout** is a framework that provides implementations of distributed machine learning algorithms.

This chapter will introduce readers to these two frameworks, which are capable of leveraging the distributed power of MapReduce.

PageRank with Apache Giraph

This recipe is primarily aimed at building and testing the default Apache Giraph PageRank example, modeled after the Google Pregel implementation. It will demonstrate the steps involved in submitting and executing a Giraph job to a pseudo-distributed Hadoop cluster.

Getting ready

For first-time Giraph users, we recommend running this recipe using a pseudo-distributed Hadoop cluster.

For the client machine, you will need Subversion and Maven installed and configured on the user environment path.

This recipe does not require a full understanding of the Giraph API, but it does assume some familiarity with **Bulk Synchronous Parallel** (**BSP**) and the design goals of vertex-centric APIs including Apache Giraph and Google Pregel.

How to do it...

Carry out the following steps to build and test the default Giraph PageRank example:

1. Navigate to a base folder and perform an SVN checkout of the latest Giraph source, located at the official Apache site:

    ```
    $ svn co https://svn.apache.org/repos/asf/giraph/trunk
    ```

2. Change the folder into a trunk and run the build:

    ```
    $ mvn compile
    ```

3. Once the build finishes, navigate to the target folder created in the trunk and you should see the JAR file `giraph-0.2-SNAPSHOT-jar-with-dependencies.jar`.

4. Run the following command:

    ```
    hadoop jar giraph-0.2-SNAPSHOT-jar-with-dependencies.jar org.
    apache.giraph.benchmark.PageRankBenchmark -V 1000 -e 1 -s 5 -w 1
    -v
    ```

5. You should see the job execute and the MapReduce command line output show success.

6. The Giraph stats counter group in the printout should show the following stats:

    ```
    INFO mapred.JobClient:    Giraph Stats
    INFO mapred.JobClient:       Aggregate edges=1000
    mapred.JobClient:        Superstep=6
    ```

```
mapred.JobClient:      Last checkpointed superstep=0
mapred.JobClient:      Current workers=1
mapred.JobClient:      Current master task partition=0
mapred.JobClient:      Sent messages=0
mapred.JobClient:      Aggregate finished vertices=1000
mapred.JobClient:      Aggregate vertices=1000
```

How it works...

First, we use Subversion to check out the latest source from the official Apache site. Once we build the JAR file, the `PageRankBenchmark` example job is available for submission. Before we are ready to test Giraph, we must set the following command line options:

- ▸ `-V`: This shows the number of total vertices to run through PageRank. We chose 1000 just for testing. For a more accurate testing we would want millions of vertices over a fully-distributed cluster.

- ▸ `-e`: This shows the number of outgoing edges defined for each vertex. This will control the number of messages that are output during each superstep to any neighboring vertices, where a neighbor is defined as a vertex connected to another vertex by one or more edges.

- ▸ `-s`: This shows the total number of supersteps to run before terminating PageRank.

- ▸ `-w`: This shows the total number of workers available to handle distinct graph partitions. Since we are running a pseudo-distributed cluster (single host), it is safe to limit this to one. In a fully-distributed cluster, we would want multiple workers spread out across different physical hosts.

- ▸ `-v`: This activates the verbose mode to follow the job progress on the console.

The job contains no additional classpath dependencies outside of core Hadoop/ZooKeeper. It can be directly submitted to the cluster via the `hadoop jar` command from the command line.

The `PageRankBenchmark` example does not output the results back to HDFS. It is designed primarily to test and expose certain cluster bottlenecks that might hinder other production Giraph jobs. Running the job against a large number of vertices with multiple edges may expose memory constraints, network I/O connectivity issues between workers, and other potential problems.

There's more...

Apache Giraph is a relatively new open source batch computation framework. The following tips will help you further your understanding:

Keep up with the Apache Giraph community

Apache Giraph has a very active developer community. The API is constantly being enhanced with new features, bug fixes, and occasional refactoring. It is a good idea to update your source from trunk at least once a week. At the time of this writing, Giraph has no public Maven artifact. This will change in the very near future, but for now SVN is required to pull source updates.

Read and understand the Google Pregel paper

Somewhere in 2009, Google published a research paper describing in high-level technical detail their proprietary software, which was made for scalable graph-centric processing based on the Bulk Synchronous Parallel (BSP) model.

Apache Giraph is an open source implementation of many of the concepts found in this research paper. Familiarity with the Pregel design will help to explain many components found in the Giraph codebase.

A basic introduction to BSP can be found on Wikipedia at `http://en.wikipedia.org/wiki/Bulk_Synchronous_Parallel`.

See also

 ▸ *Single-source shortest-path with Apache Giraph*
 ▸ *Using Apache Giraph to perform a distributed breadth-first search*

Single-source shortest-path with Apache Giraph

In this recipe, we will implement a variant of the Google Pregel shortest-path implementation between employees connected via an acyclic directed graph. The code will take a single source ID, and for all vertices in the graph, will mark the minimum number of hops required to reach each vertex from the source ID vertex. The employee network is stored in HDFS as a line-separated list of RDF triples. **Resource Description Framework** (**RDF**) is a very effective data format for representing entities and the relationships between them.

Getting ready

Make sure you have a basic familiarity with Google Pregel/BSP and the Giraph API.

You will need access to a pseudo-distributed Hadoop cluster. The code listed in this recipe uses a non-split master-worker configuration that is not ideal in fully-distributed environments. It also assumes that you have familiarity with bash shell scripting.

You will need to load the example dataset `gooftech.tsv` to an HDFS folder located at `/input/gooftech`.

You will also need to package this code inside a JAR file to be executed by the Hadoop JAR launcher from the shell. The shell script listed in the recipe shows a template for job submission with the correct classpath dependencies.

How to do it...

Carry out the following steps to implement the shortest path in Giraph:

1. First, we define our custom `InputFormat` that extends `TextInputFormat` to read the employee RDF triples from the text. Save the class as `EmployeeRDFTextInputFormat.java` in a package of your choice:

```java
import com.google.common.collect.Maps;
import org.apache.giraph.graph.BspUtils;
import org.apache.giraph.graph.Vertex;
import org.apache.giraph.graph.VertexReader;
import org.apache.giraph.lib.TextVertexInputFormat;
import org.apache.hadoop.io.*;
import org.apache.hadoop.mapreduce.InputSplit;
import org.apache.hadoop.mapreduce.RecordReader;
import org.apache.hadoop.mapreduce.TaskAttemptContext;

import java.io.IOException;
import java.util.Map;
import java.util.regex.Pattern;


public class EmployeeRDFTextInputFormat extends
            TextVertexInputFormat<Text, IntWritable,
NullWritable, IntWritable> {

  @Override
  public VertexReader<Text, IntWritable, NullWritable,
                    IntWritable>
  createVertexReader(InputSplit split, TaskAttemptContext context)
    throws IOException {
    return new EmployeeRDFVertexReader(
        textInputFormat.createRecordReader(split, context));
  }
}
```

2. We write the custom vertex reader used in the input format as a static inner class:

```
public static class EmployeeRDFVertexReader extends
    TextVertexInputFormat.TextVertexReader<Text,
IntWritable, NullWritable, IntWritable> {


    private static final Pattern TAB = Pattern.compile("[\\t]");
    private static final Pattern COLON = Pattern.compile("[:]");
    private static final Pattern COMMA = Pattern.compile("[,]");



    public EmployeeRDFVertexReader(RecordReader<LongWritable,
Text> lineReader) {
        super(lineReader);
    }
```

3. Override the `getCurrentVertex()` method. This method is where we use the line reader to parse our custom vertex objects:

```
@Override
public Vertex<Text, IntWritable, NullWritable, IntWritable>
getCurrentVertex() throws IOException, InterruptedException {
    Vertex<Text, IntWritable, NullWritable, IntWritable>
    vertex = BspUtils.<Text, IntWritable, NullWritable,
    IntWritable>
    createVertex(getContext().getConfiguration());

    String[] tokens = TAB.split(getRecordReader()
        .getCurrentValue().toString());
    Text vertexId = new Text(tokens[0]);

    IntWritable value = new IntWritable(0);
    String subtoken = COLON.split(tokens[2])[1];
    String[] subs = COMMA.split(subtoken);
    Map<Text, NullWritable> edges =
        Maps.newHashMapWithExpectedSize(subs.length);
    for(String sub : subs) {
        if(!sub.equals("none"))
            edges.put(new Text(sub), NullWritable.get());
    }

    vertex.initialize(vertexId, value, edges, null);
```

```
        return vertex;
    }

    @Override
    public boolean nextVertex() throws IOException,
InterruptedException {
        return getRecordReader().nextKeyValue();
    }
   }
  }
}
```

4. The job setup code, vertex class, and custom output format are all contained in a
    single class. Save the following code in a package of your choice to a class named
    `EmployeeShortestPath.java`:

```java
import org.apache.giraph.graph.*;
import org.apache.giraph.lib.TextVertexOutputFormat;
import org.apache.hadoop.conf.Configuration;
import org.apache.hadoop.fs.FileSystem;
import org.apache.hadoop.fs.Path;
import org.apache.hadoop.io.*;
import org.apache.hadoop.mapreduce.RecordWriter;
import org.apache.hadoop.mapreduce.TaskAttemptContext;
import org.apache.hadoop.mapreduce.lib.input.FileInputFormat;
import org.apache.hadoop.mapreduce.lib.output.FileOutputFormat;
import org.apache.hadoop.util.Tool;
import org.apache.hadoop.util.ToolRunner;

import java.io.IOException;

/**
 * Value based on number of hops. vertices receiving incoming
messages increment the message
 */
public class EmployeeShortestPath implements Tool{

    public static final String NAME = "emp_shortest_path";

    private Configuration conf;
    private static final String SOURCE_ID = "emp_source_id";

    public EmployeeShortestPath(Configuration
                                   configuration) {
        conf = configuration;
    }
```

5. The `run()` method in the following code snippet sets up the Giraph job configuration:

```
@Override
public int run(String[] args) throws Exception {
    if(args.length < 4) {
        System.err.println(printUsage());
        System.exit(1);
    }
    if(args.length > 4) {
        System.err.println("too many arguments. " +
                "Did you forget to quote the source ID
name ('firstname lastname')");
        System.exit(1);
    }
    String input = args[0];
    String output = args[1];
    String source_id = args[2];
    String zooQuorum = args[3];

    conf.set(SOURCE_ID, source_id);
    conf.setBoolean(GiraphJob.SPLIT_MASTER_WORKER,
                    false);
    conf.setBoolean(GiraphJob.USE_SUPERSTEP_COUNTERS,
                    false);
    conf.setInt(GiraphJob.CHECKPOINT_FREQUENCY, 0);
    GiraphJob job = new GiraphJob(conf, "single-source
        shortest path for employee: " + source_id);
    job.setVertexClass(EmployeeShortestPathVertex.class);
    job.setVertexInputFormatClass(EmployeeRDFTextInputFormat.
class);
    job.setVertexOutputFormatClass(EmployeeShortestPathOutputForm
at.class);
    job.setZooKeeperConfiguration(zooQuorum);

    FileInputFormat.addInputPath(job.getInternalJob(), new
Path(input));
    FileOutputFormat.setOutputPath(job.getInternalJob(),
removeAndSetOutput(output));

    job.setWorkerConfiguration(1, 1, 100.0f);
    return job.run(true) ? 0 : 1;
}
```

6. The following, method force deletes the supplied output folder in HDFS. Use it with caution. The other methods are required to conform to the `Tool` interface:

```
    private Path removeAndSetOutput(String outputDir) throws
IOException {
        FileSystem fs = FileSystem.get(conf);
        Path path = new Path(outputDir);
        fs.delete(path, true);
        return path;
    }

    private String printUsage() {
        return "usage: <input> <output> <single quoted source_id>
<zookeeper_quorum>";
    }

    @Override
    public void setConf(Configuration conf) {
        this.conf = conf;
    }

    @Override
    public Configuration getConf() {
        return conf;
    }
```

7. The `main()` method instantiates and submits the job using `ToolRunner`:

```
    public static void main(String[] args) throws Exception {
        System.exit(ToolRunner.run(new EmployeeShortestPath(new
Configuration()), args));
    }
```

8. The static inner class `EmployeeShortestPathVertex` lets us define a custom compute method to be used during each superstep:

```
    public static class EmployeeShortestPathVertex<I extends
WritableComparable,
            V extends Writable, E extends Writable, M extends
Writable> extends EdgeListVertex <Text, IntWritable, NullWritable,
IntWritable>
    {

        private IntWritable max = new IntWritable(Integer.MAX_
VALUE);
```

```
              private IntWritable msg = new IntWritable(1);

              private boolean isSource() {
                  return getId().toString().equals(
                         getConf().get(SOURCE_ID));
              }

              @Override
              public void compute(Iterable<IntWritable> messages)
                              throws IOException {
                  if(getSuperstep() == 0) {
                      setValue(max);
                      if(isSource()) {
                          for(Edge<Text, NullWritable> e :
                              getEdges()) {
                              sendMessage(e.getTargetVertexId(),
                                          msg);
                          }
                      }
                  }
                  int min = getValue().get();
                  for(IntWritable msg : messages) {
                      min = Math.min(msg.get(), min);
                  }
                  if(min < getValue().get()) {
                      setValue(new IntWritable(min));
                      msg.set(min + 1);
                      sendMessageToAllEdges(msg);
                  }
                  voteToHalt();
              }
          }
```

9. The static inner class `EmployeeShortestPathOutputFormat` lets us define a
    custom `OutputFormat`. The class `EmployeeRDFVertexWriter` lets us output our
    vertex information as `Text` key-value pairs back to HDFS:

```
    public static class EmployeeShortestPathOutputFormat extends
TextVertexOutputFormat <Text, IntWritable, NullWritable> {

        private static class EmployeeRDFVertexWriter
```

```
                    extends TextVertexWriter <Text, IntWritable,
NullWritable> {

        private Text valOut = new Text();

        public EmployeeRDFVertexWriter(
                RecordWriter<Text, Text> lineRecordWriter) {
            super(lineRecordWriter);
        }

        @Override
        public void writeVertex(
                Vertex<Text, IntWritable, NullWritable,
                        ?> vertex)
                throws IOException,
                                InterruptedException {

            valOut.set(vertex.getValue().toString());
            if(vertex.getValue().get() ==
                                Integer.MAX_VALUE)
                valOut.set("no path");
            getRecordWriter().write(vertex.getId(),
                                valOut);
        }


    }

        @Override
        public VertexWriter<Text, IntWritable, NullWritable>
        createVertexWriter(TaskAttemptContext context)
                throws IOException, InterruptedException {
            RecordWriter<Text, Text> recordWriter =
                    textOutputFormat.getRecordWriter(context);
            return new EmployeeRDFVertexWriter(recordWriter);
        }
    }
}
```

10. Create the shell script `run_employee_shortest_path.sh` using the commands
    listed in the following code snippet. Change `GIRAPH_PATH` to match your local path
    to the Giraph JAR file and change `JAR_PATH` to match your local path to the custom
    JAR file that you compiled the previous code in.

To use the alias `emp_shortest_path` your custom JAR file must use the Hadoop `Driver` class for its main class.

```
GIRAPH_PATH=lib/giraph/giraph-0.2-SNAPSHOT-jar-with-dependencies.
jar
```

```
HADOOP_CLASSPATH=$HADOOP_CLASSPATH:$GIRAPH_PATH
```

```
JAR_PATH=dist/employee_examples.jar
```

```
export HADOOP_CLASSPATH
```

```
hadoop jar $JAR_PATH emp_shortest_path -libjars $GIRAPH_
PATH,$JAR_PATH /input/gooftech /output/gooftech 'Shanae Dailey'
localhost:2181
```

11. Run `run_employee_shortest_path.sh`. The job should be submitted to the Hadoop cluster. Under `/output/gooftech` should be a single part file that lists minimum number of hops required to reach each employee from source ID, or `no path` if the employee is not reachable.

How it works...

We start with the custom input format. The Giraph API offers `TextVertexInputFormat` that wraps `TextInputFormat` and `LineReader` to read vertices stored one per line in a text file. Currently, the Giraph API requires your records to be sorted in order of the vertex ID. Our employee dataset is sorted by `firstname/lastname`, so we satisfy this requirement and can move forward. In order to create meaningful vertices from our RDF data, it is necessary that we subclass `TextVertexInputFormat` to create `EmployeeRDFTextInputFormat`. In order to control exactly how our vertices appear, we subclass `TextVertexReader` and create `EmployeeRDFVertexReader`. This allows us to override the `getRecordReader()` method in our custom input format to return an instance of our own reader subclass. The record reader delegates for an instance of the Hadoop `LineReader` and is responsible for creating the vertices from the text lines seen in each input split. From here we can override `getCurrentVertex()` and create individual vertices from each incoming RDF triple seen by the line reader. By extending `TextVertexReader` we don't have to worry about manually controlling the invocation of `getCurrentVertex()` for each line. The framework handles this for us. We simply need to tell the framework how to turn each line of text into a vertex with one or more edges.

The generic type parameters declared in the definition of `EmployeeRDFTextInputFormat` are repeatedly seen in the code. From left to right, they provide the concrete type information for the vertex ID class, vertex value class, edge value class, and message class. A quick look at the parent class shows the following generic header:

```
public abstract class TextVertexInputFormat<I extends
WritableComparable,
```

```
V extends Writable, E extends Writable, M extends Writable>
extends VertexInputFormat<I, V, E, M>
```

All four of the generic types must be `Writable`. The vertex ID class must be `WritableComparable`. Currently, Giraph does not support other serialization frameworks.

Our `getCurrentVertex()` method implementation is very basic. We set up several static final regex patterns to split the RDF triples properly. The combination `firstname/lastname` becomes our vertex ID stored as a `Text` instance. Each vertex is initialized with a vertex value of `0` stored as an `IntWritable`. Each subordinate listed in the comma-delimited list is referenced as an edge ID; however, we don't need any direct value information for each edge, and thus `NullWritable` will suffice for the edge value. For this particular job, our message types will be `IntWritable`. This class is reused in the next recipe in this chapter titled *Using Apache Giraph to perform a distributed breadth-first search*. For the sake of brevity, this input format is only explained once here.

Next, we set up our job class. The job setup borrows heavily from the Hadoop MapReduce Java API. We implement the `Tool` interface and define four arguments to read from the command line. This job requires an input folder from HDFS, and an output folder to write back to HDFS, a source ID to perform single source shortest-path, and a ZooKeeper quorum to manage the job state. Then we need to define a few other parameters as we are testing against a pseudo-distributed cluster with limited resources.

```
conf.setBoolean(GiraphJob.SPLIT_MASTER_WORKER, false);
conf.setBoolean(GiraphJob.USE_SUPERSTEP_COUNTERS, false);
conf.setInt(GiraphJob.CHECKPOINT_FREQUENCY, 0);
```

`SPLIT_MASTER_WORKER` tells Giraph whether or not the master process runs on a different host to the workers. By default, this is set to `true`, but since we are on a pseudo-distributed single node setup, this needs to be `false`. Turning off superstep counters will limit the verbosity of the MapReduce WebUI for our job. This is can be handy when testing jobs involving hundreds or potentially thousands of supersteps. Lastly, we turn off checkpointing to tell Giraph that we do not care about backing up the graph state at any superstep. This works because we are only testing and are interested in rapid job execution time. In a production job, it is recommended to checkpoint your graph state regularly at the cost of a slower overall job runtime. We then instantiate an instance of `GiraphJob` and pass our configuration instance to it along with a somewhat descriptive title for the job.

The next three lines of code are critical for the Giraph job to execute properly on your cluster.

```
job.setVertexClass(EmployeeShortestPathVertex.class);
job.setVertexInputFormatClass(EmployeeRDFTextInputFormat.class);
job.setVertexOutputFormatClass(EmployeeShortestPathOutputFormat.
class);
```

The first line tells Giraph about our custom Vertex implementation that encapsulates each vertex in the graph. This houses the application-specific `compute()` function called at each superstep. We extend the base class `EdgeListVertex` to leverage some pre-existing code for message handling, edge iteration, and member serialization.

Then, we set the ZooKeeper quorum and define a single worker to hold the graph partition. If your pseudo-distributed cluster can support multiple workers (multiple concurrent map JVMs), then feel free to increase this limit. Just remember to leave one free map slot for the master process. Finally, we are ready to submit the job to the cluster.

After the `InputFormat` handles creating the vertices from the different input splits, each vertex's `compute()` function gets invoked. We define the static inner class `EmployeeShortestPathVertex` to override the `compute()` function and implement the business logic necessary to calculate the shortest path. Specifically, we are interested in the minimum number of hops required to navigate from the source vertex to every other vertex connected by one or more pathways in the graph, or `no path` if the target vertex is not reachable by the source.

First superstep (S0)

At S0, the function immediately enters the first conditional statement and initializes every vertex value to the maximum possible integer value. As incoming messages are received, each vertex compares the integer contained in each message against the currently held minimum to see if it represents a lower value, therefore the business logic is made a bit easier by setting the initial *minimum* value to the maximum possible for the datatype. During the first superstep, it is critical that the source vertex sends a message to its edges telling the vertex along that the edge is one hop away from the source. To do this, we define a member instance `msg` just for messaging. It is reset and reused every time the vertex needs to send a message, and helps to avoid unnecessary instantiation.

We need to compare any incoming messages with the currently held minimum hops value to see if we need to update and notify our edges. Since we are only at S0 there are no messages, so the value remains as `Integer.MAX`. Since the minimum value does not change, we avoid the last conditional branch.

At the end of each superstep for our job, always invoke `voteToHalt()`. The Giraph framework will automatically have reactive vertices that have incoming messages at the next superstep, but we want to render vertices inactive that are temporarily done sending/receiving messages. Once there are no more messages to process by any vertex in the graph, the job will stop reactivating vertices and will consider itself finished.

Second superstep (S1)

After the previous superstep, every single vertex in the graph voted to halt the execution. The only vertex that messaged its edges was the source vertex, therefore the framework will reactivate only the vertices connected by the source edges. The source vertex told each edge that they were one hop away, which is less than `Integer.MAX` and immediately takes the place as the current vertex value. Each vertex receiving the message turns around and notifies its edges that they are `min + 1` hops away from the source, and the cycle continues.

Should any connected edge receive a message lower than its current vertex value, that indicates there is a path from the source ID to the current vertex that involves fewer hops, and we need to re-notify each edge connected to the current vertex.

Eventually, every vertex will know its minimum distance and no more messages will be sent at the current superstep *N*. When starting superstep *N + 1*, there will be no vertices that need to be reactivated to process incoming messages, and the overall job will finish. Now we need to output each vertex's current value denoting the minimum number of hops from the source vertex.

To write the vertex value information back to HDFS as text, we implement a static inner subclass of `TextVertexOutputFormat` named `EmployeeShortestPathOutputFormat`. This follows a similar inheritance/delegation pattern as our custom `InputFormat` defined earlier, except instead of delegating to a custom `RecordReader`, we use a custom `RecordWriter`. We set a `Text` member variable `valOut` to reuse while outputting the integer values as strings. The framework automatically handles invoking `writeVertex()` for each vertex contained in our dataset.

If the current vertex value is still equal to `Integer.MAX`, we know that the graph never received any incoming messages intended for that vertex, which implies it is not traversable by the source vertex. Otherwise, we output the minimum number of hops required to traverse to the current vertex ID from the source ID.

See also

 ▸ *Using Apache Giraph to perform a distributed breadth-first search*

Using Apache Giraph to perform a distributed breadth-first search

In this recipe, we will use the Apache Giraph API to implement a distributed breadth-first search to determine if two employees are connected in the company's network via one or more pathways. The code will rely on message passing between employee vertices to determine if a vertex is reachable.

Getting ready

Make sure you have a basic familiarity with Google Pregel/BSP and the Giraph API.

You will need access to a pseudo-distributed Hadoop cluster. The code listed in this recipe uses a split master worker configuration that is not ideal in fully-distributed environments. It also assumes familiarity with bash shell scripting.

You will need to load the example dataset `gooftech.tsv` to an HDFS folder located at `/input/gooftech`.

You will also need to package this code inside a JAR file to be executed by the Hadoop JAR launcher from the shell. The shell script listed in the recipe will show a template for job submission with the correct classpath dependencies.

How to do it...

Carry out the following steps to perform a breadth-first search in Giraph:

1. Implement `EmployeeRDFTextInputFormat.java`. See steps 1 to 3 in the *How to do it...* section of the *Single-source shortest-path with Apache Giraph* recipe.

2. The job setup code, vertex class, and custom output format are all contained in a single class. Save the following code in a package of your choice to a class with the name `EmployeeBreadthFirstSearch.java`:

```
import org.apache.giraph.graph.*;
import org.apache.giraph.lib.TextVertexOutputFormat;
import org.apache.hadoop.conf.Configuration;
import org.apache.hadoop.fs.FileSystem;
import org.apache.hadoop.fs.Path;
import org.apache.hadoop.io.*;
import org.apache.hadoop.mapreduce.RecordWriter;
import org.apache.hadoop.mapreduce.TaskAttemptContext;
import org.apache.hadoop.mapreduce.lib.input.FileInputFormat;
import org.apache.hadoop.mapreduce.lib.output.FileOutputFormat;
import org.apache.hadoop.util.Tool;
```

```
import org.apache.hadoop.util.ToolRunner;

import java.io.IOException;

/**
 * Start with specified employee, mark the target if message is
received
 */
public class EmployeeBreadthFirstSearch implements Tool{

    public static final String NAME = "emp_breadth_search";

    private Configuration conf;
    private static final String SOURCE_ID = "emp_src_id";
    private static final String DEST_ID = "emp_dest_id";

    public EmployeeBreadthFirstSearch(Configuration configuration)
{
        conf = configuration;
    }
```

3. The `run()` method in the following code sets up the Giraph job configuration:

```
@Override
public int run(String[] args) throws Exception {
    if(args.length < 5) {
        System.err.println(printUsage());
        System.exit(1);
    }
    if(args.length > 5) {
        System.err.println("too many arguments. " +"Did you
forget to quote the source or destination ID name ('firstname
lastname')");
        System.exit(1);
    }
    String input = args[0];
    String output = args[1];
    String source_id = args[2];
    String dest_id = args[3];
    String zooQuorum = args[4];

    conf.set(SOURCE_ID, source_id);
    conf.set(DEST_ID, dest_id);
    conf.setBoolean(GiraphJob.SPLIT_MASTER_WORKER,
                    false);
    conf.setBoolean(GiraphJob.USE_SUPERSTEP_COUNTERS,
```

```
                                    false);
            conf.setInt(GiraphJob.CHECKPOINT_FREQUENCY, 0);
            GiraphJob job = new GiraphJob(conf,    "determine
connectivity between " + source_id + " and " + dest_id);
            job.setVertexClass(EmployeeSearchVertex.class);
job.setVertexInputFormatClass(EmployeeRDFTextInputFormat.cl
                                ass);
            job.setVertexOutputFormatClass(BreadthFirstTextOutputForm
at.class);
            job.setZooKeeperConfiguration(zooQuorum);

            FileInputFormat.addInputPath(job.getInternalJob(),
                                    new Path(input));
            FileOutputFormat.setOutputPath(job.getInternalJob(),
                                removeAndSetOutput(output));

            job.setWorkerConfiguration(1, 1, 100.0f);

            if(job.run(true)) {
                long srcCounter = job.getInternalJob().getCounters().
                        getGroup("Search").findCounter("Source
                                Id found").getValue();
                long dstCounter =
job.getInternalJob().getCounters().getGroup("Search").
findCounter("Dest Id found").getValue();
                if(srcCounter == 0 || dstCounter == 0) {
                    System.out.println("Source and/or Dest Id not
found in dataset. Check your arguments.");
                }
                return 0;
            } else {
                return 1;
            }
        }
```

4. The following, method force deletes the supplied output folder in HDFS. Use it with caution. The other methods are required to conform to the `Tool` interface:

```
    private Path removeAndSetOutput(String outputDir) throws
IOException {
        FileSystem fs = FileSystem.get(conf);
        Path path = new Path(outputDir);
        fs.delete(path, true);
        return path;
    }
```

```
      private String printUsage() {
            return "usage: <input> <output> <single quoted source_id>
<single quoted dest_id> <zookeeper_quorum>";
      }

      @Override
      public void setConf(Configuration conf) {
            this.conf = conf;
      }

      @Override
      public Configuration getConf() {
            return conf;
      }
```

5. The `main()` method instantiates and submits the job using `ToolRunner`:

```
      public static void main(String[] args) throws Exception {
            System.exit(ToolRunner.run(new
EmployeeBreadthFirstSearch(new Configuration()), args));
      }
```

6. The static inner class, `EmployeeSearchVertex`, lets us define a custom compute method to be used during each superstep:

```
      public static class EmployeeSearchVertex<I extends
WritableComparable, V extends Writable, E extends Writable, M
extends Writable> extends EdgeListVertex<Text, IntWritable,
NullWritable, IntWritable> {

            private IntWritable msg = new IntWritable(1);

            private boolean isSource() {
                  return getId().toString().equals(
                        getConf().get(SOURCE_ID));
            }

            private boolean isDest() {
                  return getId().toString().equals(
                        getConf().get(DEST_ID));
            }

            @Override
            public void compute(Iterable<IntWritable> messages) throws
IOException {
                  if(getSuperstep() == 0) {
                        if(isSource()) {
```

```
                    getContext().getCounter("Search", "Source Id
            found").increment(1);
                        sendMessageToAllEdges(msg);
                    }  else if(isDest()){
                        getContext().getCounter("Search", "Dest Id
            found").increment(11);
                    }
                }
                boolean connectedToSourceId = false;
                for(IntWritable msg : messages) {
                    if(isDest()) {
                        setValue(msg);
                    }
                    connectedToSourceId = true;
                }
                if(connectedToSourceId)
                    sendMessageToAllEdges(msg);
                voteToHalt();
            }
        }
```

7. The static inner class, `BreadthFirstTextOutputFormat`, lets us define a custom `OutputFormat`. The `BreadtFirstTextOutputFormat` class lets us output our vertex information as `Text` key-value pairs back to HDFS:

```
    public static class BreadthFirstTextOutputFormat extends
            TextVertexOutputFormat <Text, IntWritable,
    NullWritable> {

        private static class EmployeeRDFVertexWriter
                extends TextVertexWriter <Text, IntWritable,
    NullWritable> {

            private Text valOut = new Text();
            private String sourceId = null;
            private String destId = null;

            public EmployeeRDFVertexWriter(
                    String sourceId, String destId,
    RecordWriter<Text, Text> lineRecordWriter) {
                super(lineRecordWriter);
                this.sourceId = sourceId;
                this.destId = destId;
            }

            @Override
            public void writeVertex(
                    Vertex<Text, IntWritable, NullWritable, ?>
    vertex)
                    throws IOException, InterruptedException {
```

```
                    if(vertex.getId().toString().equals(destId)) {
                         if(vertex.getValue().get() > 0) {
                              getRecordWriter().write(new Text(sourceId
+ " is connected to " + destId), new Text(""));
                         } else {
                              getRecordWriter().write(new Text(sourceId
+ " is not connected to " + destId), new Text(""));
                         }
                    }
               }
          }

          @Override
          public VertexWriter<Text, IntWritable, NullWritable>
          createVertexWriter(TaskAttemptContext context)
                    throws IOException, InterruptedException {
               RecordWriter<Text, Text> recordWriter =
                         textOutputFormat.getRecordWriter(context);
               String sourceId = context.getConfiguration().
get(SOURCE_ID);
               String destId = context.getConfiguration().get(DEST_
ID);
               return new EmployeeRDFVertexWriter(sourceId, destId,
recordWriter);
          }
     }
}
```

8. Create the shell script `run_employee_connectivity_search.sh` using the commands listed in the following code snippet. Change `GIRAPH_PATH` to match your local path to the Giraph JAR file and change `JAR_PATH` to match the local path to your own custom JAR file that you compiled using the preceding code.

> To use the alias `emp_breadth_first`, your custom JAR file must use the Hadoop `Driver` class as its main class in the JAR file.

```
GIRAPH_PATH=lib/giraph/giraph-0.2-SNAPSHOT-jar-with-dependencies.
jar
HADOOP_CLASSPATH=$HADOOP_CLASSPATH:$GIRAPH_PATH
JAR_PATH=dist/employee_examples.jar
export HADOOP_CLASSPATH
hadoop jar $JAR_PATH emp_breadth_search -libjars $GIRAPH_
PATH,$JAR_PATH /input/gooftech /output/gooftech 'Valery Dorado'
'Gertha Linda' localhost:2181
```

9. Run `run_employee_connectivity_search.sh`. You should see the job submitted to the Hadoop cluster. Upon successful completion, you should see a single part file under `/output/gooftech` saying `Valery Dorado is not connected to Gertha Linda`.

10. Open `run_employee_connectivity_search.sh`. Change the source ID to `Shoshana Gatton`. Save and close the script.

11. Run `run_employee_connectivity_search.sh`. The output should now be `Shoshana Gatton is connected to Gertha Linda`.

How it works...

To understand how the custom `InputFormat` and job setup works, check out the *How it works...* section from the recipe titled *Single-source shortest-path using Apache Giraph*. This recipe uses exactly the same input format, and the same job setup, except for the following differences:

- The job requires an additional `DEST_ID` argument to be supplied by the command line.

- The Vertex implementation is `EmployeeSearchVertex`.

- The `OutputFormat` subclass is set to the static inner class `BreadthFirstTextOutputFormat`. This is explained in more detail in the following paragraph.

- We use counters during the job execution to determine if the supplied source/destination IDs are found in the dataset.

The `compute()` function inside `EmployeeSearchVertex` is where we take advantage of Giraph message passing to determine reachability. Starting at the first superstep, we send a message to each edge from the source ID. If we find the supplied source IDs and destination IDs in the dataset vertices, we increment the counters to let the user know. This will help us quickly see any incorrectly entered command-line arguments for source/destination vertex IDs. After the first superstep, both these counters should be set to 1. We define a private constant member variable `msg` that is set to 1. The actual numeric content of the message is never used, but by keeping the vertex value as `IntWritable` we can use the already built custom `InputFormat` `EmployeeRDFTextInputFormat`. If during any superstep a vertex receives a message, we forward that message along to each of its edges. If the destination vertex ever receives a message, we set its value to the integer 1 contained in the message. By the end of the job execution, the destination vertex will have a value of 1, which means it is connected by one or more edges to the source vertex, or to the initial value of 0, meaning it never received a message and is not connected.

We define the static inner class `BreadthFirstTextOutputFormat` to handle the output formatting. This follows a similar inheritance/delegation pattern to our custom `InputFormat` defined earlier, except instead of delegating to a custom `RecordReader`, we use a custom `RecordWriter`. When we instantiate our `TextVertexWriter` subclass `EmployeeRDFVertexWriter`, we pass its references to the configured source and destination vertex IDs. The framework handles this automatically by calling the `writeVertex()` method for each vertex in our dataset. For this job, we are only interested in printing out whether or not the source vertex is connected by one or more paths to the destination vertex. If the current vertex we are processing is the destination vertex, we will printout one of two strings. If the vertex value is greater than `0`, then that destination must have received one or more messages, which is only possible if there exists at least one path of edge communication between the source and destination. Otherwise, if the value of the destination vertex is still `0`, then we can safely assume that it is not reachable by the source. For just one pair of source-destination nodes, as we have in this recipe, we could have placed this business logic directly in the job class and used counters after the execution finished, but this design is more extensible should we want to use this code to query multiple destination-source vertex pairs.

There's more...

Programs designed using the Hadoop MapReduce API usually require some additional tuning once you begin testing at scale. It is not uncommon to completely re-evaluate a chosen design pattern that simply does not scale. Working with the Giraph API requires the same diligence and patience.

Apache Giraph jobs often require scalability tuning

This is not always easy to spot initially. You may have a relatively small graph that operates very well within a given BSP design approach. Suddenly you hit scale and notice all sorts of errors you never planned for. Try to keep your `compute()` function small to avoid complications and aid with troubleshooting. At the time of this writing, Giraph workers will attempt to hold their assigned graph partitions directly in memory. Minimizing vertex memory footprint is of the upmost importance. Moreover, many people have to tune their message passing settings using the parameters located at the top of `GiraphJob`. You can control the number of messaging threads used by each worker to communicate with other workers by setting `MSG_NUM_FLUSH_THREADS`. By default, Giraph will let each worker open a communication thread to every other worker in the job. For many Hadoop clusters, this is not sustainable. Also, consider adjusting the maximum number of messages allowed to be flushed in bulk using `MAX_MESSAGES_PER_FLUSH_PUT`. The default value 2000 may not be adequate for your job.

Collaborative filtering with Apache Mahout

Collaborative filtering is a technique that can be used to discover relationships between people and items (for example, books and music). It works by examining the preferences of a set of users, such as the items they purchase, and then determines which users have similar preferences. Collaborative filtering can be used to build recommender systems. Recommender systems are used by many companies including Amazon, LinkedIn, and Facebook.

In this recipe, we are going to use Apache Mahout to generate book recommendations based on a dataset containing people's book preferences.

Getting ready

You will need to download, compile, and install the following:

- Maven 2.2 or above from `http://maven.apache.org/`
- Apache Mahout 0.6 from `http://mahout.apache.org/`
- CSV Dump of Book-Crossing Dataset from `http://www.informatik.uni-freiburg.de/~cziegler/BX/`
- Scripts for this chapter from `http://packtpub.com/support`

Once you have compiled Mahout, add the mahout binary to the system path. In addition, you must set the `HADOOP_HOME` environment variable to point to the root folder of your Hadoop installation. You can accomplish this in the bash shell by using the following commands:

```
$ export PATH=$PATH:/path/to/mahout/bin
$ export HADOOP_HOME=/opt/mapr/hadoop/hadoop-0.20.2
```

Next, extract the Book-Crossing Dataset to the folder you are currently working on. You should see three files named `BX-Books.csv`, `BX-Book-Ratings.csv`, and `BX-Users.csv`.

How to do it...

Carry out the following steps to perform Collaborative filtering in Mahout:

1. Run the `clean_book_ratings.py` script to transform the `BX-Book-Ratings.csv` file into a format the Mahout recommender can use.

    ```
    $ ./clean_book_ratings.py BX-Book-Ratings.csv cleaned_book_ratings.txt
    ```

2. Run the `clean_book_users.sh` bash script to transform the `BX-Users.csv` file into a format the Mahout recommender can use. Note that the `BX-Users.csv` file should be in the folder you are currently working on:

    ```
    $ ./clean_book_users.sh
    ```

3. Place both the `cleaned_book_ratings.txt` and the `cleaned_book_users.txt` files into HDFS:

    ```
    $ hadoop fs -mkdir /user/hadoop/books

    $ hadoop fs -put cleaned_book_ratings.txt /user/hadoop/books

    $ hadoop fs -put cleaned_book_users.txt /user/hadoop/books
    ```

4. Run the Mahout recommender using the ratings and user information we just put into HDFS. Mahout will launch multiple MapReduce jobs to generate the book recommendations:

    ```
    $ mahout recommenditembased --input /user/hadoop/books/ cleaned_
    book_ratings.txt --output /user/hadoop/books/recommended
    --usersFile /user/hadoop/books/cleaned_book_users.txt -s
    SIMILARITY_LOGLIKELIHOOD
    ```

5. Examine the results, which are in the format of `USERID [RECOMMENDED BOOK ISBN:SCORE,...]`. The output should look similar to the following:

    ```
    $ hadoop fs -cat /user/hadoop/books/recommended/part* | head -n1

    17      [849911788:4.497727,807503193:4.497536,881030392:4.497536,
    761528547:4.497536,380724723:4.497536,807533424:4.497536,310203414
    :4.497536,590344153:4.497536,761536744:4.497536,531000265:4.497536
    ]
    ```

6. Examine the results in a more human-friendly way using `print_user_summaries. py`. To print the recommendations for the first 10 users, use `10` for the last argument to `print_user_summaries.py`:

    ```
    hadoop fs -cat /user/hadoop/books/recommended/part-r-00000 | ./
    print_user_summaries.py BX-Books.csv BX-Users.csv BX-Book-Ratings.
    csv 10

    ==========
    user id =   114073
    rated:
    Digital Fortress : A Thriller  with:   9


    Angels &amp Demons with:   10


    recommended:
    Morality for Beautiful Girls (No.1 Ladies Detective Agency)
    Q Is for Quarry
    The Last Juror
    The Da Vinci Code
    Deception Point
    ```

A Walk in the Woods: Rediscovering America on the Appalachian Trail (Official Guides to the Appalachian Trail)

Tears of the Giraffe (No.1 Ladies Detective Agency)

The No. 1 Ladies' Detective Agency (Today Show Book Club #8)

The output from `print_user_summaries.py` shows which books the user rated, and then it shows the recommendations generated by Mahout.

How it works...

The first steps of this recipe required us to clean up the Book-Crossing dataset. The `BX-Book-Ratings.csv` file was in a semicolon-delimited format with the following columns:

- `USER_ID`: The user ID assigned to a person
- `ISBN`: The book's ISBN the person reviewed
- `BOOK-RATING`: The rating a person gave to the book

The Mahout recommendation engine expects the input dataset to be in the following comma-separated format:

- `USER_ID`: The `USER_ID` must be an integer
- `ITEM_ID`: The `ITEM_ID` must be an integer
- `RATING`: The `RATING` must be an integer that increases in order of preference. For example, `1` would mean that the user disliked a book intensely, `10` would mean the user enjoyed the book.

Once the transformation was completed on the `BX-Book-Ratings.csv` file, we performed a similar transformation on the `BX-Users.csv` file. We stripped away most of the information in the `BX-Users.csv` file, except for `USER_ID`.

Finally, we launch the Mahout recommendation engine. Mahout will launch a series of MapReduce jobs to determine the book recommendations for a given set of users, specified with the `–usersFile` flag. In this example, we wanted Mahout to generate book recommendations for all of the users in the dataset, so we provided the complete `USER_ID` list to Mahout. In addition to providing an input path, output path, and user list as command-line arguments to Mahout, we also specified a fourth parameter `-s SIMILARITY_LOGLIKELIHOOD`. The `-s` flag is used to specify which similarity measure we want Mahout to use, to compare similar book preferences across all users. This recipe used log likelihood because it is a simple and effective algorithm, but Mahout supports many more similarity functions. To see for yourself, run the following command, and examine the options for the `-s` flag:

```
$mahout recommenditembased
```

See also

▸ *Clustering with Apache Mahout*

▸ *Sentiment classification with Apache Mahout*

Clustering with Apache Mahout

Clustering is a technique that can be used to divide a dataset into related partitions. In this recipe, we are going to use a specific cluster method called **k-means**. K-means clustering attempts to divide a dataset into *k* clusters by minimizing the distance between points located around a central point in a cluster.

In this recipe, we will use the Apache Mahout k-means implementation to cluster the words found in Shakespeare's tragedies.

Getting ready

You will need to download, compile, and install the following:

▸ Maven 2.2 or above from `http://maven.apache.org`

▸ Apache Mahout 0.6 from `http://mahout.apache.org/`

▸ `Shakespeare.zip` file from `http://packtpub.com/support`

Extract the contents of `shakespeare.zip` into a folder named `shakespeare_text`. The `shakespeare.zip` archive should contain six works by Shakespeare. Put the `shakespeare_text` folder and its contents, into HDFS.

```
$ mkdir shakespeare_text
$ cd shakespeare_text
$ unzip shakespeare.zip
$ cd ..
$ hadoop fs -put shakespeare_text /user/hadoop
```

How to do it...

Carry out the following steps to perform clustering in Mahout:

1. Convert the Shakespeare text documents into the Hadoop SequenceFile format:

   ```
   mahout seqdirectory --input /user/hadoop/shakespeare_text --output
   /user/hadoop/shakespeare-seqdir --charset utf-8
   ```

2. Convert the text contents of the SequenceFiles into a vector:

```
mahout seq2sparse --input /user/hadoop/shakespeare-seqdir
--output /user/hadoop/shakespeare-sparse --namedVector -ml 80
-ng 2 -x 70 -md 1 -s 5 -wt tfidf -a org.apache.lucene.analysis.
WhitespaceAnalyzer
```

3. Run the k-means clustering algorithm on the document vectors. This command will launch up to ten MapReduce jobs. Also, since we are using k-means clustering, we need to specify the number of clusters we want:

```
mahout kmeans --input /user/hadoop/shakespeare-sparse/tfidf-
vectors --output /user/hadoop/shakespeare-kmeans/clusters
--clusters /user/hadoop/shakespeare-kmeans/initialclusters
--maxIter 10 --numClusters 6 --clustering –overwrite
```

4. To check the clusters identified by Mahout, use the following command:

```
mahout clusterdump --seqFileDir /user/hadoop/shakespeare-kmeans/
clusters/clusters-1-final --numWords 5 --dictionary /user/hadoop/
shakespeare-sparse/dictionary.file-0 --dictionaryType sequencefile
```

The results of the `clusterdump` tool can be overwhelming. Look for the `Top Terms:` section of the output. For example, following are the top terms for the Romeo and Juliet cluster identified by the k-means algorithm:

```
r=/romeoandjuliet.txt =]}
        Top Terms:
                ROMEO                           =>      29.15485382080078
                JULIET                          =>      25.78818130493164
                CAPULET                         =>      21.401729583740234
                the                             =>      20.942245483398438
                Nurse                           =>      20.129182815551758
```

How it works...

The initial steps required us to do some pre-processing on the raw text data prior to running the k-means algorithm with Mahout. The `seqdirectory` tool, simply converts the contents of a HDFS folder into SequenceFiles. Next, the `seq2sparse` tool converts the newly created SequenceFiles (which still contain text), into document vectors. The arguments to `seq2sparse` are described in the following list:

▸ `--input`: A folder in HDFS containing SequenceFiles formatted for Mahout.

▸ `--output`: The output HDFS folder where the document vectors will be stored.

▸ `--namedVector`: A flag to use the named vectors.

- ► `-ml`: A minimum log likelihood threshold. We set this to a high number because we only want to keep the most significant terms.
- ► `-ng`: The n-gram size.
- ► `-x`: A threshold that defines the maximum document frequency a term can appear before it is discarded. In this recipe we chose `70`, meaning that any term that appears in greater than 70 percent of the documents will be discarded. Use this setting to discard meaningless words (For example, words such as at, a, and the).
- ► `-md`: The minimum number of documents a term should occur in before it will be considered for processing. In this recipe, we used `1`, which means that a term only needs to appear in one document to be processed.
- ► `-s`: The minimum times a term needs to appear in a document before it will be considered for processing.
- ► `-wt`: The weighting algorithm that should be used. Here we chose to use `TF-IDF`. The other option is `TF`, which would not help us identify key *n*-grams.
- ► `-a`: The type of analyzer that should be used. An analyzer is used to transform a text document. The `WhitespaceAnalyzer` splits a document on whitespace into tokens. The tokens will be kept, combined, or discarded based on the other flags provided to the `seq2sparse` application.

Finally, we ran the k-means clustering algorithm on the Shakespeare dataset. Mahout will launch a series of MapReduce jobs, which are configurable. The k-means job will complete when either the k-means clusters converge, or the maximum allowed number of MapReduce jobs has been reached. The following are definitions of the parameters we used to configure the k-means Mahout job:

- ► `--input`: The folder in HDFS containing the document vectors.
- ► `--output`: The output folder in HDFS of the k-means job.
- ► `--maxIter`: The maximum number of MapReduce jobs to launch.
- ► `--numClusters`: The number of clusters we want to identify. We chose `6`, because there were six Shakespeare documents, and we wanted to identify significant bi-grams around those documents.
- ► `--clusters`: The initial setup cluster points.
- ► `--clustering`: A flag that tells Mahout to iterate over the data before clustering.
- ► `--overwrite`: A flag that tells Mahout to overwrite the output folder.

See also

- ► *Sentiment classification with Apache Mahout*

Sentiment classification with Apache Mahout

Sentiment classification is a classification process that tries to determine a person's propensity to like or dislike certain items. In this recipe, we will use a naive Bayes classifier from Apache Mahout to determine if a set of terms found in a movie review mean the movie had a negative or positive reception.

Getting ready

You will need to download, compile, and install the following:

▶ Maven 2.2 or above from `http://maven.apache.org`

▶ Apache Mahout 0.6 from `http://mahout.apache.org/`

▶ `Polarity_dataset_v2.0` from `http://www.cs.cornell.edu/people/pabo/movie-review-data/`

▶ Scripts of this chapter from `http://packtpub.com/support`

Extract the movie review dataset `review_polarity.tar.gz` to the folder you are currently working on. You should see a newly created folder named `txt_sentoken`. Within that folder there should be two more folders named `pos` and `neg`. The `pos` and `neg` folders hold text files containing the written reviews of movies. Obviously, the `pos` folder contains positive movie reviews, and the `neg` folder contains negative reviews.

How to do it...

1. Run the `reorg_data.py` script from the folder you are currently working on to transform the data into training and test sets for the Mahout classifier:

   ```
   $ ./reorg_data.py txt_sentoken train test
   ```

2. Prepare the dataset for the Mahout classifier:

   This application will read and write to the local filesystem, and not HDFS.

   ```
   $ mahout prepare20newsgroups -p train -o train_formated -a org.
   apache.mahout.vectorizer.DefaultAnalyzer -c UTF-8
   $ mahout prepare20newsgroups -p test -o  test_formated -a org.
   apache.mahout.vectorizer.DefaultAnalyzer -c UTF-8
   ```

3. Place the `train_formated` and `test_formated` folders into HDFS:

   ```
   $ hadoop fs -put train_formated /user/hadoop/
   $ hadoop fs -put test_formated /user/hadoop/
   ```

4. Train the naive Bayes classifier using the `train_formated` dataset:

```
$ mahout trainclassifier -i /user/hadoop/train_formated -o /user/
hadoop/reviews/naive-bayes-model -type bayes -ng 2 -source hdfs
```

5. Test the classifier using the `test_formated` dataset:

```
$ mahout testclassifier -m /user/hadoop/reviews/naive-bayes-model
-d prepared-test -type bayes -ng 2 -source hdfs -method sequential
```

6. The `testclassifier` tool should return a similar summary and confusion matrix. The numbers will not be exactly the same as the ones shown in the following:

```
Summary
-------------------------------------------------------------

Correctly Classified Instances          :      285        71.25%

Incorrectly Classified Instances         :      115        28.75%

Total Classified Instances               :      400


=============================================================

Confusion Matrix
-------------------------------------------------------------

a        b          <--Classified as

97       103        |   200        a      = pos

12       188        |   200        b      = neg
```

How it works...

The first two steps required us to prepare the data for the Mahout naive Bayes classifier. The `reorg_data.py` script distributed the positive and negative reviews from the `txt_sentoken` folder into a training and test set. 80 percent of the reviews were placed into the training set, and the remaining 20 percent were used as a test set. Next, we used the `prepare20newsgroups` tool to format the training and test datasets into a format compatible with the Mahout classifier. The example dataset included in Mahout has a similar format to the data produced by the `reorg_data.py` script, thus we can use the `prepare20newsgroups` tool. All that the `prepare20newsgroups` does is to combine all of the files in the `pos` and `neg` folders into a single file based on the dataset class (negative or positive). So, instead of having 1000 positive and negative files, where each file contained a single review, we now have two files named `pos.txt` and `neg.txt`, where each contains all of the positive and negative reviews.

Next, we trained a naive Bayes classifier using the n-gram size of 2, specified with the `-ng` flag, using the `train_formated` dataset in HDFS. Mahout trains the classifier by launching a series of MapReduce jobs.

Finally, we ran the `testclassifier` tool to test the classifier we created in step 4, against the `test_formated` data in HDFS. As we can see from step 6, we correctly classified 71.25 percent of the test data. It is important to note that this statistic does not mean the classifier will be accurate 71.25 percent of the time for every movie review ever. There are a number of ways in which classifiers can be trained and validated. Those techniques go beyond the scope of this book.

There's more...

The `testclassifier` tool we used in step 6, did not run a MapReduce job. It tested the classifier in local mode. If we wanted to test the classifier using MapReduce, we just need to change the `-method` parameter to `mapreduce`.

```
$ mahout testclassifier -m /user/hadoop/reviews/naive-bayes-model -d
prepared-test -type bayes -ng 2 -source hdfs -method mapreduce
```

8
Debugging

In this chapter, we will cover:

- ▸ Using Counters in a MapReduce job to track bad records
- ▸ Developing and testing MapReduce jobs with MRUnit
- ▸ Developing and testing MapReduce jobs running in local mode
- ▸ Enabling MapReduce jobs to skip bad records
- ▸ Using Counters in a streaming job
- ▸ Updating task status messages to display debugging information
- ▸ Using illustrate to debug Pig jobs

Introduction

There is an adage among those working with Hadoop that *everything breaks at scale*. Malformed or unexpected input is common. It's an unfortunate downside of working with large amounts of unstructured data. Within the context of Hadoop, individual tasks are isolated and given different sets of input. This allows Hadoop to easily distribute jobs, but leads to difficulty in tracking global events and understanding the state of each individual task. Fortunately, there are several tools and techniques available to aid in the process of debugging Hadoop jobs. This chapter will focus on applying these tools and techniques to debug MapReduce jobs.

Using Counters in a MapReduce job to track bad records

The MapReduce framework provides **Counters** as an efficient mechanism for tracking the occurrences of global events within the map and reduce phases of jobs. For example, a typical MapReduce job will kick off several mapper instances, one for each block of the input data, all running the same code. These instances are part of the same job, but run independent of one another. Counters allow a developer to track aggregated events from all of those separate instances.

A more concrete use of Counters can be found in the MapReduce framework itself. Each MapReduce job defines several standard Counters. The output of these Counters can be found in the job details of the Job Tracker web UI.

	Counter	Map	Reduce	Total
Map-Reduce Framework	Map input records	71,228,085,554	0	71,228,085,554
	Reduce shuffle bytes	0	5,419,119,866,175	5,419,119,866,175
	Spilled Records	142,174,003,132	55,141,286,320	197,315,289,452
	Map output bytes	5,513,542,463,958	0	5,513,542,463,958
	CPU_MILLISECONDS	2,658,192,290	2,352,883,960	5,011,076,250
	Combine input records	139,937,676,997	69,478,386,276	209,416,063,273
	SPLIT_RAW_BYTES	1,999,232	0	1,999,232
	Reduce input records	0	58,006,566,989	58,006,566,989
	Reduce input groups	0	3,331,430	3,331,430
	Combine output records	139,937,676,997	69,478,386,262	209,416,063,259
	PHYSICAL_MEMORY_BYTES	12,647,158,763,520	196,662,726,656	12,843,821,490,176
	Reduce output records	0	406,433,728	406,433,728
	VIRTUAL_MEMORY_BYTES	33,014,737,301,504	273,806,381,056	33,288,543,682,560
	Map output records	71,228,085,554	0	71,228,085,554
	GC time elapsed (ms)	98,623,849	342,650,729	441,274,578

The UI shows the Counter group, name, mapper totals, reducer totals, and job totals.

Counters should be limited to tracking metadata about the job. The standard Counters are good examples of this. The **Map input records** counter provides useful information about a particular execution of a job. If Counters did not exist, these kinds of statistics would have to be part of the job's main output, where they don't belong; or more likely as part of a secondary output, complicating the logic of the job.

The following recipe is a simple map-only job that filters out bad records and uses a counter to log the number of records that were filtered.

Getting ready

You will need to download the `weblog_entries_bad_records.txt` dataset from the Packt website, `http://www.packtpub.com/support`.

How to do it...

1. Copy the `weblog_entries_bad_records.txt` file from the local file system into the new folder created in HDFS:

   hadoop fs -copyFromLocal weblog_entries.txt /data/weblogs

2. Submit the `CountersExample` job:

   **hadoop jar ./CountersExample.jar com.packt.hadoop.solutions.
   CounterExample /data/weblogs/weblog_entries_bad_records.txt /data/
   weblogs/weblog_entries_clean.txt**

3. To view the counter in the Job Tracker UI, open a web browser and navigate to the Job Tracker UI. The default address is `localhost:50030`. Scroll down to the **Completed Jobs** section. Then locate the **CounterExample** job. The most recent jobs are at the bottom of the table. Once the job has been located, click on **Jobid**. This page has high-level statistics about the job, including the Counters.

com.packt.hadoop.solutions.CounterExample$BadRecords	INVALID_NUMBER_OF_COLUMNS	2	0	2
	INVALID_IP_ADDRESS	2	0	2

How it works...

Counters are defined in groups. In Java, each Counter group is an Enum. In the CounterExample job, an Enum for tracking the count of each type of bad record was defined:

```
static enum BadRecords{INVALID_NUMBER_OF_COLUMNS, INVALID_IP_ADDRESS};
```

In the map function, there are two checks for valid data. The first check splits the data delimited by tabs. For this example, if properly formed, each record should have five columns. If a record does not have five columns, a call is made to the `Context` class to get the counter for `BadRecords.INVALID_NUMBER_OF_COLUMNS`. The counter is then incremented by 1.

```
String record = value.toString();
String [] columns = record.split("\t");

// Check for valid number of columns
if (columns.length != 5) {
context.getCounter(BadRecords.INVALID_NUMBER_OF_COLUMNS).increment(1);
return;
}
```

The second check is for validating IP addresses. A regular expression, `VALID_IP_ADDRESS`, is defined. As its name implies, this regular expression will match valid IP addresses.

```
private static final String VALID_IP_ADDRESS = "^([01]?\\d\\d?|2[0-
4]\\d|25[0-5])\\.([01]?\\d\\d?|2[0-4]\\d|25[0-5])\\." +
        "([01]?\\d\\d?|2[0-4]\\d|25[0-5])\\.([01]?\\d\\d?|2[0-4]\\
d|25[0-5])$";
```

The `VALID_IP_ADDRESS` regular expression is used to check every record's IP address column for a match. For each record that does not match, the `INVALID_IP_ADDRESS` counter is incremented.

```
// Check for valid IP addresses
Matcher matcher = pattern.matcher(columns[4]);
If (!matcher.matches()) {
    context.getCounter(BadRecords.INVALID_IP_ADDRESS).increment(1);
    return;
}
```

Each increment of a counter is first stored locally by each mapper. The counter values are then sent to the Task Tracker for a second level of aggregation. Finally, the values are sent to the Job Tracker where the global aggregation takes place.

Developing and testing MapReduce jobs with MRUnit

Conceptually, MapReduce jobs are relatively simple. In the map phase, each input record has a function applied to it, resulting in one or more key-value pairs. The reduce phase receives a group of the key-value pairs and performs some function over that group. Testing mappers and reducers should be as easy as testing any other function. A given input will result in an expected output. The complexities arise due to the distributed nature of Hadoop. Hadoop is a large framework with many moving parts. Prior to the release of MRUnit by Cloudera, even the simplest tests running in local mode would have to read from the disk and take several seconds each to set up and run.

MRUnit removes as much of the Hadoop framework as possible while developing and testing. The focus is narrowed to the map and reduce code, their inputs, and expected outputs. With MRUnit, developing and testing MapReduce code can be done entirely in the IDE, and these tests take fractions of a second to run.

This recipe will demonstrate how MRUnit uses the IdentityMapper provided by the MapReduce framework in the `lib` folder. The IdentityMapper takes a key-value pair as input and emits the same key-value pair, unchanged.

Getting ready

Start with the following steps:

► Download the latest version of MRUnit from `http://mrunit.apache.org/general/downloads.html`

► Create a new Java project

► Add the `mrunit-X.Y.Z-incubating-hadoop1.jar` file and other Hadoop JAR files to the build path of the Java project

► Create a new class named `IdentityMapperTest`

► For the full source, review the `IdentityMapperTest.java` file in the source code folder of this chapter

How to do it...

Follow these steps to test a mapper with MRUnit:

1. Have the `IdentityMapperTest` class extend the `TestCase` class:

```
public class IdentityMapperTest extends TestCase
```

2. Create two private members of mapper and driver:

```
private Mapper identityMapper;
private MapDriver mapDriver;
```

3. Add a `setup()` method with a `Before` annotation:

```
@Before
public void setup() {
    identityMapper = new IdentityMapper();
mapDriver = new MapDriver(identityMapper);
}
```

4. Add a `testIdentityMapper1()` method with a `Test` annotation:

```
@Test
public void testIdentityMapper1() {
    mapDriver.withInput(new Text("key"), new Text("value"))
    mapDriver.withOutput(new Text("key"), new Text("value"))
        .runTest();
}
```

5. Run the application.

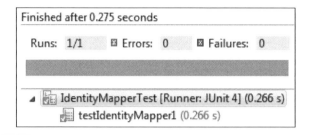

6. Add a `testIdentityMapper2()` method that would fail:

```
@Test
public void testIdentityMapper2() {
    mapDriver.withInput(new Text("key"), new Text("value"))
    mapDriver.withOutput(new Text("key2"), new Text("value2"))
    mapDriver.runTest();
}
```

7. Run the application again.

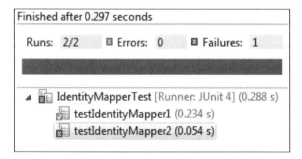

How it works...

MRUnit is built on top of the popular JUnit testing framework. It uses the object-mocking library, Mockito, to mock most of the essential Hadoop objects so the user only needs to focus on the map and reduce logic. The `MapDriver` class runs the test. It is instantiated with a `Mapper` class. The `withInput()` method is called to provide input to the `Mapper` class that the `MapDriver` class was instantiated with. The `withOutput()` method is called to provide output to validate the results of the call to the `Mapper` class. The call to the `runTest()` method actually calls the mapper, passing it the inputs and validating its outputs against the ones provided by the `withOutput()` method.

There's more...

This example only showed the testing of a mapper. MRUnit also provides a `ReduceDriver` class that can be used in the same way as `MapDriver` for testing reducers.

See also

▶ For more information on Mockito, visit `http://code.google.com/p/mockito/`

▶ The *Developing and testing MapReduce jobs running in local mode* recipe of this chapter

Developing and testing MapReduce jobs running in local mode

Developing in MRUnit and local mode are complementary. MRUnit provides an elegant way to test the map and reduce phases of a MapReduce job. Initial development and testing of jobs should be done using this framework. However, there are several key components of a MapReduce job that are not exercised when running MRUnit tests. Two key class types are `InputFormats` and `OutFormats`. Running jobs in local mode will test a larger portion of a job. When testing in local mode, it is also much easier to use a significant amount of real-world data.

This recipe will show an example of configuring Hadoop to use local mode and then debugging that job using the Eclipse debugger.

Getting ready

You will need to download the `weblog_entries_bad_records.txt` dataset from the Packt website, `http://www.packtpub.com/support`. This example will use the `CounterExample.java` class provided with the *Using Counters in a MapReduce job to track bad records* recipe.

How to do it...

1. Open the `$HADOOP_HOME/conf/mapred-site.xml` file in a text editor.

2. Set the `mapred.job.tracker` property value to `local`:

```
<property>
        <name>mapred.job.tracker</name>
        <value>local</value>
    </property>
```

3. Open the `$HADOOP_HOME/conf/core-site.xml` file in a text editor.

4. Set the `fs.default.name` property value to `file:///:`

```
<property>
    <name>fs.default.name</name>
    <value>file:///</value>
</property>
```

5. Open the `$HADOOP_HOME/conf/hadoop-env.sh` file and add the following line:

```
export HADOOP_OPTS="-agentlib:jdwp=transport=dt_socket,server=y,
suspend=y,address=7272"
```

6. Run the `CountersExample.jar` file by passing the local path to the `weblog_entries_bad_records.txt` file, and give a local path to an output file:

```
$HADOOP_HOME/bin/hadoop jar ./CountersExample.jar com.packt.
hadoop.solutions.CounterExample /local/path/to/weblog_entries_bad_
records.txt /local/path/to/weblog_entries_clean.txt
```

You'll get the following output:

```
Listening for transport dt_socket at address: 7272
```

7. Open the **Counters** project in Eclipse, and set up a new remote debug configuration.

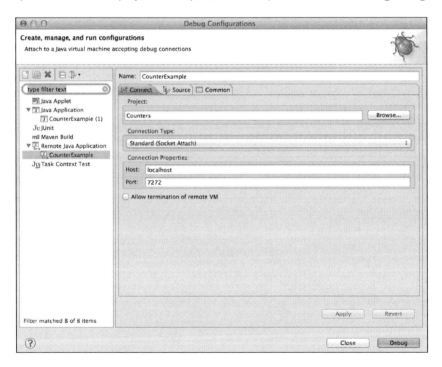

8. Create a new breakpoint and debug.

How it works...

A MapReduce job that is configured to execute in local mode runs entirely in one JVM instance. Unlike the pseudo-distributed mode, this mode makes it possible to hook up a remote debugger to debug a job. The `mapred.job.tracker` property set to `local` informs the Hadoop framework that jobs will now run in the local mode. The `LocalJobRunner` class, which is used when running in local mode, is responsible for implementing the MapReduce framework locally in a single process. This has the benefit of keeping jobs that run in local mode as close as possible to the jobs that run distributed on a cluster. One downside to using `LocalJobRunner` is that it carries the baggage of setting up an instance of Hadoop. This means even the smallest jobs will require at least several seconds to run. Setting the `fs.default.name` property value to `file:///` configures the job to look for input and output files on the local filesystem. Adding `export HADOOP_OPTS="-agentlib:jdwp=transport=dt_socket,server=y,suspend=y,address=7272"` to the `hadoop-env.sh` file configures the JVM to suspend processing and listen for a remote debugger on port `7272` on start up.

There's more...

Apache Pig also provides a local mode for development and testing. It uses the same `LocalJobRunner` class as a local mode MapReduce job. It can be accessed by starting Pig with the following command:

```
pig -x local
```

See also

▶ *Developing and testing MapReduce jobs with MRUnit*

Enabling MapReduce jobs to skip bad records

When working with the amounts of data that Hadoop was designed to process, it is only a matter of time before even the most robust job runs into unexpected or malformed data. If not handled properly, bad data can easily cause a job to fail. By default, Hadoop will not skip bad data. For some applications, it may be acceptable to skip a small percentage of the input data. Hadoop provides a way to do just that. Even if skipping data is not acceptable for a given use case, Hadoop's skipping mechanism can be used to pinpoint the bad data and log it for review.

How to do it...

1. To enable the skipping of 100 bad records in a map job, add the following to the `run()` method where the job configuration is set up:

   ```
   SkipBadRecords.setMapperMaxSkipRecords(conf, 100);
   ```

2. To enable the skipping of 100 bad record groups in a reduce job, add the following to the `run()` method where the job configuration is set up:

   ```
   SkipBadRecords.setReducerMaxSkipGroups(conf, 100);
   ```

How it works...

The process to skip bad records will trigger if skipping has been enabled. Skipping is enabled by calling the static methods on the `SkipBadRecords` class and once a task has failed twice. Hadoop will then perform a binary search through the input data to identify the bad records. Keep in mind that this is an expensive task that could require multiple attempts. A job that enables skipping will probably want to increase the number of map and reduce attempts. This can be done by using the `JobConf.setMaxMapAttempts()` and `JobConf.setMaxReduceAttempts()` methods.

There's more...

By default, the process to skip bad records will be triggered after two failed attempts. This default can be changed using the `setAttemptsToStartSkipping()` method on the `SkipBadRecords` class. The output folder of the skipped records can be controlled using the `setSkipOutputPath()` method on the `SkipBadRecords` class. By default, skipped records will be logged to the `_log/skip/` folder. These files are formatted as Hadoop sequence files. To get them into human-readable format, use the following command:

```
hadoop fs -text _log/skip/<filename>
```

Record-skipping can also be controlled using MapReduce job properties. The following table is a relevant snippet from the table provided at `http://hadoop.apache.org/common/docs/r0.20.2/mapred-default.html`.

Property	Default Value	Description
`mapred.skip.attempts.to.start.skipping`	2	The number of Task attempts *after* which skip mode will be kicked off. When skip mode is kicked off, the task reports the range of records that it will process next to the TaskTracker. This is so that, on failures, the TaskTracker knows which ones are possibly the bad records. On further executions, those are skipped.
`mapred.skip.map.auto.incr.proc.count`	true	On setting this flag to `true`, the MapRunner increments the `SkipBadRecords.COUNTER_MAP_PROCESSED_RECORDS` counter after invoking the map function. This value must be set to `false` for applications that process the records asynchronously or buffer the input records. For example, streaming. In such cases, applications should increment this counter on their own.
`mapred.skip.reduce.auto.incr.proc.count`	true	On setting this flag to `true`, the framework increments the `SkipBadRecords.COUNTER_REDUCE_PROCESSED_GROUPS` counter after invoking the reduce function. This value must be set to `false` for applications that process the records asynchronously or buffer the input records. For example, streaming. In such cases, applications should increment this counter on their own.
`mapred.skip.out.dir`		If no value is specified here, the skipped records are written to the output folder at `_logs/skip`. User can stop writing skipped records by giving the value `none`.
`mapred.skip.map.max.skip.records`	0	This is the number of acceptable skip records surrounding the bad record *per* bad record in the mapper. The number includes the bad record as well. To turn the feature of detection/skipping of bad records off, set the value to 0. The framework tries to narrow down the skipped range by retrying until this threshold is met *or* all attempts get exhausted for this task. Set the value to the value of `Long.MAX_VALUE` to indicate that the framework need not try to narrow down. Whatever records (depends on the application) get skipped, are acceptable.

Property	Default Value	Description
`mapred.skip.map.max.skip.records`	0	This is the number of acceptable skip groups surrounding the bad group *per* bad group in the reducer. The number includes the bad group as well. To turn the feature of detection/skipping of bad groups off, set the value to 0. The framework tries to narrow down the skipped range by retrying until this threshold is met *or* all attempts get exhausted for this task. Set the value to the value of `Long.MAX_VALUE` to indicate that the framework need not try to narrow down. Whatever groups (depends on the application) get skipped, are acceptable.

Using Counters in a streaming job

Hadoop is not limited to running MapReduce jobs written in Java or other JVM languages. It also provides a generic streaming interface. Using the streaming interface, any application that can read and write to `stdin` and `stdout` can be used in a MapReduce job. Since streaming jobs do not have access to the Hadoop Java classes, different approaches need to be taken to get access to the framework's features. One convenient and extremely useful feature provided by Hadoop is Counters. This recipe will use a simple Python program to show how to increment a counter from a streaming application. The Python code does not have direct access to the Java `Reporter` class used by the Hadoop framework for working with Counters. Instead, it will write data to `stderr` in a format that has special meaning. The Hadoop framework will interpret this as a request to increment the specified counter.

Getting ready

You will need to download the `weblog_entries_bad_records.txt` dataset from the Packt website, `http://www.packtpub.com/support`. This example will use the `streaming_counters.py` Python program provided in the code section of this chapter.

How to do it...

Complete the following steps to execute a Hadoop streaming job using the `streaming_counters.py` program:

1. Run the following command:

   ```
   hadoop jar $HADOOP_HOME/contrib/hadoop-*streaming*.jar \
   -file streaming_counters.py \
   -mapper streaming_counters.py \
   -reducer NONE \
   -input /data/weblogs/weblog_entries_bad_records.txt \
   -output /data/weblogs/weblog_entries_filtered.txt
   ```

2. To view the counter in the Job Tracker UI, open a web browser and navigate to the Job Tracker UI. The default address is `localhost:50030`. Scroll down to the **Completed Jobs** section. Then locate the **streaming_counters** job. The most recent jobs are at the bottom of the table. Once the job has been located, click on **Jobid**.

How it works...

The Hadoop framework constantly monitors `stderr` for entries that fit the following format:

```
reporter:counter:group,counter,value
```

If it finds a string that matches this format, the Hadoop framework will check to see if that group and counter exists. If they do exist, the current value will be incremented by that value. If they do not exist, the group and counter will be created and set to that value.

The Python code performs two validation checks on the weblog data. The first checks for an invalid number of columns:

```
if len(cols) < 5:
sys.stderr.write("reporter:counter:BadRecords,\
INVALID_NUMBER_OF_COLS,1")
    continue
```

If a line has less than five columns, the program will write to `stderr` in the format that Hadoop expects for manipulating the Counter. Similarly, the second validation verifies the IP address of each record and increments a counter each time an invalid IP address is found.

```
m = re.match(('^([01]?\\d\\d?|2[0-4]\\d|25[0-5])\\'
             '.([01]?\\d\\d?|2[0-4]\\d|25[0-5])\\'
             '.([01]?\\d\\d?|2[0-4]\\d|25[0-5])\\'
             '.([01]?\\d\\d?|2[0-4]\\d|25[0-5])$'), ip)
if not m:
sys.stderr.write("reporter:counter:BadRecords,INVALID_IP,1")
continue
```

There's more...

Streaming jobs also have access to setting the task's status message using the same basic method. Writing to `stderr` in the following format will update a task's status, setting it to `message`.

```
reporter:status:message
```

See also

▸   *Using Counters in a MapReduce job to track bad records*

Updating task status messages to display debugging information

Along with maintaining counters, another role of the `Reporter` class in Hadoop is to capture task status information. The task status information is periodically sent to the Job Tracker. The Job Tracker UI is updated to reflect the current status. By default, the task status will display its state. The task state can be one of the following:

▸   `RUNNING`

▸   `SUCCEEDED`

▸   `FAILED`

▸   `UNASSIGNED`

▸   `KILLED`

▸   `COMMIT_PENDING`

▸   `FAILED_UNCLEAN`

▸   `KILLED_UNCLEAN`

When debugging a MapReduce job, it can be useful to display a custom message that gives more detailed information on how the task is running. This recipe shows how to update the task status.

Getting ready

- ▸ Download the source code for this chapter.
- ▸ Load the `StatusMessage` project.

How to do it...

Updating a task's status message can be done using the `setStatus()` method of the job's `Context` class.

```
context.setMessage("user custom message");
```

How it works...

The source code for this chapter provides an example of using a custom task status message to display the number of rows being processed per second by the task.

```
public static class StatusMap extends Mapper<LongWritable, Text,
LongWritable, Text> {

        private int rowCount = 0;
        private long startTime = 0;

        public void map(LongWritable key, Text value, Context context)
throws IOException, InterruptedException{

            //Display rows per second every 100,000 rows
            rowCount++;
            if(startTime == 0 || rowCount % 100000 == 0)
            {
                if(startTime > 0)
{
                        long estimatedTime = System.nanoTime() - startTime;
                        context.setStatus("Processing: " + (double)rowCount /
((double)estimatedTime/1000000000.0) + " rows/second");
                        rowCount = 0;
}

                startTime = System.nanoTime();
}

            context.write(key, value);
}
}
```

Two private class variables are declared: `rowCount` for keeping track of the number of rows that are processed and `startTime` for keeping track of the time when processing started. Once the map function has processed 100,000 lines, the task status is updated with the number of rows per second that are being processed.

```
context.setStatus("Processing: " + (double)rowCount / ((double)
estimatedTime/1000000000.0) + " rows/second");
```

After the message has been updated, the `rowCount` and `startTime` variables are reset and the process starts over again. The status is stored locally in the memory of the current process. It is then sent to the Task Tracker. The next time the Task Tracker pings, the Job Tracker is also sent the updated status message. Once the Job Tracker receives the status message, this information is made available to the UI.

Using illustrate to debug Pig jobs

Generating good test data for a complex distributed job that joins, filters, and aggregates gigabytes or even terabytes of data can be one of the hardest parts of the development process, or at least one of the most tedious. Apache Pig provides an incredibly powerful tool, `illustrate`, that will seek out cases from the provided full input data that exercise different dataflow paths. The following recipe shows an example of the `illustrate` command in use.

Getting ready

Apache Pig 0.10 or a more recent version must be installed. You can download it from `http://pig.apache.org/releases.html`.

How to do it...

The following Pig code will show an example of a record with a malformed IP address:

```
weblogs = load '/data/weblogs/weblog_entries_bad_records.txt'
    as (md5:chararray, url:chararray, date:chararray, time:chararray,
ip:chararray);

ip_addresses = foreach weblogs generate ip;

bad = filter ip_addresses by not
(ip matches '^([01]?\\d\\d?|2[0-4]\\d|25[0-5])\\.([01]?\\d\\d?|2[0-4]\\
d|25[0-5])\\.([01]?\\d\\d?|2[0-4]\\d|25[0-5])\\.([01]?\\d\\d?|2[0-4]\\
d|25[0-5])$');

illustrate bad;
```

The output will look like the following:

```
-----------------------------------------------------------------------------------------------
| weblogs       | md5:chararray              | url:chararray        | date:chararray  | time:
chararray       | ip:chararray    |
-----------------------------------------------------------------------------------------------
|               | 8372babe9ebf72b32719feca7  | /ythen.html          | 2012-05-10      | 21:40
:20             | 65.392.         |
|               | baa2f0917c90342e4d7771dbfae5d9 | /fefumrfgkhqlisoke.html | 2012-05-10 | 21:24
:30             | 220.22.74.176   |
-----------------------------------------------------------------------------------------------

--------------------------------------------
| ip_addresses   | ip:chararray   |
--------------------------------------------
|                | 65.392.        |
|                | 220.22.74.176  |
--------------------------------------------

--------------------------------------------
| bad       | ip:chararray   |
--------------------------------------------
|           | 65.392.        |
--------------------------------------------
```

How it works...

In the preceding example, data is filtered on invalid IP addresses. The number of records that have an invalid IP address make up a small percentage of the total. If a traditional sampling approach was taken to create test data, chances are that the sampled data would not contain any records with an invalid IP address.

The `illustrate` algorithm makes four complete passes over a Pig script to generate its data. The first pass takes a sample of data from each input and sends it through the script. The second pass finds and removes records that followed the same path through the script. The third pass determines if any possible paths were not taken by the sampled data from the first pass. If there are paths that are not represented by the sampled data, the `illustrate` algorithm will create fake data that exercises the remaining paths. The fourth pass is similar to the second pass; it removes any redundant data created by the third pass.

See also

▶ To learn about generating example data for dataflow programs, visit
  http://i.stanford.edu/~olston/publications/sigmod09.pdf

9
System Administration

In this chapter we will cover:

- ▶ Starting Hadoop in pseudo-distributed mode
- ▶ Starting Hadoop in distributed mode
- ▶ Adding new nodes to an existing cluster
- ▶ Safely decommissioning nodes
- ▶ Recovering from a NameNode failure
- ▶ Monitoring cluster health using Ganglia
- ▶ Tuning MapReduce job parameters

Introduction

This chapter will discuss how to maintain, monitor, and tune a Hadoop cluster and MapReduce jobs. We will review the various Hadoop modes of operations, describe how to resolve problems within the Hadoop cluster, and finally review some important job tuning parameters.

Starting Hadoop in pseudo-distributed mode

Hadoop supports three different operating modes:

- ▶ **Standalone mode**: In this mode, Hadoop will run as a single process on a single node.
- ▶ **Pseudo-distributed mode**: In this mode, Hadoop will run all services in separate processes on a single node.
- ▶ **Fully-distributed mode**: In this mode, Hadoop will run all services in separate processes across multiple nodes.

This recipe will describe how to install and set up Hadoop to run in pseudo-distributed mode. In pseudo-distributed mode, all of the HDFS and MapReduce processes will start on a single node. Pseudo-distributed mode is an excellent environment to test your HDFS operations and/or your MapReduce applications on a subset of the data.

Getting ready

Ensure that you have Java 1.6, ssh, and sshd installed. In addition, the ssh daemon (sshd) should be running on the node. You can validate the installation of these applications by using the following commands:

```
$ java -version
java version "1.6.0_31"
Java(TM) SE Runtime Environment (build 1.6.0_31-b04)
Java HotSpot(TM) 64-Bit Server VM (build 20.6-b01, mixed mode)

$ ssh
usage: ssh [-1246AaCfgkMNnqsTtVvXxY] [-b bind_address] [-c cipher_spec]
           [-D [bind_address:]port] [-e escape_char] [-F configfile]
           [-i identity_file] [-L [bind_address:]port:host:hostport]
           [-l login_name] [-m mac_spec] [-O ctl_cmd] [-o option] [-p
port]
           [-R [bind_address:]port:host:hostport] [-S ctl_path]
           [-w tunnel:tunnel] [user@]hostname [command]

$ service sshd status
openssh-daemon (pid  2004) is running...
```

How to do it...

Carry out the following steps to start Hadoop in pseudo-distributed mode:

1. Create a Hadoop user account. This is not specifically required to get Hadoop running in pseudo-distributed mode, but it is a common and good security practice. Ensure that the JAVA_HOME environment property is set to the folder of the system's Java installation:

   ```
   # useradd hadoop
   # passwd hadoop
   # su - hadoop
   $ echo $JAVA_HOME
   $ /usr/java/jdk1.6.0_31
   ```

2. Generate an `ssh` public and private key pair to allow password-less login to the node using the Hadoop user account. When asked for a passphrase, hit the *Enter* key, ensuring no passphrase will be used:

```
$ su - hadoop
$ ssh-keygen -t rsa
```

3. Add the public key to the authorized key list:

 If you have more than one node, you will need to copy this key to every node in the cluster.

```
$ ssh-copy-id -i /home/hadoop/.ssh/id_rsa.pub hadoop@localhost
```

4. Test the password-less `ssh` login. You should be able to `ssh` to `localhost` using your `hadoop` account without providing a password:

```
$ ssh localhost
```

5. Download a Hadoop distribution from `http://hadoop.apache.org` using the Hadoop user account. We used Hadoop 0.20.x for this installation:

```
# su - hadoop
$ tar -zxvf hadoop-0.20.x.tar.gz
```

6. Change the following configuration files located in the `conf` folder of the extracted Hadoop distribution. These configuration changes will allow Hadoop to run in pseudo-distributed mode:

```
$ vi conf/core-site.xml
<configuration>
  <property>
    <name>fs.default.name</name>
    <value>hdfs://localhost:8020</value>
  </property>
</configuration>
$ vi conf/hdfs-site.xml
<configuration>
  <property>
    <name>dfs.replication</name>
    <value>1</value>
  </property>
</configuration>
$ vi conf/mapred-site.xml
```

```
<configuration>
  <property>
    <name>mapred.job.tracker</name>
    <value>localhost:8021</value>
  </property>
</configuration>
```

7. Format the Hadoop NameNode:

    ```
    $ bin/hadoop namenode -format
    ```

8. Start all of the Hadoop HDFS and MapReduce services:

    ```
    $ bin/start-all.sh
    ```

9. Verify all of the services started successfully by looking at the NameNode status page `http://localhost:50070/`, and the JobTracker page `http://localhost:50030/`. You can stop all of the Hadoop services by running the `bin/stop-all.sh` script.

How it works...

Steps 1 through 4 sets up a single node for a password-less login using `ssh`.

Next, we downloaded a distribution of Hadoop and configured the distribution to run in pseudo-distributed mode. The `fs.default.name` property was set to a URI to tell Hadoop where to find the HDFS implementation, which is running on our local machine and listening on port `8020`. Next, we set the replication factor of HDFS to `1` using the `dfs.replication` property. Since we are running all of the Hadoop services on a single node, there is no need to replicate any information. If we did, all of the replicated information would reside on the single node. We set the value of the last configuration property `mapred.job.tracker` to `localhost:8021`. The `mapred.job.tracker` property tells Hadoop where to find the JobTracker.

Finally, we formatted the NameNode and started the Hadoop services. You need to format the NameNode after you set up a new Hadoop cluster. Formatting a NameNode will erase all of the data in the cluster.

There's more...

By default, the Hadoop distribution comes configured to run in standalone mode. In standalone mode, there is no need to start any Hadoop service. In addition, input and output folders will be located on the local filesystem, instead of HDFS. To run a MapReduce job in standalone mode, use the configuration files that initially came with the distribution. Create an input folder on the local filesystem and use the Hadoop shell script:

```
$ mkdir input
$ cp somefiles*.txt input/
$ /path/to/hadoop/bin/hadoop jar myjar.jar input/*.txt output
```

See also

▸ *Starting Hadoop in distributed mode*

Starting Hadoop in distributed mode

As mentioned in the previous recipe, Hadoop supports three different operating modes:

▸ Standalone mode

▸ Pseudo-distributed mode

▸ Fully-distributed mode

This recipe will describe how to set up Hadoop to run in fully-distributed mode. In fully-distributed mode, HDFS and the MapReduce services will run across multiple machines. A typical architecture is to have a dedicated node run the NameNode and the JobTracker services, another dedicated node to host the Secondary NameNode service, and the remaining nodes in the cluster running both the DataNode and TaskTracker services.

Getting ready

This recipe will assume that steps 1 through 5 from the recipe *Starting Hadoop in pseudo-distributed mode* of this chapter have been completed. There should be a user named hadoop on every node in the cluster. In addition, the rsa public key generated in step 2 of the previous recipe must be distributed and installed on every node in the cluster using the ssh-copy-id command. Finally, the Hadoop distribution should be extracted and deployed on every node in the cluster.

We will now discuss the specific configurations required to get the cluster running in distributed mode. We will assume that your cluster will use the following configuration:

Server name	Purpose	Number of dedicated machines
head	Will run the NameNode and JobTracker services	1
secondary	Will run the Secondary NameNode service	1
worker(n)	Will run the TaskTracker and DataNode services	3 or greater

How to do it...

Perform the following steps to start Hadoop in fully-distributed mode:

1. Update the following configuration files on all of the nodes in the cluster:

```
$ vi conf/core-site.xml
<configuration>
  <property>
    <name>fs.default.name</name>
    <value>hdfs://head:8020</value>
  </property>
</configuration>

$ vi conf/hdfs-site.xml
<configuration>
  <property>
    <name>dfs.replication</name>
    <value>3</value>
  </property>
</configuration>

$ vi conf/mapred-site.xml
<configuration>
  <property>
    <name>mapred.job.tracker</name>
    <value>head:8021</value>
  </property>
</configuration>
```

2. Update the `masters` and `slaves` configuration files on the head node. The `masters` configuration file contains the hostname of the node which will run the Secondary NameNode. The `slaves` configuration file contains a list of the hosts which will run the TaskTracker and DataNode services:

```
$ vi conf/masters
secondary
$ vi conf/slaves
worker1
worker2
worker3
```

3. Format the Hadoop NameNode from the head node:

    ```
    $ bin/hadoop namenode -format
    ```

4. From the head node as the `hadoop` user, start all of the Hadoop services:

    ```
    $ bin/start-all.sh
    ```

5. Confirm that all of the correct services are running on the proper nodes:

    - ❑ On the master: Both the NameNode and JobTracker services should running
    - ❑ On the secondary: The Secondary NameNode service should be running
    - ❑ On the worker nodes: The DataNode and TaskTracker services should be running

How it works...

First we changed the Hadoop configuration files `core-site.xml`, `hdfs-site.xml`, and `mapred-site.xml` on every node in the cluster. These configuration files need to be updated to tell the Hadoop services running on every node where to find the NameNode and JobTracker services. In addition, we changed the HDFS replication factor to 3. Since we have three or more nodes available, we changed the replication from 1 to 3 in order to support high data availability in case one of the worker nodes experiences a failure.

There's more...

It is not necessary to run the Secondary NameNode on a separate node. You can run the Secondary NameNode on the same node as the NameNode and JobTracker, if you wish. To do this, stop the cluster, modify the `masters` configuration file on the master node, and restart all of the services:

```
$ bin/stop-all.sh
$ vi masters
head
$ bin/start-all.sh
```

Another set of configuration parameters that will come in handy when your cluster grows or when you wish to perform maintenance, are the exclusion list parameters that can be added to the `mapred-site.xml` configuration file. By adding the following lines to `mapred-site.xml`, you can list the nodes that will be barred from connecting to the NameNode (`dfs.hosts.exclude`) and/or the JobTracker (`mapred.hosts.exclude`). These configuration parameters will be used later when we discuss decommissioning of a node in the cluster:

```
<property>
    <name>dfs.hosts.exclude</name>
    <value>/path/to/hadoop/dfs_excludes</value>
```

```
            <final>true</final>
        </property>
        <property>
            <name>mapred.hosts.exclude</name>
            <value>/path/to/hadoop/mapred_excludes </value>
            <final>true</final>
        </property>
```

Create two empty files named `dfs_excludes`, and `mapred_excludes` for future use:

```
$ touch /path/to/hadoop/dfs_excludes
$ touch /path/to/hadoop/mapred_excludes
```

Start the cluster:

```
$ bin/start-all.sh
```

See also

▶ *Adding new nodes to an existing cluster*

▶ *Safely decommissioning nodes*

Adding new nodes to an existing cluster

Hadoop supports adding new nodes to an existing cluster without shutting down or restarting any service. This recipe will outline the steps required to add a new node to a pre-existing cluster.

Getting ready

Ensure that you have a Hadoop cluster up and running. In addition, ensure that you have the Hadoop distribution extracted, and the configuration files have been updated with the settings from the recipe titled *Starting Hadoop in distributed mode*.

We will use the following terms for our imaginary cluster:

Server name	Purpose	Number of dedicated machines
head	Will run the NameNode and JobTracker services	1
secondary	Will run the Secondary NameNode service	1
worker(n)	Will run the TraskTracker and DataNode services	3 or greater

How to do it...

Follow these steps to add new nodes to an existing cluster:

1. From the head node, update the `slaves` configuration file with the hostname of the new node:

   ```
   $ vi conf/slaves
   worker1
   worker2
   worker3
   worker4
   ```

2. Log in to the new node and start the DataNode and TaskTracker services:

   ```
   $ ssh hadoop@worker4
   $ cd /path/to/hadoop
   $ bin/hadoop-daemon.sh start datanode
   $ bin/hadoop-daemon.sh start tasktracker
   ```

How it works...

We updated the `slaves` configuration file on the head node to tell the Hadoop framework that a new node exists in the cluster. However, this file is only read when the Hadoop services are started (for example, by executing the `bin/start-all.sh` script). In order to add the new node to the cluster without having to restart all of the Hadoop services, we logged into the new node, and started the DataNode and TaskTracker services manually.

 The DataNode and TaskTracker services will automatically start the next time the cluster is restarted.

There's more...

When you add a new node to the cluster, the cluster is not properly balanced. HDFS will not automatically redistribute any existing data to the new node in order to balance the cluster. To rebalance the existing data in the cluster, you can run the following command from the head node:

```
# bin/start-balancer.sh
```

Rebalancing a Hadoop cluster is a network-intensive task. Imagine, we might be moving terabytes of data around, depending on the number of nodes added to the cluster. Job performance issues might arise when a cluster is in the process of rebalancing, and therefore regular rebalancing maintenance should be properly planned.

See also

▶   *Safely decommissioning nodes*

Safely decommissioning nodes

The practice of removing nodes from a Hadoop cluster is very common. Hardware might have failed, or machines might need to be upgraded. In this recipe, we will show you the steps to safely remove a worker node from a Hadoop cluster.

Getting ready

It is assumed that your cluster is up and running and you have configured the following properties in `mapred-site.xml`:

```
<property>
    <name>dfs.hosts.exclude</name>
    <value>/path/to/hadoop/dfs_excludes</value>
    <final>true</final>
</property>
<property>
    <name>mapred.hosts.exclude</name>
    <value>/path/to/hadoop/mapred_excludes </value>
    <final>true</final>
</property>
```

In addition, there should be two files located in the Hadoop `home` folder on the head node: `dfs_excludes` and `mapred_excludes`.

How to do it...

Perform the following steps to decommission a node in the Hadoop cluster:

1. Add the hostname of the node you wish to decommission to the `dfs_excludes` and `mapred_excludes` files on the head node:

    ```
    $ vi /path/to/hadoop/dfs_excludes
    ```

```
worker1
$ vi /path/to/hadoop/mapred_excludes
worker1
```

2. Notify the NameNode to re-read the exclude list and disconnect the worker node which will be decommissioned:

```
$ hadoop dfsadmin –refreshNodes
```

3. Notify the JobTracker to re-read the exclude list and disconnect the worker node which will be decommissioned:

```
$ hadoop mradmin –refreshNodes
```

4. Check the status of the decommissioning process:

```
$ hadoop dfsadmin -report
```

How it works...

First, we added the hostname of the node we wanted to decommission to the `dfs_excludes` and `mapred_excludes` files we created in a previous recipe. Next, we issued the `hadoop dfsadmin –refreshNodes` command to notify the NameNode to disconnect from all of the hosts listed in the `dfs_excludes` file. Similarly, we issued the `hadoop mradmin – refreshNodes` command to notify the JobTracker to stop using the TaskTrackers on the nodes listed in the `mapred_excludes` file.

Recovering from a NameNode failure

The NameNode is the single most important Hadoop service. It maintains the locations of all of the data blocks in the cluster; in addition, it maintains the state of the distributed filesystem. When a NameNode fails, it is possible to recover from a previous checkpoint generated by the Secondary NameNode. It is important to note that the Secondary NameNode is not a backup for the NameNode. It performs a checkpoint process periodically. The data is almost certainly stale when recovering from a Secondary NameNode checkpoint. However, recovering from a NameNode failure using an old filesystem state is better than not being able to recover at all.

Getting ready

It is assumed that the system hosting the NameNode service has failed, and the Secondary NameNode is running on a separate machine. In addition, the `fs.checkpoint.dir` property should have been set in the `core-default.xml` file. This property tells the Secondary NameNode where to save the checkpoints on the local filesystem.

How to do it...

Carry out the following steps to recover from a NameNode failure:

1. Stop the Secondary NameNode:

    ```
    $ cd /path/to/hadoop
    $ bin/hadoop-daemon.sh stop secondarynamenode
    ```

2. Bring up a new machine to act as the new NameNode. This machine should have Hadoop installed, be configured like the previous NameNode, and `ssh` password-less login should be configured. In addition, it should have the same IP and hostname as the previous NameNode.

3. Copy the contents of `fs.checkpoint.dir` on the Secondary NameNode to the `dfs.name.dir` folder on the new NameNode machine.

4. Start the new NameNode on the new machine:

    ```
    $ bin/hadoop-daemon.sh start namenode
    ```

5. Start the Secondary NameNode on the Secondary NameNode machine:

    ```
    $ bin/hadoop-daemon.sh start secondarynamenode
    ```

6. Verify that the NameNode started successfully by looking at the NameNode status page `http://head:50070/`.

How it works...

We first logged into the Secondary NameNode and stopped the service. Next, we set up a new machine in the exact manner we set up the failed NameNode. Next, we copied all of the checkpoint and edit files from the Secondary NameNode to the new NameNode. This will allow us to recover the filesystem status, metadata, and edits at the time of the last checkpoint. Finally, we restarted the new NameNode and Secondary NameNode.

There's more...

Recovering using the old data is unacceptable for certain processing environments. Instead, another option would be to set up some type of offsite storage where the NameNode can write its image and edits files. This way, if there is a hardware failure of the NameNode, you can recover the latest filesystem without resorting to restoring old data from the Secondary NameNode snapshot.

The first step in this would be to designate a new machine to hold the NameNode image and edit file backups. Next, mount the backup machine on the NameNode server. Finally, modify the `hdfs-site.xml` file on the server running the NameNode to write to the local filesystem and the backup machine mount:

```
$ cd /path/to/hadoop
$ vi conf/hdfs-site.xml
<property>
    <name>dfs.name.dir</name>
    <value>/path/to/hadoop/cache/hadoop/dfs, /path/to/backup</value>
</property>
```

Now the NameNode will write all of the filesystem metadata to both `/path/to/hadoop/cache/hadoop/dfs` and the mounted `/path/to/backup` folders.

Monitoring cluster health using Ganglia

Ganglia is a monitoring system designed for use with clusters and grids. Hadoop can be configured to send periodic metrics to the Ganglia monitoring daemon, which is useful for diagnosing and monitoring the health of the Hadoop cluster. This recipe will explain how to configure Hadoop to send metrics to the Ganglia monitoring daemon.

Getting ready

Ensure that you have Ganglia Version 3.1 or better installed on all of the nodes in the Hadoop cluster. The Ganglia monitoring daemon (`gmond`) should be running on every worker node in the cluster. You will also need the Ganglia meta daemon (`gmetad`) running on at least one node, and another node running the Ganglia web frontend.

The following is an example with modified `gmond.conf` file that can be used by the `gmond` daemon:

```
cluster {
  name = "Hadoop Cluster"
  owner = "unspecified"
  latlong = "unspecified"
  url = "unspecified"
}

host {
  location = "my datacenter"
}

udp_send_channel {
  host = mynode.company.com
  port = 8649
  ttl = 1
}
```

```
udp_recv_channel {
  port = 8649
}

tcp_accept_channel {
  port = 8649
}
```

Also, ensure that the Ganglia meta daemon configuration file includes your cluster as a data source. For example, modify the `gmeta.conf` configuration file to add the Hadoop cluster as a data source:

```
data_source "Hadoop Cluster" mynode1.company.com:8649 mynode2.company.
com:8649 mynode3.company.com:8649
```

How to do it...

Perform the following steps to use Ganglia to monitor cluster metrics:

1. Edit the `hadoop-metrics.properties` file found in the Hadoop configuration folder. If the `hadoop-metrics.properties` file does not exist, create it:

This property file will need to be updated for every node in the cluster.

```
$ vi /path/to/hadoop/hadoop-metrics.properties
dfs.class=org.apache.hadoop.metrics.ganglia.GangliaContext31
dfs.period=10
dfs.servers=mynode1.company.com:8649


mapred.class=org.apache.hadoop.metrics.ganglia.GangliaContext31
mapred.period=10
mapred.servers=mynode1.company.com 8649


jvm.class=org.apache.hadoop.metrics.ganglia.GangliaContext31
jvm.period=10
jvm.servers=mynode1.company.com:8649


rpc.class=org.apache.hadoop.metrics.ganglia.GangliaContext31
rpc.period=10
rpc.servers=mynode1.company.com 8649
```

2. Restart the Ganglia meta daemon service.

3. Restart the Hadoop cluster:

```
$ cd /path/to/hadoop
$ bin/stop-all.sh
$ bin/start-all.sh
```

4. Verify that Ganglia is collecting Hadoop metrics via the Ganglia web frontend.

How it works...

The Ganglia monitoring daemon (gmond) is responsible for collecting metric information from the nodes where it is installed. Next, all of the metrics collected by the gmond daemons are aggregated to the Ganglia meta daemon (gmetad). Finally, the Ganglia web frontend will request the aggregated metrics in the form of XML from the gmetad daemon and report that to users via the web interface.

Tuning MapReduce job parameters

The Hadoop framework is very flexible and can be tuned using a number of configuration parameters. In this recipe, we will discuss the function and purpose of different configuration parameters you can set for a MapReduce job.

Getting ready

Ensure that you have a MapReduce job which has a job class that extends the Hadoop Configuration class and implements the Hadoop Tool interface, such as any MapReduce application we have written so far in this book.

How to do it...

Follow these steps to customize MapReduce job parameters:

1. Ensure you have a MapReduce job class which extends the Hadoop Configuration class and the Tool interface.

2. Use the ToolRunner.run() static method to run your MapReduce job, as shown in the following example:

```
public static void main(String[] args) throws Exception {
        int exitCode = ToolRunner.run(new MyMapReduceJob(), args);
        System.exit(exitCode);
}
```

3. Examine the following table of Hadoop job properties and values:

Property name	Possible values	Description
mapred.reduce.tasks	Integers (0 - N)	Sets the number of reducers to launch.
mapred.child.java.opts	JVM key-value pairs	These parameters are given as arguments to every task JVM. For example, to set the maximum heap size for all tasks to 1 GB, you would set this property to '-Xmx1GB'.
mapred.map.child.java.opts	JVM key-value pairs	These parameters are given as arguments to every map task JVM.
mapred.reduce.child.java.opts	JVM key-value pairs	These parameters are given as arguments to every reduce task JVM.
mapred.map.tasks.speculative.execution	Boolean (true/false)	Tells the Hadoop framework to speculatively launch the exact same map task on different nodes in the cluster if a task is not performing well as compared to other tasks in the job. This property was discussed in *Chapter 1, Hadoop Distributed File System – Importing and Exporting Data*.
mapred.reduce.tasks.speculative.execution	Boolean (true/false)	Tells the Hadoop framework to speculatively launch the exact same reduce task on different nodes in the cluster if a task is not performing well as compared to other tasks in the job.

Property name	Possible values	Description
`mapred.job.reuse.jvm.num.tasks`	Integer (-1, 1 – N)	The number of task JVMs to be re-used. A value of 1 indicates one JVM will be started per task, a value of -1 indicates a single JVM can run an unlimited number of tasks. Setting this parameter might help increase the performance of small jobs because JVMs will be re-used for multiple tasks (as opposed to starting a JVM for each and every task).
`mapred.compress.map.output`	Boolean (true/false)	These three parameters are used to compress the output of map tasks.
`mapred.output.compression.type`	String (NONE, RECORD, or BLOCK)	
`mapred.map.output.compression.codec`	String (Name of compression codec class)	
`mapred.output.compress`	Boolean (true/false)	These three parameters are used to compress the output of a MapReduce job.
`mapred.output.compression.type`	String (NONE, RECORD, or BLOCK)	
`mapred.output.compression.codec`	String (Name of compression codec class)	

4. Execute a MapReduce job with a custom Hadoop property. For example, we will launch a job using five reducers:

```
$ cd /path/to/hadoop
$ bin/hadoop -jar MyJar.jar com.packt.MyJobClass -Dmapred.reduce.tasks=5
```

How it works...

When a job class extends the Hadoop `Configuration` class and implements the Hadoop `Tool` interface, the `ToolRunner` class will automatically handle the following generic Hadoop arguments:

Argument/Flag	Purpose
`-conf`	Takes a path to a parameter configuration file.
`-D`	Used to specify Hadoop key/value properties which will be added to the job configuration
`-fs`	Used to specify the host port of the NameNode
`-jt`	Used to specify the host port of the JobTracker

In the case of this recipe, the `ToolRunner` class will automatically place all of the parameters specified with the `-D` flag into the job configuration XML file.

10

Persistence Using Apache Accumulo

In this chapter, we will cover:

- ▶ Designing a row key to store geographic events in Accumulo
- ▶ Using MapReduce to bulk import geographic event data into Accumulo
- ▶ Setting a custom field constraint for inputting geographic event data in Accumulo
- ▶ Limiting query results using the regex filtering iterator
- ▶ Counting fatalities for different versions of the same key using SumCombiner
- ▶ Enforcing cell-level security on scans using Accumulo
- ▶ Aggregating sources in Accumulo using MapReduce

Introduction

Storage of big data is a topic of ever-increasing popularity. Software projects facing concerns over data scalability frequently find themselves having to shell out top dollar for expensive RDBMS commercial licenses, or worse, having to rely on solutions in which scalability was an afterthought. In the last couple of years, we have seen the introduction of many viable open source database solutions to help manage massive amounts of structured and unstructured data. Apache Accumulo was inspired by the Google **BigTable** design approach, and offers scalable, distributed columnar persistence of data backed over Apache Hadoop. The Google BigTable design is explained in detail at `http://research.google.com/archive/bigtable.html`. This chapter will show several recipes that tackle common database query/load tasks, and also shows how many of Accumulo's unique features help to streamline the implementation.

Designing a row key to store geographic events in Accumulo

The **Armed Conflict Location Event Data** (**ACLED**) dataset is a collection of individual events that occurred across a wide range of geographic areas. This recipe will show how we can leverage Accumulo's sorted key ordering to group ACLED event records into geographic ranges. Furthermore, each geographic range will be subgrouped in the descending order of event occurrence. Specifically, the code in this recipe shows the generation logic that we can turn around and use to build ACLED keys from our records. To verify that the key generator works as expected, we will build and run unit tests with some sample row data.

Getting ready

To run the unit tests, you will need TestNG (`testng-jdk15.jar`) on the environment classpath. Some basic familiarity with the TestNG testing API will help make sense of the unit tests.

This recipe makes use of a specific type of quadtree data structure that is useful for grouping geospatial data into indexed ranges. It will help to have some familiarity with a Z-order curve (a.k.a. Morton curve) to build this type of quadtree for use over 2D geospatial data.

How to do it...

Follow these steps to implement a geospatial, reverse chronological row key generator:

1. Open the Java IDE editor of your choice.

2. Create the package `example.accumulo` and create the interface `RowIDGenerator.java` with the following content:

   ```
   package examples.accumulo;

   import javax.security.auth.login.Configuration;
   import java.io.IOException;

   public interface RowIDGenerator {
   public String getRowID(String[] parameters)
           throws IllegalArgumentException;
   }
   ```

3. Under the same package `example.accumulo`, create a class named `ACLEDRowIDGenerator.java` with the following content:

   ```
   package examples.accumulo;

   import java.text.DateFormat;
   import java.text.ParseException;
   ```

```
import java.text.SimpleDateFormat;
import java.util.Date;
import java.util.regex.Pattern;

public class ACLEDRowIDGenerator implements RowIDGenerator {

    private DateFormat dateFormat = new
                            SimpleDateFormat("yyyy-MM-dd");
    private static final Pattern decimalPattern =
                            Pattern.compile("[.]");
```

4. We write the method `getRowID()` to take a list of `String[]` parameters.

```
@Override
public String getRowID(String[] parameters)
        throws IllegalArgumentException {
    if(parameters.length != 3)
        throw new IllegalArgumentException("Required:
                                    {lat, lon, dtg}")
    StringBuilder builder = new StringBuilder();
    builder.append(getZOrderedCurve(parameters[0],
                                parameters[1]));
    builder.append("_");
    builder.append(getReverseTime(parameters[2]));
    return builder.toString();
}
```

5. We add the public method `getZOrderedCurve()` to build the geospatial portion of our rowID. The public accessibility will help with unit testing:

```
public String getZOrderedCurve(String lat, String lon)
        throws IllegalArgumentException {
    StringBuilder builder = new StringBuilder();
    lat = cleanAndValidatePoint(lat);
    lon = cleanAndValidatePoint(lon);
    int ceiling = Math.max(lat.length(), lon.length());
    for (int i = 0; i < ceiling; i++) {
        if(lat.length() <= i) {
            builder.append("0");
        } else {
            builder.append(lat.charAt(i));
        }
        if(lon.length() <= i) {
            builder.append("0");
        } else {
            builder.append(lon.charAt(i));
        }
    }
    return builder.toString();
}
```

6. The private method `cleanAndValidatePoint()` will help validate and sanitize `lat/lon` points into an appropriate form for Z-order shuffling:

```java
private String cleanAndValidatePoint(String point)
        throws IllegalArgumentException {

    String[] pointPieces = decimalPattern.split(point);
    if(pointPieces.length > 2) {
        throw new IllegalArgumentException("Malformed
                                    point: " + point);
    }
    String integralStr = null;
    int integral = 0;
    try {
        //offset any negative integral portion
        integral = Integer.parseInt(pointPieces[0]) + 90;
        if(integral > 180 | integral < 0) {
            throw new IllegalArgumentException("Invalid
integral: " + integral + " for point: " + point);
        }
        integralStr = "" + integral;
        if(pointPieces.length > 1)
            integralStr +=
                            Integer.parseInt(pointPieces[1]);
        if(integral < 10)
            integralStr = "00" + integralStr;
        else if (integral >= 10 && integral < 100)
            integralStr = "0" + integralStr;
        return  integralStr;
    } catch (NumberFormatException e) {
        throw new IllegalArgumentException("Point: " +
            point + " contains non-numeric characters");
    }
}
```

7. The public method `getReverseTime()` helps build the timestamp portion of the row key. The public accessibility will help with unit testing:

```java
public long getReverseTime(String dateTime)
        throws IllegalArgumentException {
    Date date = null;
    try {
        date = dateFormat.parse(dateTime);
    } catch (ParseException e) {
        throw new IllegalArgumentException(dateTime +
                        "Could not be parsed to a " +
```

```
                    "valid date with the supplied DateFormat " +
dateFormat.toString());
        }
        return Long.MAX_VALUE - date.getTime();
    }
}
```

8. In the package `examples.accumulo`, create a TestNG unit test class named `ValidatingKeyGenTest.java` with the following content:

```java
package examples.accumulo;

import org.apache.hadoop.hbase.thrift.generated.IllegalArgument;
import org.testng.annotations.BeforeClass;
import org.testng.annotations.Test;
import static org.testng.Assert.*;

import java.text.ParseException;
import java.text.SimpleDateFormat;
import java.util.Date;

public class ValidatingKeyGenTest {

    private ACLEDRowIDGenerator keyGen;
    private SimpleDateFormat dateFormatter = new
                        SimpleDateFormat("yyyy-MM-dd");
```

9. Use the `@BeforeClass` annotation to create an instance of `ACLEDRowIDGenerator`.

```java
@BeforeClass
public void setup() {
    keyGen = new ACLEDRowIDGenerator();
}
```

10. Add the `validZOrder()` unit test method.

```java
@Test
public void validZOrder() {
    try {
        // +90 = 123.22,134.55
        String zpoint = keyGen.getZOrderedCurve("33.22",
                    "44.55");
        assertEquals(zpoint, "1123342525");

        // +90 = 123, 134.55
        zpoint = keyGen.getZOrderedCurve("33", "44.55");
```

```
            assertEquals(zpoint, "1123340505");

            // +90 = 123.55, 134
            zpoint = keyGen.getZOrderedCurve("33.55", "44");
            assertEquals(zpoint, "1123345050");


            // +90 = 123.1234, 134.56
            zpoint =
            keyGen.getZOrderedCurve("33.1234","44.56");
            assertEquals(zpoint, "11233415263040");

            // +90 = 00.11, 134.56
            zpoint = keyGen.getZOrderedCurve("-90.11",
                                             "44.56");
            assertEquals(zpoint, "0103041516");

            // +90 = 005.11, 134.56
            zpoint = keyGen.getZOrderedCurve("-85.11",
                                             "44.56");
            assertEquals(zpoint, "0103541516");

            // +90 = 011.11, 134.56
            zpoint = keyGen.getZOrderedCurve("-79.11",
                                             "44.56");
            assertEquals(zpoint, "0113141516");

            // +90 = 095, 134.56
            zpoint = keyGen.getZOrderedCurve("5", "44.56");
            assertEquals(zpoint, "0193540506");

        } catch (Exception e) {
            fail("EXCEPTION fail: " + e.getMessage());
        }

    }
```

11. Add the `invalidZOrder()` unit test method.

```
    @Test
    public void invalidZOrder() {
        String zpoint = null;
        try {
            zpoint = keyGen.getZOrderedCurve("98.22",
                                             "33.44");
```

```
        fail("Should not parse. Too big an integral
               value.");
    } catch (IllegalArgumentException e) {
        assertTrue(e.getMessage().contains("invalid
integral"));
    }

    try {
        zpoint = keyGen.getZOrderedCurve("78.22",
                                    "-91.44");
        fail("Should not parse. Too big an integral
               value.");
    } catch (IllegalArgumentException e) {
        assertTrue(e.getMessage().contains("invalid
integral"));
    }

    try {
        zpoint =
    keyGen.getZOrderedCurve("332.22.33","33.44.33.22");
        fail("Should not parse. Too many split values.");
    } catch (IllegalArgumentException e) {
        assertTrue(e.getMessage().contains("Malformed
                                        point"));
    }

    try {
        zpoint = keyGen.getZOrderedCurve("33.22a",
                                    "33.33");
        fail("Should not parse. Contains bad characters.");
    } catch (IllegalArgumentException e) {
        assertTrue(e.getMessage().contains("contains non-
numeric characters"));
    }

    try {
        zpoint = keyGen.getZOrderedCurve("33.22",
                                    "3c.33");
        fail("Should not parse. Contains bad characters.");
    } catch (IllegalArgumentException e) {
        assertTrue(e.getMessage().contains("contains non-
numeric characters"));
    }
}
```

12. Add the `testValidReverseTime()` unit test method.

```
@Test
public void testValidReverseTime() {
    String dateStr = "2012-05-23";
    long reverse = keyGen.getReverseTime(dateStr);
    try {
        Date date = dateFormatter.parse(dateStr);
        assertEquals(reverse, (Long.MAX_VALUE -
                        date.getTime()));
    } catch (ParseException e) {
        fail(e.getMessage());
    }
}
```

13. Add the `testInvalidReverseTime()` unit test method.

```
@Test
public void testInvalidReverseTime() {
    try {
        long reverse = keyGen.getReverseTime("201a-22-
                                            22");
        fail("Should not reverse invalid date for
                DateFormat");
    } catch (IllegalArgumentException e) {
        assertTrue(e.getMessage().contains("could not be
parsed to a valid date with the supplied DateFormat"));
    }
}
```

14. Add the `testFullKey()` unit test method.

```
@Test
public void testFullKey() {
    try {
        String dateStr = "2012-03-13";
        Date date = dateFormatter.parse(dateStr);
        long reverse = Long.MAX_VALUE - date.getTime();

        // +90 = 123.55, 156.77
        String key = keyGen.getRowID(new String[]{"33.55",
"66.77", dateStr});
        assertEquals(key, "1125365757_" + reverse);
    } catch (ParseException e) {
        fail(e.getMessage());
    } catch (IllegalArgumentException e) {
        fail(e.getMessage());
    }
}
```

15. Run the unit tests in your environment. Every test should pass.

How it works...

This code will serve as the basis for generating geospatial/reverse chronological row keys. It exists as an independent component outside of any code that loads data to Accumulo. It is designed specifically to build row keys that will sort in a very particular order once persisted to an Accumulo table.

First, we define a general interface `RowIDGenerator.java` that could be re-used to build different key generator implementations. All implementing classes must fulfill a simple contract for `getRowID()`. It takes an array of arbitrary strings and returns a single string representing the rowID. Should any errors occur, throw an `IllegalArgumentException` exception. The class `ACLEDRowIDGenerator.java` requires an array of at least three strings for input. We then start to build the Z-order structure necessary for the rowID strategy.

The `getZOrderedCurve()` method takes `lat` and `lon` strings as arguments. Building an effect quadtree using the `lat/lon` point requires the points to adhere to strict formatting guidelines, thus before we shuffle the points, we must validate and format the points using the function `cleanAndValidatePoint()`.

The function `cleanAndValidatePoint()` first separates the integral portion to the left-hand side of the decimal from the fractional portion to the right-hand side of the decimal. A point is not required to contain a decimal portion, but it must at least contain an integral portion. Additionally, there should not be multiple fraction portions. Therefore, we throw an `IllegalArgumentException` exception if splitting the point on decimal does not return a one- or two-element array. Moving on, we offset each point by +90 to avoid negative numbers, which would otherwise corrupt the Z-order interpretation. If after applying the offset we contain a point with integral greater than 180 or less than 0, we can conclude that the point either started at a number greater than 90 or a number less than -90. Both these conditions flag an invalid point, and we throw an `IllegalArgumentException` exception indicating such. If after these checks our point is still considered valid, it is time to start formatting it for proper Z-order interpretation. Depending on the length of the point, we want to zero-pad the beginning such that the integral portion is always of length 3. This will make more sense when we examine how `getZOrderCurve()` uses the result. If applicable, add the fractional portion back to the reformatted string representation without the decimal place. If at any time we get a `NumberFormatException` exception, throw an `IllegalArgumentException` exception.

Once both latitude and longitude points have been properly formatted, we are ready to start shuffling the numbers to build the quadtree. As our loop control variable, we'll take the greater of the two lengths when comparing latitude and longitude, and use that as our loop's max variable. As we cycle through `i` going from 0 to max, we start with `lat` and print the ith character, followed by the ith character of `lon`. Should we reach the length of `lat` before `lon`, or vice versa, print 0 for an interleaved spot in the iteration. This helps generate a consistent key for a given `lat/lon` pair no matter the discrepancy in precision between the latitude and longitude (that is, `lat/lon`: 1.23/4.56789 can be interpreted as 1.23000/4.56780).

The general idea is to interleave the points such that the most significant digits are arranged in the left-to-right order. Accumulo will maintain the sorted order of our geospatial keys using lexicographical byte-order sorting. This means that the points pertaining to similar geographic regions will be arranged contiguously for effective range scans. We can quickly look up the given points for a particular `lat/lon` bounding region by building the offset Z-order representation of both the lower and bound bounding parameters and setting the start and end key ranges to the lower and upper bounding parameters respectively. For example, searching for all of the points between `lat/lon`: 30.1/60.2 and 40.8/70.9 would produce 120.1/150.2 and 130.8/160.9 (offset +90). The Z-order representation would thus have the lower-bound (start-key) value of 11250012 and an upper-bound (end-key) value of 11360089. This is why it is critical to zero-pad the integral portion of the `lat/lon` points. Without doing so, the application would incorrectly place 1.23 near 10.3 in the table, since the Z-order shuffle for both points would yield a row key that started with 1.

The geospatial portion is only half of our rowID. When storing ACLED event data, we would like to arrange events that lie in similar `lat/lon` regions in reverse chronological order. The function `getReverseTime()` achieves this by appending a reverse timestamp for the given item to the already calculated Z-order curve, separated by an underscore token. This allows us to use the same table in Accumulo to further restrict queries by temporal ranges (that is, 100 most recent, last 3 months', and so on). Events with the exact same `lat/lon` values will sort the records in the Accumulo table in the ascending order, but more recent events when converted to milliseconds from epoch will have larger long values. To counter this, we subtract the long value from the maximum possible long value. If incoming date strings do not match the simple date format yyyy-MM-dd, throw an exception.

The resulting keys take the form of `zOrderPoint_reverseTimestamp`.

The unit tests are designed to test the error handling of `getZOrderCurve()` and `getReverseTime()` as well as validate the expected output. We run this suite of tests to perform a stress test on our rowID generator before using it to load new ACLED event records into our Accumulo table.

There's more...

The rowID generation strategy listed in this recipe is designed to accommodate `lat/lon` geospatially bound queries with an optional time restriction for events. While this sounds very open-ended, there really is no one-size-fits-all solution for rowIDs when it comes to BigTable-designed columnar datastores. Depending on the types of queries you wish to perform over Accumulo, your rowID strategy might differ entirely. The following are a few sections that further expand on the design choices made in this recipe.

Lexicographic sorting of keys

Accumulo arranges key-value pairs stored in a table in the lexicographical sorted order of the key contents. This means that keys are arranged in terms of their respective byte contents, which does not always conform to an expected natural ordering pattern. For example, consider that we wanted to persist the sequence {1,2,10} as rowIDs. The lexicographic order would sort 10 after 1, but before 2, which is not what we expected for our sequence. This recipe circumvents this limitation by using zero-padding points to create a fixed-length string representation where the byte sorted order matches the expected natural ordering. Zero-padding the mentioned sequence produces 01, 02, and 10; which, when sorted lexicographically, maintains the sequence 01, 02, and 10.

This technique plays a key role in the previous recipe. Without using fixed-length points, the Z-order shuffle of the points 1.23, 9.88 and 10.23, 9.88 would order them closer in an overall sorted order of the dataspace than they technically belong. The Z-order representation would produce 192838 and 19082830 respectively, which gives an inaccurate appearance of the two points being close together. In this recipe, the offset of `+90` means that no point can exceed `180`, implying a maximum integral length of three digits. By zero-padding every integral out to three characters (001.23 instead of 1.23, 010.23 instead of 10.23, and so on), the left-to-right digit ordering of the rowID more accurately reflects the point separation.

Z-order curve

Z-order curve is a technique to generate quadtrees that represent a flattened, 2-dimensional view of geospatial data. A more in-depth explanation can be found in Wikipedia at `http://en.wikipedia.org/wiki/Z-order_curve`

Specifically, this recipe uses the technique to produce rowIDs that are flexible for range queries involving `lat/lon` points where the precision of the upper/lower bounding parameters can vary. The left-to-right placement of significant digits in the rowID means that a shorter Z-order queryID will match on more rows that begin with the supplied queryID pattern than would a longer queryID pattern. Take, for example, the `lat/lon` bounded query 30.1/40.2 and 50.7/60.8; when interleaved, this produces a start-key of 340012 and an end-key of 560078. However, the same table could be used for a more precise bounded range query such as 30.123/40.234 and 50.789/60.891, which yields start keys 3400122334 and 5600788991. The former, less verbose start- or end-key range will return more rows than the latter, which is what you would expect.

See also

> ▸ *Using MapReduce to bulk import geographic event data into Accumulo*

Using MapReduce to bulk import geographic event data into Accumulo

This recipe will use MapReduce to load tab-separated ACLED event data directly into an Accumulo table.

Getting ready

This recipe will be the easiest to test over a pseudo-distributed Hadoop cluster with Accumulo 1.4.1 and Zookeeper 3.3.3 installed. The shell script in this recipe assumes that Zookeeper is running on the host `localhost` on port `2181`; you can change this to suit your environment needs. The Accumulo installation's `bin` folder needs to be on your environment path.

For this recipe, you'll need to create an Accumulo instance named `test` with the user as `root` and password as `password` (top-notch security, I know...).

You will need the dataset `ACLED_nigeria_cleaned.tsv` loaded into HDFS at the path `/input/acled_cleaned/`.

It is also highly recommended that you complete the *Designing a row key to store geographic events in Accumulo* recipe earlier in this chapter. This recipe will use the classes `AccumuloTableAssistant.java` and `ACLEDRowIDGenerator.java`, and its parent interface `RowIDGenerator.java` to help with the setup.

How to do it...

Follow these steps to bulk load events into Accumulo using MapReduce:

1. Open the Java IDE editor of your choice.
2. Create a build template that produces a JAR file named `accumulo-examples.jar`.
3. Create the package `example.accumulo` and add `RowIDGenerator.java`, `AccumuloTableAssistant.java`, and `ACLEDRowIDGenerator.java`.
4. You will need to configure the Accumulo core and Hadoop classpath dependencies.
5. Create the class `ACLEDIngest.java` with the following content:

```
package examples.accumulo;

import org.apache.accumulo.core.client.mapreduce.
AccumuloFileOutputFormat;
import org.apache.accumulo.core.client.mapreduce.lib.partition.
RangePartitioner;
import org.apache.accumulo.core.data.Key;
import org.apache.accumulo.core.data.Value;
```

```
import org.apache.accumulo.core.util.CachedConfiguration;
import org.apache.hadoop.conf.Configuration;
import org.apache.hadoop.conf.Configured;
import org.apache.hadoop.fs.FileSystem;
import org.apache.hadoop.fs.Path;
import org.apache.hadoop.io.LongWritable;
import org.apache.hadoop.io.Text;
import org.apache.hadoop.mapreduce.Job;
import org.apache.hadoop.mapreduce.Mapper;
import org.apache.hadoop.mapreduce.Reducer;
import org.apache.hadoop.mapreduce.lib.input.FileInputFormat;
import org.apache.hadoop.mapreduce.lib.input.TextInputFormat;
import org.apache.hadoop.util.GenericOptionsParser;
import org.apache.hadoop.util.Tool;
import org.apache.hadoop.util.ToolRunner;

import java.io.IOException;
import java.util.regex.Pattern;

public class ACLEDIngest extends Configured implements Tool {


    private Configuration conf;

    public ACLEDIngest(Configuration conf) {
        this.conf = conf;
    }
```

6. The `run()` method is where we create and submit the job.

```
    @Override
    public int run(String[] args) throws Exception {

        if(args.length < 8) {
            System.err.println(printUsage());
            System.exit(0);
        }

        Job job = new Job(conf, "ACLED ingest
                            to Accumulo");
        job.setInputFormatClass(TextInputFormat.class);
        job.setMapperClass(ACLEDIngestMapper.class);
        job.setMapOutputKeyClass(Text.class);
        job.setMapOutputValueClass(Text.class);
        job.setReducerClass(ACLEDIngestReducer.class);
```

```
job.setPartitionerClass(RangePartitioner.class);
job.setJarByClass(getClass());

String input = args[0];
String outputStr = args[1];
String instanceName = args[2];
String tableName = args[3];
String user = args[4];
String pass = args[5];
String zooQuorum = args[6];
String localSplitFile = args[7];

FileInputFormat.addInputPath(job, new Path(input));
AccumuloFileOutputFormat.setOutputPath(job,
                            clearOutputDir(outputStr));
job.setOutputFormatClass(
                    AccumuloFileOutputFormat.class);
```

7. Create the `AccumuloTableAssistant` instance to help create and presplit the `acled` table.

```
AccumuloTableAssistant tableAssistant = new
                AccumuloTableAssistant.Builder()
 .setInstanceName(instanceName)
 .setTableName(tableName).setUser(user)
 .setPassword(pass)
 .setZooQuorum(zooQuorum)
 .build();

String splitFileInHDFS = "/tmp/splits.txt";
int numSplits = 0;
tableAssistant.createTableIfNotExists();
if(localSplitFile != null) {
    numSplits = tableAssistant.
presplitAndWriteHDFSFile(conf, localSplitFile, splitFileInHDFS);
}
RangePartitioner.setSplitFile(job, splitFileInHDFS);
job.setNumReduceTasks(numSplits + 1);

if(job.waitForCompletion(true)) {
    tableAssistant.loadImportDirectory(conf, outputStr);
}
return 0;
}
```

8. Create `printUsage()` and `clearOutputDir()` to show argument order and to automatically clear the supplied output directory.

```
private String printUsage() {
    return "<input> <output> <instance_name> <tablename> +
            "<username> <password> <zoohosts> <splits_file_
path>";
}

private Path clearOutputDir(String outputStr)
        throws IOException {
    FileSystem fs = FileSystem.get(conf);
    Path path = new Path(outputStr);
    fs.delete(path, true);
    return path;
}
```

9. Create a static nested map class called `ACLEDIngestMapper.java`.

```
public static class ACLEDIngestMapper
        extends Mapper<LongWritable, Text, Text, Text> {

    private Text outKey = new Text();
    private static final Pattern tabPattern =
                            Pattern.compile("[\\t]");
    private ACLEDRowIDGenerator gen = new
                            ACLEDRowIDGenerator();

    protected void map(LongWritable key, Text value,
                    Context context) throws IOException,
InterruptedException {

        String[] values =
                    tabPattern.split(value.toString());
        if(values.length == 8) {
            String [] rowKeyFields = new String[]
            // lat,lon,timestamp
            {values[4], values[5], values[1]};

            outKey.set(gen.getRowID(rowKeyFields));
            context.write(outKey, value);
        } else {
            context.getCounter("ACLED Ingest",
                    "malformed records").increment(1l);
        }
    }
}
```

10. Create a static nested reduce class called `ACLEDIngestReducer.java`.

```java
public static class ACLEDIngestReducer
        extends Reducer<Text, Text, Key, Value> {

    private Key outKey;
    private Value outValue = new Value();
    private Text cf = new Text("cf");
    private Text qual = new Text();
    private static final Pattern tabPattern =
                        Pattern.compile("[\\t]");

    @Override
    protected void reduce(Text key, Iterable<Text> values,
                        Context context) throws
                IOException, InterruptedException {

        int found = 0;
        for(Text value : values) {
            String[] cells =
                    tabPattern.split(value.toString());
            if(cells.length == 8) {
             // don't write duplicates
                if(found < 1) {
                write(context,  key, cells[3],"atr");
                write(context,  key, cells[1], "dtg");
                write(context,  key, cells[7], "fat");
                write(context,  key, cells[4], "lat");
                write(context,  key, cells[0], "loc");
                write(context,  key, cells[5], "lon");
                write(context,  key, cells[6], "src");
                write(context,  key, cells[2],"type");
                } else {
                    context.getCounter("ACLED Ingest",
                            "duplicates").increment(1l);
                }
            } else {
                context.getCounter("ACLED Ingest",
    "malformed records missing a field").increment(1l);
            }
            found++;
        }
    }
}
```

11. Create the following method inside the reduce class to help output key-value pairs:

```
private void write(Context context, Text key,
                         String cell, String qualStr)
          throws IOException, InterruptedException {
    if(!cell.toUpperCase().equals("NULL")) {
        qual.set(qualStr);
        outKey = new Key(key, cf, qual,
                    System.currentTimeMillis());
        outValue.set(cell.getBytes());
        context.write(outKey, outValue);
    }
}

}

@Override
public void setConf(Configuration conf) {
    this.conf = conf;
}

@Override
public Configuration getConf() {
    return conf;
}
```

12. Add the main class to submit an instance of your job to the `ToolRunner` class.

```
public static void main(String[] args) throws Exception {
    Configuration conf =
                    CachedConfiguration.getInstance();
    args = new GenericOptionsParser(conf,
                            args).getRemainingArgs();
    ToolRunner.run(new ACLEDIngest(conf), args);
}
}
```

13. Save the code and build `accumulo-examples.jar` to the base working directory.

14. Create a file named `splits.txt` in the base working folder with the following strings: 00, 01, 10, 11; each on their own line in the file.

15. Create a launcher shell script named `bulk_ingest.sh` in the base working folder that has the following contents:

```
tool.sh accumulo_examples.jar examples.accumulo.ACLEDIngest\
/input/acled_cleaned/\
/output/accumulo_acled_load/\
test\
acled\
root\
password\
localhost:2181\
splits.txt
```

16. Run the script. You should see the job execute in the MapReduce WebUI. Upon completion, the ACLED data should be available for scan under the table `acled` in Accumulo.

How it works...

The program takes in eight arguments, each of which is very important. The input location is where MapReduce will find the ACLED data. The output folder is where it will output data in Accumulo's native RFile format. The string `test` is our testing Accumulo instance name stored in Zookeeper. The string `acled` is our desired table name in Accumulo. We authenticate with the Accumulo instance using the strings `root:password`. For this execution, we supplied one Zookeeper host on `localhost:2181`. Finally, `splits.txt` is used to help presplit our newly created `acled` table.

The program clears any previous folder located in our output location. We configure the `AccumuloFileOutputFormat` to write to this location. For this job, the mapper will output the type `Text` for both the key and the value.

`AccumuloTableAssistant` utilizes the `Builder` pattern to chain setter calls for object instantiation and helps avoid accidentally misplacing the arguments during construction time. We'll create the table `acled` if it does not exist, and will use the assistant to presplit the table based on our locally supplied `splits.txt` file. Without presplitting the table at creation time, the `RangePartitioner` class would force all of the intermediate key-value pairs to a single reducer. It is much more efficient to create presplit tablets based on expected row-key distribution and to allow multiple reducers to build RFiles in parallel. We set the number of reducers to the number of entries in our `splits.txt` file plus 1 to handle keys that fall above our highest split point (`11`). Finally, we are ready to submit the job and to examine the map and reduce phases.

Each map task JVM creates an internal instance of `ACLEDRowIDGenerator`. See the *Designing a row key to store geographic events in Accumulo* recipe in this chapter for an in-depth explanation of how this class works. Our data is tab-delimited and follows a very strict column ordering, thus we can hand-pick the column indices to read the values for `lat`, `lon`, and `dtg` in that respective order. The key generator needs these fields to make a valid composite geospatial and reverse timestamp rowID. We output the generated row key with the text value that was read for the line. This produces a distinct intermediate key for every unique rowID we wish to insert into Accumulo.

The reducer is responsible for taking our generated rowID and reading through any other delimited lines that output an equivalent rowID. The rowID generator in the map phase builds unique rowIDs based on the composite of `lat`, `lon`, and `dtg`. By definition, an ACLED event that took place in the exact same `lat/lon` with the same reverse timestamp, would be grouped to the same intermediate key for the reducer. However, having multiple ACLED events with the exact same rowID means that we have duplicate entries we wish to ignore. Therefore, we only want to preserve the first value collected in the `Iterable` object. This job does not do any duplicate merging. We use a counter to keep track of duplicate occurrences, as well as invalid lines that don't split properly. Since we are directly writing instances of `Key/Value` as RFiles, Accumulo requires `key/value` objects to be inserted in a sorted order. The rowIDs are naturally the same for each qualifier, and the column family is a static label `cf`, but it's very important that we maintain lexicographical ordering while considering the write order for our qualifier labels. Fortunately, our data is very predictable, and we hardcode the column value reads based on the alphabetic ordering of our qualifier labels.

Once the job is finished, and we have all of the RFiles for the presplit tablets, we use the assistant instance to read all of the files produced to the output directly and place them in the appropriate tablet. The data is immediately available for querying in the `acled` table in Accumulo.

There's more...

Here is a bit more explanation on some of the design choices you see in this recipe:

AccumuloTableAssistant.java

This class is designed for re-use across different Accumulo data loading and management applications. Since it requires five input strings for operation, the `Builder` pattern was an obvious choice to prevent accidental variable assignment constructions. See *Effective Java 2.0* by Joshua Block for more detail on the `Builder` design pattern.

Split points

The choice of `00`, `01`, `10`, and `11` as split points was entirely arbitrary. It was more to emphasize the importance of presplitting Accumulo tables during creation. Choosing the right split points really depends on the distribution of your rowID ranges. Too few split points and job throughput will bottleneck at the reduce stage. Too many, and you may start to waste resources and spin up time on underutilized reduce task JVMs.

AccumuloOutputFormat versus AccumuloFileOutputFormat

If you need to ingest data at a massive volume, `AccumuloFileOutputFormat` is the obvious choice. Producing RFiles for direct insert into tablets is not subject to the `AccumuloOutputFormat` overhead of writing mutations directly to the Accumulo table. On the other hand, if your MapReduce job is not write-intensive, it can be easier to work directly with `Mutation` instances instead of RFiles. Moreover, if your job does not require reduction and is map-only, `AccumuloOutputFormat` and writing direct mutations would be a much simpler design choice.

See also

> ▸ *Designing a row key to store geographic events in Accumulo*

Setting a custom field constraint for inputting geographic event data in Accumulo

In this recipe, we will build a custom `Constraint` class to limit the types of mutations we can apply to event date values in an Accumulo table. Specifically, we want newly entered values to conform to a particular `SimpleDateFormat` pattern, but these values should not be in the *future* according to the system time on the TabletServer.

Getting ready

This recipe will be the easiest to test over a pseudo-distributed Hadoop cluster with Accumulo 1.4.1 and Zookeeper 3.3.3 installed. The shell script in this recipe assumes that Zookeeper is running on the host `localhost` and on the port `2181`; you can change this to suit your environment needs. The Accumulo installation's `bin` folder needs to be on your environment path.

For this recipe you'll need to create an Accumulo instance named `test` with user as `root` and password as `password`.

You will need a table by the name `acled` to exist in the configured Accumulo instance.

It is also highly recommended that you go through the *Using MapReduce to bulk import geographic event data into Accumulo* recipe of this chapter. This will give you some sample data with which you can experiment.

How to do it...

Follow these steps to implement and install a constraint in Accumulo:

1. Open the Java IDE editor of your choice. You will need to configure the Accumulo core and Hadoop classpath dependencies.

2. Create a build template that produces a JAR file named `accumulo-examples.jar`.

3. Create the package `example.accumulo` and create the class `DtgConstraint.java` with the following content:

```java
package examples.accumulo;

import org.apache.accumulo.core.constraints.Constraint;
import org.apache.accumulo.core.data.ColumnUpdate;
import org.apache.accumulo.core.data.Mutation;

import java.text.DateFormat;
import java.text.ParseException;
import java.text.SimpleDateFormat;
import java.util.ArrayList;
import java.util.List;

public class DtgConstraint implements Constraint {


    private static final short DATE_IN_FUTURE = 1;
    private static final short MALFORMED_DATE = 2;
    private static final byte[] dtgBytes = "dtg".getBytes();
    private static final DateFormat dateFormatter = new
                    SimpleDateFormat("yyyy-MM-dd");

    public String getViolationDescription(short violationCode) {
        if (violationCode == DATE_IN_FUTURE) {
            return "Date cannot be in future";
        } else if (violationCode == MALFORMED_DATE) {
            return "Date does not match simple date format
                    yyyy-MM-dd";
        }
        return null;
    }
```

4. Implement the `check()` method.

```
@Override
public List<Short> check(Environment env, Mutation mutation) {
    List<Short> violations = null;
    try {
        for(ColumnUpdate update : mutation.getUpdates()) {
            if(isDtg(update)) {
                long dtgTime = dateFormatter.parse(new
                    String(update.getValue())).getTime();
                long currentMillis =
                                System.currentTimeMillis();
                if(currentMillis < dtgTime) {
                    violations = checkAndAdd(
                            violations, DATE_IN_FUTURE);
                }
            }
        }
    } catch (ParseException e) {
        violations = checkAndAdd(violations,
                                    MALFORMED_DATE);
    }
    return violations;
}
```

5. Do a byte comparison to check if the update is for the qualifier `dtg`.

```
private boolean isDtg(ColumnUpdate update) {
    byte[] qual = update.getColumnQualifier();
    if(qual.length != dtgBytes.length)
        return false;
    for (int i = 0; i < qual.length; i++) {
        if(!(qual[i] == dtgBytes[i])) {
            return false;
        }
    }
    return true;
}

private List<Short> checkAndAdd(List<Short> violations,
                                short violationCode) {
    if(violations == null)
        violations = new ArrayList<Short>();
    violations.add(violationCode);
    return violations;
}
}
```

6. Save the class.

7. In the same package, `examples.accumulo`, create the class `DtgConstraintMain.java` with the following content:

```
package examples.accumulo;

import org.apache.accumulo.core.client.*;
import org.apache.accumulo.core.conf.Property;
import org.apache.accumulo.core.data.ConstraintViolationSummary;
import org.apache.accumulo.core.data.Mutation;
import org.apache.accumulo.core.data.Value;
import org.apache.hadoop.io.Text;

import java.util.List;

public class DtgConstraintMain {

    public static final long MAX_MEMORY= 10000L;
    public static final long MAX_LATENCY=1000L;
    public static final int MAX_WRITE_THREADS = 4;
    public static final String TEST_TABLE = "acled";
    public static final Text COLUMN_FAMILY = new Text("cf");
    public static final Text DTG_QUAL = new Text("dtg");
```

8. The `main()` method tries to insert both valid and invalid `dtg` values to test our constraint.

```
    public static void main(String[] args) throws Exception {
        if(args.length < 6) {
System.err.println("examples.accumulo.DtgConstraintMain <row_id>
<dtg> <instance_name> <user> <password> <zookeepers>");
            System.exit(0);
        }
        String rowID = args[0];
        byte[] dtg = args[1].getBytes();
        String instanceName = args[2];
        String user = args[3];
        String pass = args[4];
        String zooQuorum = args[5];
        ZooKeeperInstance ins;
        Connector connector = null;
        BatchWriter writer = null;
        try {

            ins = new ZooKeeperInstance(instanceName,
                                        zooQuorum);
```

```
                connector = ins.getConnector(user, pass);
                writer = connector.createBatchWriter(TEST_TABLE, MAX_
    MEMORY,
                            MAX_LATENCY, MAX_WRITE_THREADS);
    connector.tableOperations().setProperty(TEST_TABLE, Property.
    TABLE_CONSTRAINT_PREFIX.getKey() + 1, DtgConstraint.class.
    getName());
                Mutation validMutation = new Mutation(new
                                    Text(rowID));
                validMutation.put(COLUMN_FAMILY, DTG_QUAL,
                            new Value(dtg));
                writer.addMutation(validMutation);
                writer.close();
            } catch (MutationsRejectedException e) {
                List<ConstraintViolationSummary> summaries =
                    e.getConstraintViolationSummaries();
                for (ConstraintViolationSummary sum : summaries) {
                    System.err.println(sum.toString());
                }
            }
        }
    }
```

9. Build the JAR file, `accumulo-examples.jar`.

10. Navigate to your local Accumulo installation folder, `$ACCUMULO_HOME/conf`, and edit the file `accumulo-site.xml`.

11. Edit the `general.classpaths` property in the `accumulo-site.xml` file to include the path to `accumulo-examples.jar`.

12. Restart the local TabletServer for Accumulo using `$ACCUMULO_HOME/bin/tdown.sh` and `tup.sh`.

13. Issue the following command to test whether the JAR file is on the Accumulo classpath:

    ```
    $ accumulo classpath
    ```

    You should see a file `//printout` with `accumulo-examples.jar`.

14. In the base working folder where `accumulo-examples.jar` is located, create a new shell script named `run_constraint_test.sh` with the following commands. Be sure to change ACCUMULO-LIB, HADOOP_LIB, and ZOOKEEPER_LIB to match your local paths.

    ```
    ACCUMULO_LIB=/opt/cloud/accumulo-1.4.1/lib/*
    ```

    ```
    HADOOP_LIB=/Applications/hadoop-0.20.2-cdh3u1/*:/Applications/
    hadoop-0.20.2-cdh3u1/lib/*
    ```

```
ZOOKEEPER_LIB=/opt/cloud/zookeeper-3.4.2/*
java -cp $ACCUMULO_LIB:$HADOOP_LIB:$ZOOKEEPER_LIB:accumulo-
examples.jar examples.accumulo.DtgConstraintMain\
  00993877573819_9223370801921575807\
  2012-08-07\
  test\
  root\
  password\
  localhost:2181
```

15. Save and run the script. It should silently complete.

16. Edit the script `run_constraint_test.sh` and change the value of the `dtg` parameter from `2012-08-07` to `2030-08-07`.

17. Save and re-run the script. You should see a constraint error printed to the console indicating `Date cannot be in future`.

How it works...

Our `Constraint` class looks through every mutation and determines if the column qualifier matching `dtg` is involved. If the `ColumnUpdate` object mutates a key-value pair containing the qualifier `dtg`, examine the value for errors. This constraint has the following two violation conditions:

1. The date does not match the Java `SimpleDateFormat` pattern, yyyy-MM-dd. So 1970-12-23 and 2012-02-11 will pass, but 70-12-23 or 12-20-22 will generate an error and add a constraint violation.

2. The date is in the future. At the time of this writing, `2030-08-07` was 18 years in the future. If the column update contains a future date, add a constraint violation.

The main class takes all of the required parameters to connect to the Accumulo instance and adds the `Constraint` class to the table. It then attempts to perform a mutation on the supplied rowID using the argument value for `dtg`. If the mutation is rejected for any reason, print out the constraint violations to see if the `DtgConstraint` was violated.

We can modify the `dtg` argument in the shell script to see the different constraint violation errors our class generated.

There's more...

Constraints are a powerful feature for data policy enforcement in Accumulo. The following headings discuss a few additional things you should know.

Bundled Constraint classes

The Accumulo core offers numerous constraint implementations out of the box. They cover a variety of common checked conditions and are already on the TabletServer classpath. Check out the example implementations in the `simple` example's module located at the package `org.apache.accumulo.examples.simple.constraints`. Cell visibility and other core system checks in Accumulo use constraint implementations behind the scenes.

Installing a constraint on each TabletServer

If after installing a custom constraint to your Accumulo instance, you'll notice every mutation being rejected; it's likely that, for whatever reason, the TabletServer server did not find your `Constraint` class on the classpath. Check the TabletServer logs for `ClassNotFoundExceptions`. This can happen if the table configuration has the `Constraint` class listed but cannot find a class matching the fully qualified name. In a fully-distributed setup, make sure to restart every TabletServer after modifying each general classpath.

See also

▸ *Using MapReduce to bulk import geographic event data into Accumulo*

▸ *Enforcing cell-level security on scans using Accumulo*

Limiting query results using the regex filtering iterator

This recipe will use the built-in `RegExFilter` class in Accumulo to return only key-value pairs, where the qualifier is of a particular source value. The filtering will be distributed across the different TabletServers that house the table `acled`.

Getting ready

This recipe will be the easiest to test over a pseudo-distributed Hadoop cluster with Accumulo 1.4.1 and Zookeeper 3.3.3 installed. The shell script in this recipe assumes that Zookeeper is running on the host `localhost` and on the port `2181`; you can change this to suit your environment needs. The Accumulo installation's `bin` folder needs to be on your environment path.

For this recipe you'll need to create an Accumulo instance named `test` with the user as `root` and password as `password`.

To see the filtered results from this recipe, you will need to complete the *Using MapReduce to bulk import geographic event data into Accumulo* recipe listed earlier in this chapter. This will give you some sample data to experiment with.

How to do it...

Follow these steps to use the Regex filtering iterator:

1. Open your Java IDE of choice. You will need to configure the Accumulo core and Hadoop classpath dependencies.

2. Create a build template that produces a JAR file named `accumulo-examples.jar`.

3. Create the package `example.accumulo` and add the class `SourceFilterMain.java` with the following content:

```java
package examples.accumulo;

import org.apache.accumulo.core.client.Connector;
import org.apache.accumulo.core.client.IteratorSetting;
import org.apache.accumulo.core.client.Scanner;
import org.apache.accumulo.core.client.ZooKeeperInstance;
import org.apache.accumulo.core.data.Key;
import org.apache.accumulo.core.data.Value;
import org.apache.accumulo.core.iterators.user.RegExFilter;
import org.apache.accumulo.core.security.Authorizations;
import org.apache.hadoop.io.Text;

import java.util.HashMap;
import java.util.Map;

public class SourceFilterMain {

    public static final String TEST_TABLE = "acled";

    public static final Text COLUMN_FAMILY = new Text("cf");
    public static final Text SRC_QUAL = new Text("src");
```

4. The `main()` method handles argument parsing and querying with the filter:

```java
public static void main(String[] args) throws Exception {
    if(args.length < 5) {
        System.err.println("usage: <src> <instance
            name> <user> <password> <zookeepers>");
        System.exit(0);
    }
    String src = args[0];
    String instanceName = args[1];
    String user = args[2];
    String pass = args[3];
    String zooQuorum = args[4];
```

```
                  ZooKeeperInstance ins = new
                          ZooKeeperInstance(instanceName, zooQuorum);
                  Connector connector = ins.getConnector(user, pass);
                  Scanner scan = connector.createScanner(TEST_TABLE,
                                  new Authorizations());
                  scan.fetchColumn(COLUMN_FAMILY, SRC_QUAL);
                  IteratorSetting iter = new IteratorSetting(15,
                                  "regexfilter", RegExFilter.class);
                  iter.addOption(RegExFilter.VALUE_REGEX, src);
                  scan.addScanIterator(iter);
                  int count = 0;
                  for(Map.Entry<Key, Value> row : scan) {
                    System.out.println("row: " +
                                  row.getKey().getRow().toString());
                    count++;
                  }
                  System.out.println("total rows: " + count);
              }
      }
```

5. Save and build the JAR file `accumulo-examples.jar`.

6. In the base working folder where `accumulo-examples.jar` is located, create a new shell script named `run_src_filter.sh` with the following commands. Be sure to change `ACCUMULO-LIB`, `HADOOP_LIB`, and `ZOOKEEPER_LIB` to match your local paths:

    ```
    ACCUMULO_LIB=/opt/cloud/accumulo-1.4.1/lib/*

    HADOOP_LIB=/Applications/hadoop-0.20.2-
    cdh3u1/*:/Applications/hadoop-0.20.2-cdh3u1/lib/*

    ZOOKEEPER_LIB=/opt/cloud/zookeeper-3.4.2/*

    java -cp $ACCUMULO_LIB:$HADOOP_LIB:$ZOOKEEPER_LIB:accumulo-
    examples.jar examples.accumulo.SourceFilterMain\
      'Panafrican News Agency'\
      test\
      root\
      password\
      localhost:2181
    ```

7. Save and run the script. You should see 49 rows returned for the source `Panafrican News Agency`.

How it works...

The script takes in the required parameters necessary to connect to the Accumulo table `acled`, plus an additional parameter for a source qualifier value to filter on. We set up a `Scanner` instance with blank authorizations and configure an `IteratorSetting` of type `RegExFilter` to do the regex comparison on the TabletServer. Our regex is a very simple direct match on the supplied source argument.

We then iterate over the result set and printout the rowID for any matching key-value pairs. At the end, we print a tally of how many key-value pairs were found matching that source.

The responsibility of filtering key-value pairs based on the value is distributed across the various TabletServers that hold tablets for the `acled` table. The client only sees rows that match the filter, and can immediately begin processing.

See also

- ▸ *Using MapReduce to bulk import geographic event data into Accumulo*
- ▸ *Enforcing cell-level security on scans using Accumulo*

Counting fatalities for different versions of the same key using SumCombiner

This recipe will use the built-in SumCombiner in Accumulo to treat the cell value associated with the qualifier `fat` as long and for each key in the `acled` table, to sum the total for all versions of the key.

Getting ready

This recipe will be easiest to test over a pseudo-distributed Hadoop cluster with Accumulo 1.4.1 and Zookeeper 3.3.3 installed. The shell script in this recipe assumes that Zookeeper is running on the host `localhost` and on the port `2181`; you can change this to suit your environment needs. The Accumulo installation's `bin` folder needs to be on your environment path.

For this recipe, you'll need to create an Accumulo instance named `test` with user as `root` and password as `password`.

You will need a table by the name `acled` to exist in the configured Accumulo instance. If you have an existing table by that name from an earlier recipe, delete and recreate it.

It is also highly recommended that you complete the *Using MapReduce to bulk import geographic event data into Accumulo* recipe earlier in this chapter. This will give you some sample data to experiment with.

How to do it...

Follow these steps to issue a query using SumCombiner:

1. Open your Java IDE of choice. You will need to configure the Accumulo core and Hadoop classpath dependencies.

2. Create a build template that produces a JAR file named `accumulo-examples.jar`.

3. Create the package `example.accumulo` and add the class `TotalFatalityCombinerMain.java` with the following content:

```java
package examples.accumulo;

import org.apache.accumulo.core.client.*;
import org.apache.accumulo.core.client.Scanner;
import org.apache.accumulo.core.data.*;
import org.apache.accumulo.core.iterators.Combiner;
import org.apache.accumulo.core.iterators.LongCombiner;
import org.apache.accumulo.core.iterators.user.SummingCombiner;
import org.apache.accumulo.core.security.Authorizations;
import org.apache.hadoop.io.Text;

import java.util.*;

public class TotalFatalityCombinerMain {

    public static final long MAX_MEMORY= 10000L;
    public static final long MAX_LATENCY=1000L;
    public static final int MAX_WRITE_THREADS = 4;
    public static final String TEST_TABLE = "acled";
    public static final Text COLUMN_FAMILY = new Text("cf");
    public static final Text FATALITIES_QUAL = new Text("fat");
```

4. The `main()` method handles the argument parsing:

```java
    public static void main(String[] args) throws Exception {
        if(args.length < 4) {
            System.err.println("usage: <instance name>
                        <user> <password> <zookeepers>");
            System.exit(0);
        }
        String instanceName = args[0];
        String user = args[1];
        String pass = args[2];
        String zooQuorum = args[3];
        ZooKeeperInstance ins = new
```

```
            ZooKeeperInstance(instanceName, zooQuorum);
         Connector connector = ins.getConnector(user, pass);
         if(!connector.tableOperations().exists(TEST_TABLE))
             connector.tableOperations().create(TEST_TABLE);

         BatchWriter writer = connector.createBatchWriter(TEST_
    TABLE, MAX_MEMORY, MAX_LATENCY, MAX_WRITE_THREADS);
```

5. Write some sample data with the exact same rowID eventA, column family, and qualifier:

```
         Mutation m1 = new Mutation("eventA");
         m1.put(COLUMN_FAMILY, FATALITIES_QUAL, new
             Value("10".getBytes()));

         Mutation m2 = new Mutation("eventA");
         m2.put(COLUMN_FAMILY, FATALITIES_QUAL, new
             Value("5".getBytes()));
```

6. Write an additional key with rowID eventB:

```
         Mutation m3 = new Mutation("eventB");
         m3.put(COLUMN_FAMILY, FATALITIES_QUAL, new
             Value("7".getBytes()));

         writer.addMutation(m1);
         writer.addMutation(m2);
         writer.addMutation(m3);
         writer.close();
```

7. Configure an IteratorSetting for the scanner to use the combiner:

```
         IteratorSetting iter = new IteratorSetting(1,
                             SummingCombiner.class);
         LongCombiner.setEncodingType(iter,
                             SummingCombiner.Type.STRING);
         Combiner.setColumns(iter,
                     Collections.singletonList(new
                     IteratorSetting.Column(COLUMN_FAMILY,
                                 FATALITIES_QUAL)));
         Scanner scan = connector.createScanner(TEST_TABLE,
                     new Authorizations());
         scan.setRange(new Range(new Text("eventA"), new
                             Text("eventB")));
         scan.fetchColumn(COLUMN_FAMILY, FATALITIES_QUAL);
         scan.addScanIterator(iter);
         for(Map.Entry<Key, Value> item : scan) {
```

```
                        System.out.print(item.getKey().getRow().toString() +
    ":
                    fatalities: ");
            System.out.println(new
                            String(item.getValue().get()));
        }
      }
    }
```

8. Save and build the JAR file `accumulo-examples.jar`.

9. In the base working folder where the `accumulo-examples.jar` file is located, create a new shell script named `run_combiner.sh` with the following commands. Be sure to change `ACCUMULO-LIB`, `HADOOP_LIB`, and `ZOOKEEPER_LIB` to match your local paths:

    `ACCUMULO_LIB=/opt/cloud/accumulo-1.4.1/lib/*`

    `HADOOP_LIB=/Applications/hadoop-0.20.2-cdh3u1/*:/Applications/hadoop-0.20.2-cdh3u1/lib/*`

    `ZOOKEEPER_LIB=/opt/cloud/zookeeper-3.4.2/*`

    `java -cp $ACCUMULO_LIB:$HADOOP_LIB:$ZOOKEEPER_LIB:accumulo-examples.jar examples.accumulo.TotalFatalityCombinerMain\`

    `test\`

    `root\`

    `password\`

    `localhost:2181`

10. Save and run the script.

11. You should see the following console printout when the application finishes:

    ```
    eventA: fatalities: 15
    eventB: fatalities: 7
    ```

12. Re-run the script.

13. You should now see twice the count for each event:

    ```
    eventA: fatalities: 30
    eventB: fatalities: 14
    ```

How it works...

The class `TotalFatalityCombinerMain` reads the required arguments to connect to Accumulo and instantiates a `BatchWriter` instance to write out test data to the `acled` table. We write two mutations for two different versions of the same key containing the rowID `eventA`. One contains the qualifier `fat` with value `10` and the other a value of `5`. We also write one mutation with the key containing the rowID `eventB` with a value of `7` for the qualifier `fat`.

We then use a `Scanner` instance to apply the SumCombiner at scan time over the key-value pairs in the table. The combiner's job is to collect different long values associated with the exact same key and emit the sum of those long values. The values `5` and `10` are both associated with the same key for the rowID `eventA`, and are combined to produce a value `15`. There is only one key version associated with the rowID `eventB`, so the single value `7` remains the total sum for that key.

If we re-run this application, the previous mutations are still stored in the same Accumulo table. Re-running the application applies the same mutations once more, adding the values `10` and `5` as key-value entries for the rowID `eventA`, and `7` for `eventB`.

Re-running the `Combiner` scanner now shows four entries for the rowID `eventA` (5, 10, 5, and 10) as well as two entries for the rowID `eventB` (7, 7). The result is double the count from our previous execution. For each time we re-run this application without clearing the table, the results are increased by +15 and +7.

This happens because at the raw key-value level, our mutations are inserting new key-value pairs to the table with different timestamps every time the application is called. Our combiner sees all timestamped versions of every distinct key.

There's more...

Here are some more helpful tips regarding combiners:

Combiners are on a per-key basis, not across all keys

This can cause confusion with new Accumulo users. Combiners use the Accumulo iterator pattern for key-value aggregation, but only a per-key basis across different versions of that key. If you have a requirement to do table-wide aggregation for the values of a common qualifier, you will likely still want to use MapReduce. See the *Aggregating sources in Accumulo using MapReduce* recipe in this chapter.

Combiners can be applied at scan time or applied to the table configuration for incoming mutations

This recipe uses the combiner to aggregate the qualifier values at scan time. Accumulo also supports persistent combiners stored in the table configuration that combine values during mutation writes.

See also

▸ *Using MapReduce to bulk import geographic event data into Accumulo*

▸ *Limiting query results using the regex filtering iterator*

▸ *Aggregating sources in Accumulo using MapReduce*

Enforcing cell-level security on scans using Accumulo

Accumulo offers the ability to apply cell visibility labels for each unique key/value in a table, which is arguably its most distinguishing feature from other BigTable implementations. This recipe will demonstrate one way to apply cell-level security. The code in this recipe will write several mutations that can only be scanned and read with the proper authorizations.

Getting ready

This recipe will be the easiest to test over a pseudo-distributed Hadoop cluster with Accumulo 1.4.1 and Zookeeper 3.3.3 installed. The shell script in this recipe assumes that Zookeeper is running on the host `localhost` and on the port `2181`; you can change this to suit your environment needs. The Accumulo installation's `bin` folder needs to be on your environment path.

For this recipe you'll need to create an Accumulo instance named `test` with user as `root` and password as `password`.

You will need a table by the name `acled` to exist in the configured Accumulo instance. If you have an existing table by that name from an earlier recipe, delete, and recreate it.

It is also highly recommended that you go through the *Using MapReduce to bulk import geographic event data into Accumulo* recipe earlier in this chapter. This will give you some sample data to experiment with.

How to do it...

The following are the steps to read/write data to Accumulo using cell visibility controls:

1. Open the Java IDE of your choice. You will need to configure the Accumulo core and Hadoop classpath dependencies.

2. Create a build template that produces a JAR file named `accumulo-examples.jar`.

3. Create the package `example.accumulo` and add the class `SecurityScanMain.java` with the following content:

```
package examples.accumulo;


import org.apache.accumulo.core.client.*;
import org.apache.accumulo.core.data.Key;
import org.apache.accumulo.core.data.Mutation;
import org.apache.accumulo.core.data.Value;
import org.apache.accumulo.core.security.Authorizations;
import org.apache.accumulo.core.security.ColumnVisibility;
import org.apache.hadoop.io.Text;

import java.util.Map;

public class SecurityScanMain {

    public static final long MAX_MEMORY= 10000L;
    public static final long MAX_LATENCY=1000L;
    public static final int MAX_WRITE_THREADS = 4;
    public static final String TEST_TABLE = "acled";
    public static final Text COLUMN_FAMILY = new Text("cf");
    public static final Text THREAT_QUAL = new
                                        Text("trt_lvl");


    public static void main(String[] args)throws Exception {
        if(args.length < 4) {
            System.err.println("usage: <instance name>  <user>
<password> <zookeepers>");
            System.exit(0);
        }
        String instanceName = args[0];
        String user = args[1];
        String pass = args[2];
        String zooQuorum = args[3];
```

4. Create a `Connector` instance for our `user` or `pass` variable to the `test` Accumulo instance.

```
ZooKeeperInstance ins = new
        ZooKeeperInstance(instanceName, zooQuorum);
Connector connector = ins.getConnector(user, pass);
if(!connector.tableOperations().exists(TEST_TABLE))
    connector.tableOperations().create(TEST_TABLE);
```

5. Get the root user's current authorizations.

```
Authorizations allowedAuths =
connector.securityOperations().getUserAuthorizations(user);
BatchWriter writer =
connector.createBatchWriter(TEST_TABLE, MAX_MEMORY,
                    MAX_LATENCY, MAX_WRITE_THREADS);
```

6. Write the test mutations.

```
Mutation m1 = new Mutation(new Text("eventA"));
m1.put(COLUMN_FAMILY,
        THREAT_QUAL,
        new ColumnVisibility("(p1|p2|p3)"),
        new Value("moderate".getBytes()));
Mutation m2 = new Mutation(new Text("eventB"));
m2.put(COLUMN_FAMILY,
        THREAT_QUAL,
        new ColumnVisibility("(p4|p5)"),
        new Value("severe".getBytes()));
writer.addMutation(m1);
writer.addMutation(m2);
writer.close();
```

7. Create a scanner with our user's authorizations, and fetch any key-value pairs where the key contains the qualifier `threat`.

```
Scanner scanner = connector.createScanner(TEST_TABLE,
allowedAuths);
scanner.fetchColumn(COLUMN_FAMILY, THREAT_QUAL);
boolean found = false;
for(Map.Entry<Key, Value> item: scanner) {
    System.out.println("Scan found: " + item.getKey().
getRow().toString() + " threat level: " + item.getValue().
toString());
    found = true;
}
```

8. If this condition matches, our user is not authorized to see any event threats.

    ```
    if(!found)
            System.out.println("No threat levels are visible with
    your current user auths: " + allowedAuths.serialize());
        }
    }
    ```

9. Save and build the JAR file `accumulo-examples.jar`.

10. In the base working folder where `accumulo-examples.jar` is located, create a new shell script named `run_security_auth_scan.sh` with the following commands. Be sure to change `ACCUMULO-LIB`, `HADOOP_LIB`, and `ZOOKEEPER_LIB` to match your local paths.

    ```
    ACCUMULO_LIB=/opt/cloud/accumulo-1.4.1/lib/*
    ```

    ```
    HADOOP_LIB=/Applications/hadoop-0.20.2-cdh3u1/*:/Applications/
    hadoop-0.20.2-cdh3u1/lib/*
    ```

    ```
    ZOOKEEPER_LIB=/opt/cloud/zookeeper-3.4.2/*
    ```

    ```
    java -cp $ACCUMULO_LIB:$HADOOP_LIB:$ZOOKEEPER_LIB:accumulo-
    examples.jar examples.accumulo.SecurityScanMain\
    ```

    ```
     test\
    ```

    ```
     root\
    ```

    ```
     password\
    ```

    ```
     localhost:2181
    ```

11. Save and run the script.

12. You should see the following output in the console:

    ```
    no threat levels are visible with your current user auths:
    ```

13. Launch the Accumulo shell.

    ```
    accumulo shell -u root -p password
    ```

14. Run the `setauths` command to see a list of options.

    ```
    $ root@test> setauths
    ```

15. Run the following command:

    ```
    $ root@test> setauths -s p1
    ```

16. Re-run the script `run_security_auth_scan.sh`.

17. You should see the following output in the console:

    ```
    Scan found: eventA threat level: moderate
    ```

18. Re-enter the Accumulo shell and run the following command:

```
$ root@test> setauths -s p1,p4
```

19. Re-run the script `run_security_auth_scan.sh`.

20. You should see the following output in the console:

```
Scan found: eventA threat level: moderate
Scan found: eventB threat level: severe
```

How it works...

The class `SecurityScanMain` reads the required arguments to connect to Accumulo and instantiates a `BatchWriter` instance to write out test data to the `acled` table. We write two mutations to the table. The first is for rowID `eventA` and the column visibility expression (p1|p2|p3). The second is for rowID `eventB` and the column visibility (p4|p5). The column visibility expressions are very simple Boolean expressions. Before a scan can occur over an Accumulo table, the client must supply authorization tokens for the connected user. Accumulo will compare the given tokens against the column visibility label on each key to determine visibility for that user over the given key/value. The expression (p1|p2|p3) implies that a scanner reading the key must present an `Authorizations` object that supplies p1, p2, or p3. By default, the root user does not have any scanning authorization tokens. The call to the `getUserAuthorizations(user)` method on the connector currently returns no authorization tokens. To view `eventA`, we need to present p1, p2, or p3; none of which are currently listed for the root user. To view `eventB`, we need to present p4 or p5; which the root user also does not have. Once we go into the shell and add p1 for the root user, our scan will present the authorization p1 and find a successful Boolean match to `eventA`. Once we set the scan tokens for the root user to p1,p4, we can view both `eventA` and `eventB`.

There's more...

Cell visibility is a feature with more complexity than you might think. Here are some things to know about cell security in Accumulo:

Writing mutations for unauthorized scanning

Authorization tokens restrict what users can see during scans, but not what column visibility expressions they can write on mutations.

This is the default behavior and, for many systems, is undesirable. If you would like to enforce this policy in your Accumulo installation, you can add the `Constraint` class implementation `org.apache.accumulo.core.security.VisibilityConstraint` as a system-wide constraint. Once applied to the Accumulo installation, users will be barred from writing mutations containing column visibility labels they themselves are not authorized to read.

ColumnVisibility is part of the key

Different keys containing the exact same rowID, column-family, and qualifier may have different `ColumnVisibility` labels. If the most recent timestamped version of a key contains a `ColumnVisibility` key that is not viewable by the current scan, the user will see the next oldest version of that key for which a column visibility token matches, or none if they are not authorized to see any of the versions.

The normal scanning logic for key/value presentation has the scanner returning the most recent version of a given key. The cell visibility system adjusts that logic with one additional condition. The scanner will return the most recently timestamped version of a given key that matches the supplied authorization tokens.

Supporting more complex Boolean expressions

This recipe shows two very simple disjunction examples of the `ColumnVisibilty` Boolean expression. You can apply more complicated expressions, should your application require them. For example, (((A & B)|C) & D) would match for authorizations that supplied the label D and either label C or labels A and B.

See also

> ▶ *Using MapReduce to bulk import geographic event data into Accumulo*
> ▶ *Setting a custom field constraint for inputing geographic event data in Accumulo*

Aggregating sources in Accumulo using MapReduce

In this recipe, we will use MapReduce and the `AccumuloInputFormat` class to count occurrences of each unique source stored in an Accumulo table.

Getting ready

This recipe will be the easiest to test over a pseudo-distributed Hadoop cluster with Accumulo 1.4.1 and Zookeeper 3.3.3 installed. The shell script in this recipe assumes that Zookeeper is running on the host `localhost` and on the port `2181`; you can change this to suit your environment needs. The Accumulo installation's `bin` folder needs to be on your environment path.

For this recipe you'll need to create an Accumulo instance named `test` with user as `root` and password as `password`.

You will need a table by the name `acled` to exist in the configured Accumulo instance.

To see the filtered results from this recipe, you will need to go through the *Using MapReduce to bulk import geographic event data into Accumulo* recipe seen earlier in this chapter. This will give you some sample data to experiment with.

How to do it...

The following are the steps to count occurrences of different sources using MapReduce:

1. Open the Java IDE of your choice. You will need to configure the Accumulo core and Hadoop classpath dependencies.

2. Create a build template that produces a JAR file named `accumulo-examples.jar`.

3. Create the package `example.accumulo` and add the class `SourceCountJob.java` with the following content:

```java
package examples.accumulo;

import org.apache.accumulo.core.client.mapreduce.
AccumuloInputFormat;
import org.apache.accumulo.core.data.Key;
import org.apache.accumulo.core.data.Value;
import org.apache.accumulo.core.security.Authorizations;
import org.apache.accumulo.core.util.CachedConfiguration;
import org.apache.accumulo.core.util.Pair;
import org.apache.hadoop.conf.Configuration;
import org.apache.hadoop.conf.Configured;
import org.apache.hadoop.fs.FileSystem;
import org.apache.hadoop.fs.Path;
import org.apache.hadoop.io.IntWritable;
import org.apache.hadoop.io.Text;
import org.apache.hadoop.mapreduce.Job;
import org.apache.hadoop.mapreduce.Mapper;
import org.apache.hadoop.mapreduce.Reducer;
import org.apache.hadoop.mapreduce.lib.output.FileOutputFormat;
import org.apache.hadoop.mapreduce.lib.output.TextOutputFormat;
import org.apache.hadoop.util.GenericOptionsParser;
import org.apache.hadoop.util.Tool;
import org.apache.hadoop.util.ToolRunner;

import java.io.IOException;
import java.lang.Override;
import java.util.HashSet;
public class SourceCountJob extends Configured implements Tool {

    private Configuration conf;
    private static final Text FAMILY = new Text("cf");
    private static final Text SOURCE = new Text("src");

    public SourceCountJob(Configuration conf) {
        this.conf = conf;
    }
```

4. Add the `run()` method to conform to the `Tool` interface and parse the arguments from the command line.

```
@Override
public int run(String[] args) throws Exception {

    args = new GenericOptionsParser(conf,
            args).getRemainingArgs();
    if(args.length < 6) {
        System.err.println(printUsage());
        System.exit(0);
    }

    String tableName = args[0];
    String outputStr = args[1];
    String instanceName = args[2];
    String user = args[3];
    String pass = args[4];
    String zooQuorum = args[5];
```

5. Configure the Accumulo input settings.

```
    AccumuloInputFormat.setInputInfo(conf, user, pass.
getBytes(), tableName, new Authorizations());
    AccumuloInputFormat.setZooKeeperInstance(conf,
instanceName, zooQuorum);
    HashSet<Pair<Text, Text>> columnsToFetch = new
HashSet<Pair<Text,Text>>();
    columnsToFetch.add(new Pair<Text, Text>(FAMILY, SOURCE));
    AccumuloInputFormat.fetchColumns(conf, columnsToFetch);
```

6. Set up the job, map/reduce classes, and the output location.

```
    Job job = new Job(conf, "Count distinct sources in
                            ACLED");
    job.setInputFormatClass(AccumuloInputFormat.class);
    job.setMapperClass(ACLEDSourceMapper.class);
    job.setMapOutputKeyClass(Text.class);
    job.setMapOutputValueClass(IntWritable.class);
    job.setReducerClass(ACLEDSourceReducer.class);
    job.setCombinerClass(ACLEDSourceReducer.class);
    job.setJarByClass(getClass());
    job.setOutputFormatClass(TextOutputFormat.class);
    FileOutputFormat.setOutputPath(job,
                            clearOutputDir(outputStr));
    job.setNumReduceTasks(1);
    return job.waitForCompletion(true) ? 0 : 1;


}
```

```
            private String printUsage() {
                return "<tablename> <output> <instance_name>
                        <username> <password> <zoohosts>";
            }

            private Path clearOutputDir(String outputStr)
                    throws IOException {
                FileSystem fs = FileSystem.get(conf);
                Path path = new Path(outputStr);
                fs.delete(path, true);
                return path;
            }
```

7. Add the static inner class `ACLEDSourceMapper`.

```
            public static class ACLEDSourceMapper
                    extends Mapper<Key, Value, Text, IntWritable> {

                private Text outKey = new Text();
                private IntWritable outValue = new IntWritable(1);

                @Override
                protected void map(Key key, Value value,
                                    Context context) throws IOException,
        InterruptedException {

                    outKey.set(value.get());
                    context.write(outKey, outValue);
                }
            }
```

8. Add the static inner class `ACLEDSourceReducer`.

```
            public static class ACLEDSourceReducer
                    extends Reducer<Text, IntWritable, Text,
                            IntWritable> {

                private IntWritable outValue = new IntWritable();

                @Override
                protected void reduce(Text key,
                                    Iterable<IntWritable> values,
                                Context context) throws
                            IOException, InterruptedException {

                int count = 0;
                for(IntWritable value : values) {
```

```
            count += value.get();
        }
        outValue.set(count);
        context.write(key, outValue);
    }
}

@Override
public void setConf(Configuration conf) {
    this.conf = conf;
}

@Override
public Configuration getConf() {
    return conf;
}
```

9. Define a `main()` method to submit the job as a `Tool` instance.

```
public static void main(String[] args) throws Exception {
    Configuration conf =
                    CachedConfiguration.getInstance();
    args = new GenericOptionsParser(conf,
                        args).getRemainingArgs();
    ToolRunner.run(new SourceCountJob(conf), args);
    }
}
```

10. Save and build the JAR file `accumulo-examples.jar`.

11. In the base working folder where `accumulo-examples.jar` is located, create a new shell script named `source_count.sh` with the following commands. Be sure to change `ACCUMULO-LIB`, `HADOOP_LIB`, and `ZOOKEEPER_LIB` to match your local paths:

```
tool.sh accumulo_examples.jar examples.accumulo.SourceCountJob\
 -Dmapred.reduce.tasks=4\
 acled\
 /output/accumulo_source_count/\
 test\
 root\
 password\
 localhost:2181
hadoop fs -cat /output/accumulo_source_count/part* > source_count.
txt
```

12. Save and run the script. You should see the MapReduce job start executing over your pseudo-distributed cluster.

13. Upon successful completion of the job, you should see the file `source_count.txt` in your base working folder. Type in the `cat` command to see the counts for each source.

How it works...

We define the `SourceCountJob` class to implement the `Tool` interface for ease of remote submission with the `ToolRunner` class. The `CachedConfiguration.getInstance()` static method sends our `Tool` instance the correct Accumulo configuration on the classpath.

The `run()` method parses the arguments necessary to connect to the Accumulo instance using `AccumuloInputFormat`. For this job we're only interested in retrieving the column qualifier `src` from the column family `cf` for each key. By default, the scanner will only return the most recent versions of each key containing the qualifier `src`. If we wanted to count source occurrences across every key-value pair in the table for every version, we would have to configure `maxVersions` in the input format.

We then set up our job instance with the `AccumuloInputFormat` and map/reduce classes required to count each source. As our reducer class is simply adding integers together, we can re-use the sample implementation for a combiner. We clear any existing output folders and set the number of reduce tasks to 1 as we are running a pseudo-distributed cluster. Now we are ready to submit the job to the cluster.

The business logic operates in a very similar manner to the traditional WordCount example.

The `AccumuloInputFormat` class handles scanning and returning of only key-value pairs for the qualifier `src`. Therefore, any key/value instances that enter our `ACLEDSourceMapper` class's `map()` function are already restricted to the data we're interested in aggregating, and we can simply output 1 to represent one occurrence of that source value in our dataset. The output key is simply the value of the incoming source.

The reduce class `ACLEDSourceReducer` simply tallies occurrences for each source, and outputs the results back to HDFS.

At the end of the shell script, we download and concatenate the different part files together into one file, `source_counts.txt`. We now have one single file with newline-separated source listings and the total number of occurrences for each source.

Index

used, for transforming geographical
    event data 84-88
using to build per-month report of fatalities,
    over geographic event data 159-161
using, to create tables from weblog query
    results 108-110
using to intersect weblog IPs and determine
    country 113, 114
Hive date UDFs
using to sort event dates, from geographic
    event data 156, 157
using to transform event dates, from
    geographic event data 156, 157
Hive query language 165
Hive string UDFs
using, to concatenate fields in weblog
    data 110, 111

I

IdentityMapper 51, 212
IdentityMapperTest class 213
IllegalArgumentException exception 253
illustrate
using, to debug Apache Pig 224
InputFormat
creating, to read geographical event
    data 98-104
input splits 43
InputStream object 42
INVALID_IP_ADDRESS counter 212
invalidZOrder() unit test method 250
io.compression.codecs property 45
ip field 80
isSplitable() method 104
IsUseragentBot class 70, 71, 72

J

JAVA_HOME environment property 228
Java Virtual Machine (JVM) 92
JobConf documentation
URL 13
JobConf.setMaxMapAttempts() method 218
**JobConf.setMaxReduceAttempts() method
    218**
Job Tracker UI 222-224

JOIN statement 135
JOIN table 115

K

keys
Lexicographic sorting 255
key.toString() method 97
key-value store
used, for joining data 144
k-means 203

L

LineReader 188
LineRecordReader class 104
loadRedis() method 146, 148
LocalJobRunner class 217
local mode
MapReduce running jobs,
    developing 215-217
MapReduce running jobs, testing 215-217
LOCATION keyword 107
location_regains_mapper.py file 92
LZO
codec implementation, downloading 43
DistributedLzoIndexer 45
io.compression.codecs property 45
setting up, steps for 43
used, for data compressing 42-45
working 45
LzoIndexer 45
LzoTextInputFormat 45

M

Mahout. *See* **Apache Mahout**
main() method 185, 195
MapDriver class 214
map() function 118, 123, 152, 154
Map input records counter 210
map() method 131
map-only jobs 48
Mapper class 124
col_pos 154
outKey 154
outValue 154
pattern 154

Python streaming
using, to perform time series analytic 89-93

Q

QL statement 88
Quantile UDF 174, 175
query
issuing, SumCombiner used 274, 277
query results
limiting, regex filtering iterator used 270-273

R

read compression option 49
Record class 62
record-skipping 218
Redis
about 144
URL 148
used, for joining data in MapReduce 145
reduce() function 153
reduce() method 154
Reducer class 154
reduce-side join 128, 132
regex filtering iterator
used, for limiting query results 270-273
removeAndSetOutput() method 117
removeAndSetPath() method 120
replicated join, Apache Pig
used, for joining data 132, 133
replication factor
setting, for HDFS 63
replication factor setting 39
request_date field 110
request_time field 110
Resource Description Framework (RDF) 180
rowCount variable 224
row key
designing, to store geographic events in
Accumulo 246-254
run() method 97, 119, 124, 151, 184, 218,
257, 285
runTest() method 214

S

scans
cell-level security enforcing, Accumulo used
278-282
Sqoop
configuring, for Microsoft SQL Server 25, 26
Secondary NameNode 40
secondary sort
using, to calculate page views 78-82, 83, 84
select() method 148
SELECT statement 158
SELECT TRANSFORM 170
seq2sparse arguments 204
-a arguments 205
–input arguments 204
-md arguments 205
-ml arguments 205
–namedVector arguments 204
-ng arguments 205
–output arguments 204
-s arguments 205
-wt arguments 205
-x arguments 205
seqdirectory tool 204
SequenceFileInputFormat.class 48
SequenceFiles
about 49
block compression option 49
data, reading to 46, 47
data, writing to 46, 47
read compression option 49
uncompressed option 49
SequenceWriter class 48
SerDe 107
sessionize web server log data
viewing, Apache Pig used 74, 76
setAttemptsToStartSkipping() method 218
setJarByClass() method 119, 154
set() method 148
setNumReduceTasks() method 12
setSkipOutputPath() method 218
setStatus() method 223
setup() method 124, 131, 213
setup() routine 123
shell commands
URL 9

Thank you for buying
Hadoop Real-World Solutions Cookbook

About Packt Publishing

Packt, pronounced 'packed', published its first book "*Mastering phpMyAdmin for Effective MySQL Management*" in April 2004 and subsequently continued to specialize in publishing highly focused books on specific technologies and solutions.

Our books and publications share the experiences of your fellow IT professionals in adapting and customizing today's systems, applications, and frameworks. Our solution based books give you the knowledge and power to customize the software and technologies you're using to get the job done. Packt books are more specific and less general than the IT books you have seen in the past. Our unique business model allows us to bring you more focused information, giving you more of what you need to know, and less of what you don't.

Packt is a modern, yet unique publishing company, which focuses on producing quality, cutting-edge books for communities of developers, administrators, and newbies alike. For more information, please visit our website: www.packtpub.com.

About Packt Open Source

In 2010, Packt launched two new brands, Packt Open Source and Packt Enterprise, in order to continue its focus on specialization. This book is part of the Packt Open Source brand, home to books published on software built around Open Source licenses, and offering information to anybody from advanced developers to budding web designers. The Open Source brand also runs Packt's Open Source Royalty Scheme, by which Packt gives a royalty to each Open Source project about whose software a book is sold.

Writing for Packt

We welcome all inquiries from people who are interested in authoring. Book proposals should be sent to author@packtpub.com. If your book idea is still at an early stage and you would like to discuss it first before writing a formal book proposal, contact us; one of our commissioning editors will get in touch with you.

We're not just looking for published authors; if you have strong technical skills but no writing experience, our experienced editors can help you develop a writing career, or simply get some additional reward for your expertise.

Hadoop Beginner's Guide

ISBN: 978-1-849517-30-0   Paperback: 340 pages

Learn how to crunch Big data to extract meaning from the data avalanche

1. Learn tools and techniques that let you approach Big data with relish and not fear

2. Shows how to build a complete infrastructure to handle your needs as your data grows

3. Hands-on examples in each chapter give the big picture while also giving direct experience

Hadoop MapReduce Cookbook

ISBN: 978-1-849517-28-7   Paperback: 308 pages

Recipes for analyzing large and complex datasets with Hadoop MapReduce

1. Learn to process large and complex datasets, starting simply, then diving in deep

2. Solve complex Big data problems such as classifications, finding relationships, online marketing and recommendations

3. More than 50 Hadoop MapReduce recipes, presented in a simple and straightforward manner, with step-by-step instructions and real-world examples

Please check **www.PacktPub.com** for information on our titles

HBase Administration Cookbook

ISBN: 978-1-849517-14-0   Paperback: 332 pages

Master HBase configuration and administration for optimum database performance

1. Move large amounts of data into HBase and learn how to manage it efficiently

2. Set up HBase on the cloud, get it ready for production, and run it smoothly with high performance

3. Maximize the ability of HBase with the Hadoop eco-system including HDFS, MapReduce, Zookeeper, and Hive

Cassandra High Performance Cookbook

ISBN: 978-1-849515-12-2   Paperback: 310 pages

Over 150 recipes to design and optimize large-scale Apache Cassandra deployments

1. Get the best out of Cassandra using this efficient recipe bank

2. Configure and tune Cassandra components to enhance performance

3. Deploy Cassandra in various environments and monitor its performance

Please check **www.packtpub.com** for information on our titles

Made in the USA
Lexington, KY
16 August 2013